MANAGEMENT ACCOUNTING FOR FEE-FOR-SERVICE/PREPAID MEDICAL GROUPS

Eldon L. Schafer, PhD, CPA
Dwight J. Zulauf, PhD, CPA
Michael E. Gocke, MBA, CPA

CENTER FOR RESEARCH
IN AMBULATORY
HEALTH CARE ADMINISTRATION

RESEARCH ARM OF THE
MEDICAL GROUP MANAGEMENT ASSOCIATION
ENGLEWOOD, COLORADO
1992

The preparation of this text was assisted by a grant from the W. K. Kellogg Foundation, Battle Creek, Michigan.

The opinions, conclusions, and proposals in the text are those of the authors and do not necessarily represent the views of either the W. K. Kellogg Foundation or the Medical Group Management Association.

CENTER FOR RESEARCH IN AMBULATORY HEALTH CARE ADMINISTRATION
104 Inverness Terrace East
Englewood, Colorado 80112
(303) 799-1111

ISBN 0-933948-88-3

Printed in the United States of America.

Outline and Table of Contents

Table of Exhibits

Foreword

Management Accounting for Fee-for-Service/Prepaid Medical Groups was developed by the Center for Research in Ambulatory Health Care Administration (CRAHCA) as one product of the W. K. Kellogg Foundation supported grant, "Financial Information Systems for Medical and Dental Group Management." Funding for the project was through the Hospital Research and Educational Trust, Chicago, Illinois, to the Center for Research in Ambulatory Health Care Administration and to Hospital Administrative Services (HAS), an affiliate of the American Hospital Association.

Other major components of the project are:

- ***Management Accounting for Health Maintenance Organizations***—developed by CRAHCA.
  Written for the administrators of staff, group, and IPA model Health Maintenance Organizations, this hardbound text instructs how to better manage and control the financial systems inherent in the HMO. A chart of accounts and model financial statements are presented; additionally, the text instructs the administrator in using cost accounting, financial planning and control, and how to develop HMO premium rates.

- ***Practical Financial Management for Dental Practice Administration***—developed by CRAHCA.
  A four-volume text containing a complete financial information system for the practicing dentist. The financial information system described provides the dentist or dental administrator with the technical instruction for income tax reporting, forecasting revenue, cost accounting, income distribution, short-term cash management, capital equipment purchasing, and long-range planning decisions.

- ***A Primer on Financial Information Systems for Your Dental Practice***—developed by CRAHCA.
  A monograph, published by the American Dental Association, directed to the dentist establishing a practice. The primer addresses the doctor's immediate financial information needs and instructs how to use a financial information system for better financial management.

- ***The Group Practice Performance Evaluator and the Dental Practice Performance Evaluator***—developed jointly by CRAHCA and HAS.
These products are productivity and performance comparison reports for managers of medical groups and dental practices. Each data system provides comparisons among similar health care organizations as well as an evaluation of trends in the subscribing group or practice.

- **Educational Programs**—developed by CRAHCA.
Integral to the development of the other products are educational programs instructing physicians, dentists, and health care administrators in the use of financial information in their practices. Educational programs created by the Center for Research in conjunction with the project are: Use of Comparative Financial/Statistical Data, Decision Making with Microcomputers: Using Lotus 1-2-3, Financial Management of the Fee-for-Service/ Prepaid Medical Group, and Financial Management for Dental Practices.

The W. K. Kellogg Foundation provided assistance to the Center for Research to undertake this project as a follow-up to a financial text produced earlier. This text, *Practical Financial Management for Medical Groups*, also developed with support from the W. K. Kellogg Foundation, was published in 1979, with immediate acceptance as the de facto standard chart of accounts and financial handbook for medical groups. The financial information system and instruction in this text were directed to the needs of a fee-for-service medical group. Specific revenue accounts were reserved for prepaid activity; however, *Practical Financial Management for Medical Groups* did not address the sizeable information needs of the fee-for-service medical group that contracts to provide prepaid health care.

The financial information system presented in ***Management Accounting for Fee-for-Service/Prepaid Medical Groups*** complements the system of the earlier text and is designed for installation into the group's management and computer information systems with minimal conversion. Medical groups that are hybrid organizations combining an HMO and a medical group practice as a single entity should reference both this text and *Management Accounting for Health Maintenance Organizations* to satisfy their total information needs.

Major changes are underway in the financial information needs of health care organizations. To direct a successful and viable organization in the future, the group practice administrator will require more than technical skill; equally important will be the ability to manage the expenses of providing care. ***Management Accounting for Fee-for-Service/Prepaid Medical Groups*** is the source of information to better manage the financial aspects of the group today and in the changing environment to come.

For further information about the project or to obtain copies of the texts produced through this project, contact the Center for Research in Ambulatory Health Care Administration, 104 Inverness Terrace East, Englewood, Colorado 80112, phone (303) 799-1111.

Denver, Colorado
October 15, 1985

Mary Alice Krill, PhD
Director of Research
and Administrative Director
CRAHCA

Preface

The purpose of this text is to furnish medical groups who have, or are considering adding, a prepaid component with the financial tools required to provide management, owners, and creditors with relevant financial information. This new book adapts the information presented in the 1979 financial text, *Practical Financial Management for Medical Groups*, for the changes brought about by the entry of groups into prepaid medicine.

The major emphasis of this text is on the financial controls necessary to support a prepaid component. As long as the prepaid component is small (less than about 15 percent of the total practice), the financial information system presented in *Practical Financial Management for Medical Groups* will probably serve the group adequately. However, as the prepaid component grows in importance, a subtle but critical change takes place. The financial information system must change from an emphasis on utilization and high production to an emphasis on financial controls to serve the practice effectively. This new text provides an expansion of the CRAHCA Chart of Accounts and information on financial controls as well as on the use of financial information in the prepaid environment.

This text complements other texts published by the Center for Research in Ambulatory Health Care Administration in the *Going Prepaid* series and *Management Accounting for Health Maintainence Organizations*. In developing the text, the authors drew upon the experience of many medical groups as well as sound theory. The long period of research, the extensive testing, and the thorough review and critique of the text by practitioners should assure its relevance to the needs of medical groups entering prepaid practice.

Tacoma, Washington
October 15, 1985

Eldon L. Schafer, PhD, CPA
Dwight J. Zulauf, PhD, CPA
Michael E. Gocke, MBA, CPA

Acknowledgments

The Center for Research in Ambulatory Health Care Administration (CRAHCA), an affiliate of the Medical Group Management Association, would like to express its gratitude to the W. K. Kellogg Foundation, Battle Creek, Michigan, for its assistance in developing the Financial Information Systems for Medical and Dental Group Management project. ***Management Accounting for Fee-for-Service/Prepaid Medical Groups*** is one of the six major elements resulting from the project.

Members of the Medical Group Management Association (MGMA) played a crucial role in developing this text. After a survey of fee-for-service/prepaid medical groups in the United States, office interviews of MGMA members from fee-for-service/prepaid medical groups provided the authors the background material and examples required to structure the CRAHCA Prepaid Group Chart of Accounts.

Appreciation is extended to the members of the task force who assisted in development of the text and reviewed manuscripts prior to publication. Members of the task force were:

Dale J. Anderson, FACMGA
Administrator
Littleton Clinic Medical Center, PC
Littleton, Colorado

Richard H. Cooper
Associate Director
Everett Clinic
Everett, Washington

Martin A. Hadelman
Executive Director
Atlanta Medical Associates
Atlanta, Georgia

Jeffrey B. Milburn
Financial Management Consultant
Colorado Springs, Colorado

Robert G. Shouldice, DBA
Professor of Health Services Administration
George Washington University
Washington, D.C.

Steven N. Sorensen, CPA
Certified Public Accountant
Minneapolis, Minnesota

Fred C. Smith, Jr., FACMGA
Regional Administrator
Manhattan Medical Group, PC
Health Insurance Plan of Greater New York, Inc.
New York, New York

The Center for Research staff prepared the authors' manuscript for publication and supervised the typesetting and printing of the text.

The staff involved were:
Mary Alice Krill, PhD, CRAHCA Administrative Director and
Director of Research
Mary Jo Ross, CRAHCA Administrative Assistant
Ann M. Madden, Project Secretary
Particia J. Doty, word processing support.

There were many others involved in producing the final text; their assistance is greatly appreciated.

Denver Colorado
October 20, 1985

David N. Gans
Project Director

About CRAHCA and MGMA

The Center for Research in Ambulatory Health Care Administration (CRAHCA) is a Section 501(c)(3) tax-exempt charitable organization as defined by the Internal Revenue Code. Founded in 1973, the purpose of CRAHCA is to improve ambulatory health care in general and group practice in particular through better administration. Its work focuses on new and innovative publications; education, research, and data services; and demonstration programs. CRAHCA is an affiliate of the Medical Group Management Association (MGMA). MGMA is a Section 501(c)(6) professional association. Founded in 1926, MGMA, which today comprises over 5,600 members and 2,800 medical groups involving about 65,000 physicians, is the oldest and largest membership organization representing group practice administration. MGMA serves its individual and organizational members and their patients and promotes the group practice of medicine as an effective and efficient form of healthcare delivery.

About the Authors

Eldon L. Schafer, PhD, CPA, is Professor of Accounting at Pacific Lutheran University in Tacoma, Washington. He holds BS, MA, and PhD degrees from the University of Nebraska and is a certified public accountant in Nebraska. He has taught previously at the University of Washington, Syracuse University, San Jose State University, the University of Nebraska, and as a visiting professor at Massey University in New Zealand; and is a member of the Technical Advisory Committee of the Washington State Hospital Commission. He coauthored *Management Accounting* and *Ambulatory Care Organization and Management*, published by John Wiley and Sons; *Practical Financial Management for Medical Groups, Practical Financial Management for Dental Practice Administration, Management Accounting for Health Maintenance Organizations,* and *Evaluating the Performance of a Prepaid Medical Group*, published by the Center for Research in Ambulatory Health Care Administration. He is a member of American Accounting Association, National Association of Accountants, and Washington Society of Certified Public Accountants. He has been active in professional development programs in management accounting throughout the United States.

Dwight J. Zulauf, PhD, CPA, is a Professor of Accounting at Pacific Lutheran University in Tacoma, Washington, and is a certified public accountant in the state of Washington. He holds a BS from the University of Oregon, an MS from Columbia University, and a PhD from the University of Minnesota. During 1983-84 he was a Visiting Professor at California State University at Long Beach. In 1985 he returned to Pacific Lutheran where he initiated the Dwight J. Zulauf Alumni Chair of Business Administration. He coauthored *Practical Financial Management for Medical Groups* and *Practical Financial Management for Dental Practice Administration*, published by the Center for Research in Ambulatory Health Care Administration. He has been active in a variety of health care organizations as a consultant and volunteer for over a decade.

Michael E. Gocke, MBA, CPA, is a shareholder in Phillips, Schmechel, and Gocke, CPA PS, in Tacoma, Washington. He holds a BS in Accounting from California State University in Sacramento, California, an MBA from Pacific Lutheran University in Tacoma, Washington, and an MS in Taxation from

Golden Gate University in Seattle, Washington. He is a certified public accountant and a certified financial planner. He coauthored *Management Accounting for Health Maintenance Organizations* and *Evaluating the Performance of a Prepaid Medical Group*. He has provided professional and management-level services to medical groups, health maintenance organizations, and hospitals. He is a member of the American Institute of Certified Public Accountants, Washington Society of Certified Public Accountants, National Association of Accountants, Institute of Certified Financial Planners, and Group Health Association of America.

PART I

FINANCIAL INFORMATION SYSTEM DESIGN

Chapter 1

Introduction to Part I

The medical group administrator faces many challenges in the day-to-day operations of a medical group. He or she must be adept at managing human and physical resources, marketing the health care services provided by group physicians, and—most importantly—must have a firm knowledge of finance and accounting. While the need for good management is often less apparent than the need for good clinical skills, the long-term viability of a medical group may well be dependent on the quality and timeliness of the administrator's financial decisions. ***Management Accounting for Fee-for-Service/Prepaid Medical Groups*** is written to provide the fee-for-service/prepaid medical group administrator with a comprehensive financial information system and instruction on how better to manage the group financially.

Medical groups entering into contracts to deliver prepaid health care face a new set of financial risks. The extent of these financial risks depends upon the nature of the contract with the prepaid plan or HMO. A survey by the authors of medical groups with a prepaid component indicated that 68 percent of their contracts provided for capitation payments, 19 percent compensated the groups on a discounted fee-for-service basis, 7 percent compensated the groups on a fee-for-service basis similar to any other reimbursement organization or patient, and 6 percent of the contracts contained another reimbursement method, such as a flat payment. Responding groups using the last type of contract generally indicated that the contract represented a temporary or unusual arrangement with an HMO or employer.

Those groups accepting prepaid patients on a capitation basis face a dramatic change in financial risks. Where revenue was uncertain and expenses were relatively certain in their fee-for-service practices, now revenue is certain and collected in advance but expenses, particularly the cost of outside referrals and hospitalization, are uncertain. The amount of financial risk depends upon whether the group is capitated only for primary care, for primary care and referrals, or for the complete health care of the patient. Fee-for-service behavior, which rewards utilization and high production, may now have drastic financial results. The group will need new utilization data and controls as well as new financial controls to practice effectively.

Finally, those groups forming their own prepaid plans or HMOs undertake not only an expanded role in health care delivery but also undertake an indemnity insurance role requiring administration, marketing, and actuarial skills not possessed by many groups.

This text is prepared for the medical group participating in prepaid health care. A group limiting its involvement to fee-for-service or discounted fee-for-service reimbursement will find that the 1979 CRAHCA text, *Practical Financial Management for Medical Groups,*[1] should meet its needs in designing and using a financial information system. The added financial risks associated with capitation payments require a different frame of reference. The chart of accounts in *Practical Financial Management for Medical Groups* has been expanded and tailored to the needs of a group with both fee-for-service and prepaid practice. Although the basic structure remains largely unchanged, new accounts have been added, some titles changed, and explanations revised to make it easier to understand the accounting for prepayment. Additionally, this text provides information on financial control and the use of the financial information in the prepaid environment.

HMO plan administrators and medical groups operating an HMO are directed to a companion CRAHCA text, *Management Accounting for Health Maintenance Organizations,*[2] which presents a chart of accounts for HMOs and a discussion of how it may be used to provide financial information needed to manage HMOs' needs. Although the chart of accounts developed for HMOs has a structure similar to the chart of accounts in this text, HMOs require a number of additional accounts for transactions that are not faced by medical groups.

Overview of Text

Part I presents the chart of accounts for a medical group offering care on a prepaid basis. The chart of accounts is the heart of a financial information system. It provides the structure for accumulation and retrieval of financial data. The chart of accounts in this text, although largely unchanged from the chart of accounts in *Practical Financial Management for Medical Groups*, is tailored to prepaid care with an expansion of accounts and new explanations. Part I also presents a discussion of accounting principles and financial statements

[1]*Practical Financial Management for Medical Groups*, Center for Research in Ambulatory Health Care Administration, Denver, Colorado, 1979.

[2]*Management Accounting for Health Maintenance Organizations*, Center for Research in Ambulatory Health Care Administration, Denver, Colorado, 1984.

for prepaid medical groups. Because of the critical need for financial information that cannot be met on the cash basis of accounting, accrual basis accounting measurements are stressed. Many of the unsuccessful experiences of medical groups in prepaid care can be traced to a lack of both current financial information showing group performance and good utilization data including referrals and hospitalizations. As the level of prepaid care and its financial risks grow, the group must use accrual measurements to evaluate performance.

Part II, *Cost Accounting for Prepaid Medical Groups*, describes and illustrates techniques to measure the cost of providing service. Knowledge and control of costs is essential in a prepaid practice. In addition to financial control, good cost information will provide the base for contract negotiations with the prepaid plan or HMO.

Part III, *Financial Planning and Control*, builds upon the first two parts. It provides an approach to budgeting and illustrates the development of a budget for a group with both fee-for-service and prepaid practice. Three different levels of evaluation of performance are examined and illustrated: first, evaluation of the performance of the group as a whole; second, evaluation of a department or specialty, using the fee-for-service equivalents to measure the prepaid service in the department; and third, evaluation of the prepaid component of the practice by comparing the revenue from prepaid contracts with the fee-for-service equivalent of service provided plus the cost of referrals and hospitalization.

Outline of Part I

The major purpose of Part I is to present the structure of a financial information system, including a detailed chart of accounts, that will serve the financial information needs of a medical group with a prepaid component. This section will provide information and illustrations that describe and depict general purpose financial statements and the principles that guide their preparation. Understandable and reliable financial statements benefit outside users such as bankers as well as serve present and prospective owners, policy committees, governing boards, and group practice administrators.

The chart of accounts presented in this text has its origins in the previously published CRAHCA Chart of Accounts for Medical Groups,[1] which was designed to accommodate a broad range of financial information needs. It has been accepted and implemented widely by medical groups in the United States. In the authors' survey of 442 medical groups with a prepaid component, 48

[1]Volume IIA, Data Accumulation System for Groups with Limited Objectives and Volume IIB, Data Accumulation System for Groups with Complex Objectives, *Practical Financial Management for Medical Groups*, Center for Research in Ambulatory Health Care Administration, Denver, Colorado, 1979.

percent of the responding groups indicated they had adopted the CRAHCA Chart of Accounts. The chart of accounts presented in this volume is an adaption of the experience-proven CRAHCA Chart of Accounts.

Chapter 2 provides an overview of the structure and explains the numerical coding system of the CRAHCA Prepaid Group Chart of Accounts. Described in this chapter is the relationship between the flexible nature of the coding structure and the financial information needs of the group.

Chapter 3 describes in detail the CRAHCA Prepaid Group Chart of Accounts. Summary and detail accounts are delineated and explained fully. The account titles and explanations have been tailored to medical groups with both prepaid and fee-for-service components.

Chapter 4 describes accounting principles underlying the development of general purpose financial statements for medical group practices with a prepaid component. Cash and accrual bases of accounting are examined and briefly compared. The chapter closes with a discussion of accounting for prepayment.

The next three chapters discuss and illustrate the three general purpose financial statements that have evolved as a result of years of experience: Chapter 5, the statement of financial position (balance sheet); Chapter 6, the income statement; and Chapter 7, the statement of changes in financial position (funds flow or cash flow statement).

The final chapter, Chapter 8, provides a summary of Part I.

Chapter 2

Structure of the Chart of Accounts

The major purpose of this text is to develop a financial information system to serve many financial information objectives. It is intended to meet the needs of a broad spectrum of medical groups, including those who provide all of their care on a prepaid basis. Part I, *Financial Information System Design*, presents the framework for accumulating financial data. The heart of any data accumulation system is a chart of accounts, a systematic prenumbering of financial accounts. The structure of this chart of accounts is flexible, allowing groups of differing sizes and complexities to meet their financial information objectives. Should a group expand in size or complexity, its increased information needs can be met by expanding within the system rather than rebuilding the entire system. In addition, participation in comparative data studies, such as the Medical Group Management Association's Cost Survey or Group Practice Performance Evaluator, is facilitated, and the amount and quality of information available to participating groups will be increased.

An explanation of the numerical coding system is presented in this chapter. Emphasis is placed on the relationship between the expandable nature of the coding structure and financial information objectives of the user.

As the prepaid component of the practice expands, more data are required to analyze the profitability of prepaid contracts. For example, medical groups participating in a prepaid plan on a discounted fee-for-service basis would require very little financial information beyond that required for their fee-for-service practice; they would need information on the amount of service they are providing for plan members. Groups providing prepaid care on a capitation basis, however, would need data by individual prepaid plan as well as cost and utilization data within the group. This would include, as a minimum for each prepaid plan, the fee-for-service equivalent value of services provided, the cost of referrals for outside medical services, the cost of drugs and supplies, and the cost of hospitalization of prepaid patients.

This need for increased information can be met from two basic sources: the financial information system and the utilization or billing system. Utilization data are maintained by both the group and the HMO. The HMO must accumulate utilization data to identify errors in its actuarial assumptions, to determine profitability by contract, to revise premiums and capitation rates, and to pinpoint areas where costs of contracts could be better controlled. The HMO will share the data with contracting groups. The amount of utilization data accumulated within the group will depend upon the billing system. If the group has maintained its fee-for-service billing system, it may be accumulating only production type data for income distribution purposes. If the group has seriously considered the added information needs of prepaid practice, it may be accumulating the following data from patient encounter forms in the billing system:

- The physician providing the service
- Procedures ordered
- Diagnosis code
- Referrals to outside physicians or other providers
- Outpatient use of urgent care facilities, ambulatory surgical units, and hospitals
- Inpatient use of hospitals.

Once captured, the data may be summarized at any desired level ranging from individual patient or physician profiles to totals for the prepaid practice or for the group as a whole.

The CRAHCA Prepaid Group Chart of Accounts is designed to meet the needs of the medical group to determine the overall profitability of its prepaid component. Detailed analysis, such as the number of referrals by doctor, requires data from the utilization system. If the prepaid component is essentially discounted fee-for-service, this chart of accounts will accumulate actual revenue by contract and the fee-for-service equivalent of these same medical services. For capitation plans, data may also be accumulated on the cost of referrals and hospitalization for each prepaid plan.

Coding Structure

The numerical coding system used in the chart of accounts has four fields. Each field represents a different purpose for accumulating information. The four fields are: entity field, allowing the same basic structure to be used for more than one entity; basic field, presenting the basic structure of accounts common to all groups; responsibility center field, allowing data to be accumulated by responsibility center; and provider field, allowing data to be accumulated by health care provider. The four fields can be illustrated as follows:

Entity Field	Basic Field	Responsibility Center Field	Provider Field
0	0 0 0 0	0 0	0 0
1 Digit	4 Digits	2 Digits	2 Digits

When a group's financial information objectives are not met completely by the basic field, three additional fields are available. These fields provide for different entities, responsibility centers, and individual health care providers. Use of these additional fields provides information for financial planning, short-range decisions, increased management control, and capital budgeting. The coding system may be fully expanded to nine digits. The addition of one digit to the left of the basic field designates the entity. The addition of digits to the right of the basic field designates the responsibility center and the health care provider.

The overall structure of the chart of accounts is presented in Exhibit 2-1.

Entity Field

A digit representing the entity precedes those of the basic field. This single-digit field permits the use of the same basic structure for more than one legal entity. For example, the professional corporation, a realty corporation, independent satellite clinics, and a research corporation could all be identified. Another example would be a professional corporation for fee-for-service patients and a second one for the operation of a prepaid plan (HMO) by the group. This system allows the financial statements of two or more entities to be consolidated into a set of financial statements for the total organization. When systems are computerized, a single program could be used for all related entities.

Basic Field

The whole system centers around the basic field. It consists of four digits and describes the fundamental nature of the accounts (for example, assets, liabilities, revenues, or expenses). The basic field always is used in the chart of accounts and meets the information objectives of general purpose financial statements, some reports for internal use, tax reports, and distribution of income to physicians. As information requirements of management grow, more fields are added to give the system the capability of providing additional information to facilitate planning, budgeting, decision making, and financial control.

First Digit. The first digit in the basic field identifies the major financial statement category.

1000	Assets
2000	Liabilities and owners' equity
3000	Revenues
4000	Adjustments and allowances
5000	Human resource expenses
6000	Physical resource expenses
7000	Purchased services and general and administrative expenses
8000	Nonoperating revenues and expenses

Second Digit. The second digit in the basic field identifies the primary classification of accounts within the major financial statement categories. These classifications follow the sequence in which the information is normally presented in financial statements, such as current assets and current liabilities in the statement of financial position. In the income statement, the second digit provides the minimum breakdown for uniformity among groups. If uniformity at this level is maintained, adequate information for most comparisons will be provided.

Statement of Financial Position Accounts

1000	Assets
1100-1300	Current assets
1400	Investments and long-term receivables
1500-1800	Noncurrent tangible assets
1900	Intangible and other assets
2000	Liabilities and owners' equity
2100-2300	Current liabilities
2400	Long-term liabilities
2500-2700	Owners' equity

Income Statement Accounts

3000	Revenues
3100	Gross charges—fee-for-service
3200	Adjusted gross charges—fee-for-service
3300	Gross charges—fee-for-service for prepaid practice
3400	Cash collected from patients—fee-for-service
3500	Cash collected from prepaid plan—discounted fee-for-service
3600-3700	Gross charges—prepaid contract
3800	Prepaid contract revenues
3900	Other revenues
4000	Adjustments and allowances to gross charges
4100-4500	Adjustments
4600-4800	Allowances and write-offs
4900	Provision for cash basis conversion

5000	Human resource expenses
5100	Physician salaries, distributions, and bonuses
5200	Physician benefits—owner/stockholder
5300	Physician extender salaries
5400	Ancillary department salaries
5500	Medical support salaries
5600	Administrative salaries
5700	Housekeeping, maintenance, and security salaries
5800	Other salaries
5900	Nonphysician employee benefits
6000	Physical resource expenses
6100-6300	Supplies and cost of goods sold
6400-6500	Occupancy and use—buildings and grounds
6600-6800	Occupancy and use—furniture, fixtures, and equipment
6900	Other occupancy and use expenses
7000	Purchased services and general and administrative expenses
7100	Purchased services—nonprepaid professional and medical
7200	Purchased services—prepaid professional and medical
7300	General and administrative expenses—purchased services
7400	General and administrative expenses—employee-related
7500	General and administrative expenses—liability insurance
7600-7700	Other general and administrative expenses
7800	Interest expenses
8000	Nonoperating revenues and expenses, income taxes, and extraordinary items
8100	Nonoperating revenues
8200	Nonoperating expenses
8300	Income taxes
8400	Extraordinary gains
8500	Extraordinary losses

Third Digit. The third digit in the basic field provides the maximum breakdown a smaller group should need for any purpose. For the group that does not use the additional fields, this digit also may be used to identify certain expenses with ancillary departments (such as laboratory and radiology).

Fourth Digit. The fourth digit in the basic field identifies subaccounts for groups that need more detail for control. For example, Account 6110 is entitled "Drugs and Medications." The fourth digit allows the group to accumulate the cost of up to nine classes of drugs and medications, if necessary.

By using the last two digits of the basic field, a variety of classification combinations can be obtained. Classification of revenue transactions by location of service or patient pay type are two suggested alternatives.

Suggested Location Breakdown

10	Group practice
20	Hospital
30	Patient residence
40	Nursing home
50	Ambulance
60	Urgent care facility
70	Ambulatory surgery unit
80-90	Other locations

Suggested Pay Type Breakdown

10	Private pay
20	Blue Cross/Blue Shield
30	Commercial insurance
40	Medicare
50	Medicaid
60	Workers' Compensation
70	Other state agencies
80	Collection agencies
90	Other pay types

For prepaid revenue, the last two digits in the basic field may be used to indicate the type of revenue by the third digit and the specific prepaid plan, if more than one, by the fourth digit.

Suggested Prepaid Revenue Type Breakdown

10-30	Capitation
40	Risk-sharing—hospitalization
50	Risk-sharing—outside referrals
60	Copayments
70	Coordination of benefits
80	Reinsurance recoveries
90	Other prepaid revenue types

Suggested Prepaid Plan Breakdown

01	HMO 1
02	HMO 2
03	HMO 3

Responsibility Center Field

This field is used to identify the responsibility centers (organizational units within medical groups having responsibility for revenues and/or expenses). The two-digit field provides for the accumulation of revenue and expense data by responsibility center and allows identification of up to 99 centers.

There are two major purposes for accumulating revenues and expenses by department: information for control and information for decision making. The cost accounting system described in Part II identifies costs relevant to each of these two major purposes. First, for control and for some decisions, only those costs incurred by a responsibility center and traceable to that center are relevant. Such costs are termed direct costs. Costs incurred in one responsibility center and allocated to another responsibility center cannot be controlled by the center receiving the allocation. Although the allocated costs may be useful for some decisions, they are not useful for control.

Second, for purposes of decision making (such as setting premiums or fees), it is necessary to know the full cost of providing the service. Full cost is determined by a two-step process. First, all costs are traced to the centers responsible for their incurrence (for example, to revenue-producing responsibility centers such as internal medicine, pediatrics, general surgery, laboratory, and radiology; and to service responsibility centers such as administration, data processing, and occupancy). Then, the costs of the service-only responsibility centers are allocated to the revenue-producing responsibility centers. Costs incurred in one responsibility center and allocated to another responsibility center are termed indirect costs of the second responsibility center. The full cost of providing a service includes the direct costs of the responsibility center providing the service as well as a fair share of the indirect costs incurred by other responsibility centers that support the revenue-producing centers.

Because each cost must be traceable to some responsibility center, responsibility centers must be identified carefully. It should not be necessary to prorate or allocate any cost for purposes of control. When a full cost is to be determined, manual worksheets or computer work files should be used to allocate the costs of service-only responsibility centers to revenue-producing responsibility centers. A detailed discussion of responsibility centers and determining full cost is contained in Part II, *Cost Accounting for Prepaid Medical Groups.*

Many smaller groups may want to develop limited cost information for a few ancillary departments without employing the responsibility center field for all transactions. The basic field of the account structure allows for vertical expansion, providing space to accumulate several categories of costs for a limited number of ancillary departments. Vertical expansion of the basic field can accommodate responsibility center information on salaries, supplies, cost of goods sold to patients, equipment rental, equipment depreciation, and maintenance of equipment.

Horizontal and vertical expansions of the account structure are illustrated below with the account used for salaries of ancillary department personnel as an example. Account 5400—Ancillary Department Salaries covers the salaries and bonuses of all employees in the medical group's ancillary departments, such as laboratory, radiology, physical therapy, and optical. Horizontal expansion

EXHIBIT 2-1
CHART OF ACCOUNTS STRUCTURE

Entity Field (1 Digit)	Basic Field (4 Digits): First Digit		Second Digit		Third Digit		Fourth Digit		Responsibility Center Field (2 Digits)	Provider Field[1] (2 Digits)
	BALANCE SHEET									
1-9	1	Assets	1-3	Current Assets	1-9	Minimum breakdown of items in primary classification	1-9	Optional maximum breakdown of items in primary classification	01-99	01-99
			4	Investments						
			5-8	Noncurrent Tangible Assets						
			9	Intangible and Other Assets						
	2	Liabilities and Owners' Equity	1-3	Current Liabilities	1-9	Minimum breakdown of items in primary classification	1-9	Optional maximum breakdown of items in primary classification		
			4	Long-Term Liabilities						
			5	Partners' Equity						
			6	Stockholders' Equity						
			7	Not-for-Profit Equity						
			8	Revenue and Expense Summary						
			9	Open						
	INCOME STATEMENT									
	3	Revenues	1	Gross Charges—FFS	1-9	Minimum breakdown of items in primary classification	1-9	Optional maximum breakdown of items in primary classification		
			2	Adjusted Gross Charges—FFS						

		3	Gross Charges—FFS for Prepaid Practice				
		4	Cash Collected—FFS				
		5	Cash Collected from Prepaid Plan—Discounted FFS				
		6-7	Gross Charges—Prepaid Contract				
		8	Prepaid Contract Revenues				
		9	Other Revenues				
4	Adjustments and Allowances to Gross Charges	1-9	Types of Adjustments and Allowances	1-9	Minimum breakdown of items in primary classification	1-9	Optional maximum breakdown of items in primary classification
5	Human Resource Expenses	1	Physician Salaries	1-9	Minimum breakdown of items in primary classification	1-9	Optional maximum breakdown of items in primary classification
		2	Physician Benefits				
		3	Physician Extender Salaries				
		4	Ancillary Department Salaries				
		5	Medical Support Salaries				
		6	Administrative Salaries				
		7	Housekeeping, Maintenance, and Security Salaries				
		8	Other Salaries				
		9	Nonphysician Employee Benefits				

continued

EXHIBIT 2-1
CHART OF ACCOUNTS STRUCTURE (continued)

Entity Field (1 Digit)	Basic Field (4 Digits)								Responsibility Center Field (2 Digits)	Provider Field[1] (2 Digits)
	First Digit		Second Digit		Third Digit		Fourth Digit			
	6	Physical Resource Expenses	1	Supplies Expense	1-9	Minimum breakdown of items in primary classification	1-9	Optional maximum breakdown of items in primary classification		
			2	Ancillary Department Supplies Expense						
			3	Cost of Goods Sold—Ancillary Departments						
			4	Occupancy and Use—Bldgs. and Grounds						
			5	Occupancy and Use—Bldg. Depreciation						
			6	Occupancy and Use—Rent/Lease—Furniture Fixtures, & Equipment						
			7	Occupancy and Use—Depr.—F, F, & E						
			8	Occupancy and Use Expenses—Other F, F, & E						
			9	Other Occupancy and Use Expenses						

7	Purchased Services and General and Administrative	1	Purchased Services—Nonprepaid Professional and Medical	1-9	Minimum breakdown of items in primary classification	1-9	Optional maximum breakdown of items in primary classification
		2	Purchased Services—Prepaid Professional and Medical				
		3	General and Administrative—Purchased Services				
		4	G & A Expenses—Employee-related				
		5	G & A—Liability Insurance				
		6-7	Other G & A Expenses				
		8	Interest Expenses				
8	Nonoperating Revenues and Expenses, Income Taxes, and Extraordinary Items	1	Nonoperating Revenues	1-9	Minimum breakdown of items in primary classification	1-9	Optional maximum breakdown of items in primary classification
		2	Nonoperating Expenses				
		3	Income Taxes				
		4	Extraordinary Gains				
		5	Extraordinary Losses				

[1] Can be expanded

of the account structure by using the responsibility center field provides the following accounts for salaries in these four ancillary departments:

5400-50	Salaries—laboratory
5400-51	Salaries—radiology
5400-52	Salaries—physical therapy
5400-53	Salaries—optical

This example relates only to ancillary department salaries. Other costs would be traced to medical and surgical departments as well as to cost centers such as administration, data processing, and occupancy. Each group must determine its own responsibility center designations.

Salaries for each ancillary department may be further detailed according to group needs by using the third and fourth digits of the basic field. The structure can accomodate the identification of up to 99 salary types. The following illustration expands laboratory salaries to five types by using the fourth digit.

5401-50	Salaries of professional technicians—laboratory
5403-50	Salaries of nurses—laboratory
5404-50	Salaries of medical receptionists and appointments—laboratory
5405-50	Salaries of medical records personnel—laboratory
5409-50	Other salaries—laboratory

On the other hand, vertical expansion of the basic field provides information for up to nine ancillary departments for six categories of cost. The accounts for salaries in the four ancillary departments would be as follows:

5410	Salaries—laboratory
5420	Salaries—radiology
5430	Salaries—physical therapy
5440	Salaries—optical

If necessary, an even further breakdown of ancillary salaries is possible by using the fourth digit. Laboratory salaries may be expanded as follows:

5411	Salaries of professional technicians—laboratory
5413	Salaries of nurses—laboratory
5414	Salaries of medical receptionists and appointments—laboratory
5415	Salaries of medical records—laboratory
5416	Other salaries—laboratory

Each medical group should use the fourth digit of the basic field to best serve its own needs. Only the first three digits (and in some cases, only the first two digits) are required for uniform accumulation and reporting of data.

Additional information contained in Part II of this text describes and illustrates a cost accounting system developed around the chart of accounts. Both horizontal and vertical expansion of the accounts are explained.

Provider Field

The last field is used to identify revenues and expenses by health care provider (physician or physician extender). Through the use of this field, operating reports may be prepared according to health care provider. This field can also be used to indicate type of provider instead of each provider. As an example, this information would indicate the total cost of purchasing specific specialty physician services outside of the group and, in conjunction with other information, would help in making a decision on adding a particular type of physician to the group. Use of the provider field is further illustrated in Part II.

Summary Accounts

A feature of this chart of accounts is the use of summary accounts. A zero in the fourth digit of the basic field, or zeros in the third and fourth digits, indicate a summary account that may represent the total of a number of related subaccounts. For example, Account 6480 accumulates the cost of utilities. If no greater detail is desired, Account 6480 can be used to accumulate all utilities. If greater detail is required, the fourth digit may be used to identify types of utilities as follows:

6481	Water
6482	Electricity
6483	Gas
6484	Fuel oil
6485	Steam
6486	Waste disposal
6487-6489	Other utilities

The amount of detail required is left up to the groups using the chart of accounts. The only requirement that must be observed in creating additional accounts is that these accounts conform to the summary accounts as defined in the chart of accounts.

Summary

The chart of accounts outlined in this chapter is flexible, allowing multiple objectives to be achieved for a wide range of medical groups. The numerical coding structure is based upon four fields providing for: entity, nature of classification (such as expenses), responsibility center, and provider. The group may select only those fields needed to meet its financial information objectives.

By specifying only three digits in the basic field showing nature of classification, the group may accumulate extra detail through the fourth digit.

Chapter 3

CRAHCA Prepaid Group Chart of Accounts

The financial position of a medical group is presented in a statement of financial position (balance sheet) showing the group's assets, liabilities, and owners' equity (capital) on a given date. The income statement is used to summarize results of group operations for a period of time to determine if the group is operating efficiently. This chapter outlines the basic accounts that may be used for accumulation of information for financial position presentation and to summarize the results of group operations for a period of time.

STATEMENT OF FINANCIAL POSITION ACCOUNTS

1000 ASSETS

1100-1300 Current Assets

Cash and other assets that are expected to be converted to cash, sold, or consumed in the normal course of operations within one year.

1110-1140—Cash—Unrestricted—Banks Cash on deposit in banks that is immediately available for general operating purposes. Cash restricted for other than general operating purposes should be included in Account 1410—Cash—Restricted.

1110—General Checking Accounts Cash on deposit in banks that is immediately available for general operating purposes.

1120—Payroll Checking Accounts Cash on deposit in banks that is immediately available for payroll transactions.

1130-1140—Other Checking Accounts Cash on deposit in banks that is immediately available for other disbursements.

1150-1160—Cash—Unrestricted—On Hand

1150—Change Fund

1160—Petty Cash Cash on hand that is reimbursed periodically for amounts expended.

1170—Marketable Securities and Short-Term Investments Short-term investments intended to be used to finance current operations, including savings accounts,marketable securities, U.S. Government securities, certificates of deposit, and other securities that are traded regularly. Securities not intended to be used to finance current operations should be included in Account 1430—Investments in Securities.

1210—Accounts Receivable—Fee-for-Service Amounts owed to the group by patients, third parties, employer groups, unions, individuals, subscribers, and others. This account is usually a control account for individual accounts receivable balances that may be contained in a subsidiary ledger.

1211-1219	Groups using the fourth digit of the basic field to break down payors should use the pay types specified in Chapter 2. Additionally, groups receiving discounted fee-for-service payments from an IPA type prepaid plan(s) or preferred provider organization(s) should designate an account for each plan or PPO.

1220—Accounts Receivable—Prepaid Contracts Amounts owed to the group by HMOs and other prepaid plans. This account is usually a control account for individual accounts receivable balances that may be contained in a subsidiary ledger.

1221	Accounts Receivable—Capitation—HMO (Plan A)
1222	Accounts Receivable—Capitation—HMO (Plan B)
1223	Accounts Receivable—Capitation—Medicare
1224	Accounts Receivable—Capitation—Medicaid
1225	Accounts Receivable—Capitation—State, County, City
1226	Accounts Receivable—Capitation—Individual (nongroup)
1227	Accounts Receivable—Reinsurance Claims
1228	Accounts Receivable—Copayments and Coordination of Benefits
1229	Accounts Receivable—Other Prepaid Contracts

1230—Allowance for Uncollectible Receivables Estimated amount of uncollectible receivables. An aging schedule of accounts receivable is usually required to determine the periodic credits to this account.

1231	Allowance for Estimated Uncollectible Receivables —Private Pay

---

1240—Allowance for Contractual Adjustments Estimated adjustments for third-party agencies.

1241-1249	The fourth digit of the basic field should parallel the account classification of payers in Accounts 1211-1219, plus accounts for collection agencies employed by the group and an interim clearing account.

1250—Allowance for Conversion to Cash Basis An account used only with cash basis accounting to convert accounts receivable (Accounts 1210-1220) from accrual basis to cash basis. This allowance reduces the accounts receivable balance to zero. This account is used in conjunction with Account 4900—Provision for Cash Basis Conversion.

1260—Notes Receivable—Short-Term Amounts owed to the group by other entities where the obligation is represented by a note with a maturity of one year or less.

1280-1290—Other Short-Term Receivables Short-term receivables such as interest that has been earned but not yet received.

1281	Interest Receivable

1310-1330—Supply Inventories Costs of unused supplies. The group should establish an inventory policy defining which items are charged to an inventory account at the date of purchase and which items are expensed as acquired.

1311	Drugs and Medications
1312	Medical Supplies
1313	Administrative Supplies

1314 Forms
1315 Housekeeping and Maintenance Supplies
1316 Linen Supplies
1317-1339 Other Supplies

1340-1370—Ancillary Department Supplies Costs of unused supplies and inventory of goods held for resale that are distinct to an ancillary department. The type of department may be identified either by using Account 1340 with specific department designated by the responsibility center field or by designating Accounts 1340-1370 as specific ancillary service department accounts.

Example: Assignment of responsibility field codes to each department.
1340-50 Laboratory Supplies
1340-51 Radiology Supplies
1340-52 Optical Supplies
In this case, radiology supplies (film, special materials) would be charged to Account 1340-51. Office supplies inventoried in the radiology department would be charged to Account 1313-51.

For the group that does not use the responsibility center field, Accounts 1340-1370 may be used to identify supplies in ancillary departments.
1340—Laboratory Supplies
1350—Radiology Supplies
1360—Optical Supplies
1370—Other Ancillary Supplies

1380—Prepaid Expenses Payments for goods or services that will benefit future operations.

1381 Prepaid Interest
1382 Prepaid Insurance
1383 Prepaid Rent
1384 Prepaid Taxes
1385 Prepaid Dues
1386-1389 Other Prepaid Expenses

1390—Other Current Assets

1400 **Investments and Long-Term Receivables**
Long-term investments in securities, restricted cash, property (not used for operations), and receivables due beyond one year. Assets recorded in these accounts will not be used to finance operations.
1410—Cash—Restricted Cash restricted for other than general operating purposes.
1420—Long-Term Receivables Receivables that will mature beyond one year.
1430—Investments in Securities Investments held for long-term or restricted purposes not included in Account 1170—Marketable Securities and Short-Term Investments.
1440—Investments in Affiliates Investments in affiliated companies.
1450—Property Held for Future Use Investments in land and buildings not currently used in group operations but held for future use.

1500-1800 **Noncurrent Tangible Assets**
Long-lived, tangible assets used in the operations of the group. Assets recorded in these accounts generally have a useful life in excess of one year.

1500 **Real Property**
1510—Land Acquisition value or cost of land owned by a group. If land is purchased, this account includes the purchase price and other costs, such as legal fees and excavation costs, that may be necessary to put the land in condition for its intended use. This account also should include the costs of off-site improvements or assessments, such as charges for sewer and water lines, assessments for paving and sidewalks, and any other land-related expenditures of a nondepreciable nature. Land does not deteriorate with use or with the passage of time; therefore, no depreciation is charged. If land is acquired by gift, this account reflects its appraised value at the time of acquisition.
1530—Land Improvements All land-related expenditures for group operations that are amortized to Account 6530—Amortization— Land Improvements, over their useful lives. For example, the cost of on-site sewer and water lines, parking lots, shrubbery, fences, and sidewalks may be charged to this account.
1540—Buildings Acquisition value or cost of buildings plus the cost of any subsequent additions. Architectural, consulting, and legal fees applicable to acquisition or construction should be charged to this account.
1560—Capital Leases—Buildings Initial cost measured by the

present value of future lease payments, not in excess of fair market value and excluding all interest, financing charges, maintenance, and taxes, for building acquired under a capital lease.

A capital lease meets any of the following criteria.

Lease transfers ownership to lessee during lease term.
Lease contains a bargain purchase option.
Lease term is 75 percent or more of estimated economic life of property.
Present value of minimum lease payments equals 90 percent or more of fair market value of leased property, minus lessor investment tax credit.[1]

The initial cost of a depreciable asset capitalized under a capital lease should be amortized to its residual value over the term of the lease or over the life of the asset if the lease transfers title.
1570—Leasehold Improvements Costs of any depreciable improvements to leased land or buildings. Depreciation should be charged for the estimated life of the improvement or the remaining term of the lease, whichever is shorter.
1580—Construction in Progress Costs pertaining to new structures that have not yet been placed in service. At the time the structure is placed in service, its cost is transferred to the appropriate asset account.
1590—Other Real Property Real property that does not fit the above categories and is used in the operations of the group.

1600 Accumulated Depreciation—Real Property
Contra-asset accounts used to accumulate the sum of depreciation recorded for real property. (Note that the last two digits of each accumulated depreciation account match the last two digits of the related asset account.)
1630—Accumulated Depreciation—Land Improvements
1640—Accumulated Depreciation—Buildings
1660—Accumulated Depreciation—Capital Leases—Buildings
1670—Accumulated Depreciation—Leasehold Improvements
1680-1690—Accumulated Depreciation—Other Real Property

---

[1]FASB Statement No. 13, *Accounting for Leases,* November, 1976.

1700 Furniture, Fixtures, and Equipment

Costs of furniture, fixtures, and equipment. A common criterion for capitalization is a unit cost of $250 or more, with smaller items expensed in the supplies accounts (6100 and 6200). Each group should determine rules for the capitalizing or expensing of the costs of furniture, fixtures, and equipment. Other criteria for capitalization are:

A unit cost sufficiently large to justify the cost of control incident to an equipment or property ledger.

Depreciable life of two years or more but less than the life of buildings to which the equipment or fixtures may be affixed

Used in group operations

Sufficient individuality and size to make control feasible by means of identification tags or numbers.

Leased Equipment: In this chart of accounts, equipment acquired under a lease and capitalized as an asset is included with owned equipment. For external reporting, it may be necessary to maintain additional records of capital lease equipment and purchased equipment. The addition of separate equipment and accumulated depreciation accounts for categories of equipment requires the use of the fourth digit.

1710—Furniture, Fixtures, and Equipment—Group Services
Furniture, fixtures, and equipment used by the medical group for the direct provision of services to patients. Includes reception room furniture and fixtures.

1711	Medical Equipment
1712	Reception Room Furniture and Fixtures

1720-1740—Furniture, Fixtures, and Equipment—Ancillary Departments Furniture, fixtures, and equipment used in ancillary departments, that is, laboratory, radiology, or other departments. For the group that does not use the responsibility center field, Accounts 1720-1740 may be used to identify equipment for various ancillary departments.

1720—Furniture, Fixtures, and Equipment—Laboratory

1730—Furniture, Fixtures, and Equipment—Radiology

1740—Furniture, Fixtures, and Equipment—Other Ancillary Departments

1750—Furniture, Fixtures, and Equipment—Office

1760—Furniture, Fixtures, and Equipment—Data Processing

1770—Furniture, Fixtures, and Equipment—Transportation

1780—Furniture, Fixtures, and Equipment—Maintenance
1790—Furniture, Fixtures, and Equipment—Other

1800 **Accumulated Depreciation—Furniture, Fixtures, and Equipment**
Contra-asset accounts used to accumulate the sum of depreciation recorded for furniture, fixtures and equipment.
1810—Accumulated Depreciation—Furniture, Fixtures, and Equipment—Group Services
1820—Accumulated Depreciation—Furniture, Fixtures, and Equipment—Laboratory
1830—Accumulated Depreciation—Furniture, Fixtures, and Equipment—Radiology
1840—Accumulated Depreciation—Furniture, Fixtures, and Equipment—Other Ancillary Departments
1850—Accumulated Depreciation—Furniture, Fixtures, and Equipment—Office
1860—Accumulated Depreciation—Furniture, Fixtures, and Equipment—Data Processing
1870—Accumulated Depreciation—Furniture, Fixtures, and Equipment—Transportation
1880—Accumulated Depreciation—Furniture, Fixtures, and Equipment—Maintenance
1890—Accumulated Depreciation—Furniture, Fixtures, and Equipment—Other

1900 **Intangible and Other Assets**
Costs of property rights without physical substance that will benefit future operations of the group. Intangible assets are purchased from external sources, provide future benefit, and are relatively long-lived. Other assets include long-term prepayments, deferred charges, and assets not included in other categories.
1910—Organization Costs Costs incurred in the original incorporation of a professional corporation. These costs are generally amortized over a period of five years.
1920—Goodwill Excess of costs over the fair market value of identifiable assets in the purchase of an entire practice. These costs are generally amortized over a period not to exceed 40 years.
1930—Relocation Costs Costs of moving the group practice or a material segment of it that will benefit future operations. These costs are amortized over a reasonable period of time.
1940—Other Intangible Assets

1950—Noncurrent Prepaid Expenses Costs incurred (payments) for goods or services that will benefit future operations (beyond a year).

1951	Noncurrent Prepaid Interest
1952	Noncurrent Prepaid Insurance
1953	Noncurrent Prepaid Rent
1954	Noncurrent Prepaid Taxes
1955	Noncurrent Prepaid Dues
1956-1959	Other Noncurrent Prepaid Expenses

1960-1990—Other Assets

2000 LIABILITIES AND OWNERS' EQUITY

2100-2300 Current Liabilities

2100 Current Liabilities—Payables

Liabilities that mature and require payment from current assets or the creation of other current liabilities within one year.

2110-2120—Accounts Payable Amounts on open account owed by the group to outside persons or organizations for goods and services received by the group. These accounts are usually control accounts for individual accounts payable balances that may be contained in a subsidiary ledger.

2130—Contract Claims Payable Amounts owed by the group to providers outside the group for medical services to HMO patients assigned to the group. If desired, this account may be combined with Account 2350—Estimated Contract Claims Payable.

2131	Accrued Referral Liability. This account is used to record the group's liability for unpaid referral care provided to prepaid patients for whom the group receives capitation payments. Additional accounts can be used to designate specific ancillary or physician services.
2135	Accrued Hospitalization Liability. This account is used to record the group's liability for unpaid hospitalization amounts.

2140—Notes and Loans Payable Liabilities of the group as evidenced by promissory notes to various creditors due and payable within one year.

2141	Notes and Loans Payable—Vendors
2142	Notes and Loans Payable—Banks
2143	Notes and Loans Payable—Physicians
2144	Notes and Loans Payable—Stockholders/Partners
2145-2149	Other Notes and Loans Payable

2150—Long-Term Debt—Current Portion Long-term debt that matures in one year or less and is to be paid out of current assets. Long-term debt that is to be refunded or paid out of a sinking fund should be classified as a noncurrent liability.

2160—Capital Lease Obligation—Current Portion Present value of future lease payments, excluding interest and finance charges, to be made within one year on long-term leases that have been capitalized. The present value of lease payments beyond one year is included in Account 2440—Capital Lease Obligations—Long-Term Portion. Refer to Account 1560—Capital Leases—Buildings, for capitalization criteria.

2170—Construction Contracts Payable

2180—Bank Overdrafts Payable Overdrafts on banks having no other free balances in amounts sufficient to offset.

2190—Other Current Liabilities Payable

2200 **Current Liabilities—Payroll**

Liabilities related to payroll for amounts withheld from employees or otherwise accrued.

2210-2240—Payroll Withholdings Actual liabilities for payroll withholdings. These accounts are credited for amounts withheld from employees and are debited when payment is made to the appropriate agency or authority.

2210—Federal and State Tax Withholdings Payable

2211	Federal Income Tax Withholdings Payable
2212	State Income Tax Withholdings Payable
2213	FICA Tax Withholdings Payable
2214-2219	Other Tax Withholdings Payable

2220—Insurance Withholdings Payable

2221	Health Insurance Withholdings Payable
2222	Life Insurance Withholdings Payable
2223	State Disability Insurance Withholdings Payable
2224-2229	Other Insurance Withholdings Payable

2230-2240—Other Payroll Withholdings Payable United Way, savings programs, union dues, parking fees, and other payroll withholdings.

2250—Accrued Payroll Liabilities Actual or estimated liabilities for payroll obligations. These accounts are credited when the payroll expense is incurred and are debited when payment is made to the appropriate employee, agency, or authority.

2251	Accrued Payroll
2252	Accrued Vacation, Holiday, and Sick Pay (compensated absences)
2253	Other Accrued Salary, Bonuses, and Wages
2254	Accrued FICA Taxes Payable
2255	Accrued State Unemployment Taxes Payable
2256	Accrued Federal Unemployment Taxes Payable
2257	Accrued State Workers' Compensation Payable
2258-2259	Other Accrued Payroll Liabilities

If desired, Account 2254 may be combined with 2213.

2260-2290—Other Payroll Liabilities

2300 Current Liabilities—Other

Current liabilities not included in Accounts 2100 and 2200.

2310-2320—Accrued Liabilities—Nonpayroll Current liabilities accrued at the end of an accounting period to reflect the proper amount of expenses for the group under the accrual basis of accounting. Generally, no invoices or other billings are received within the accounting period, and the liability for these items is estimated or obtained from other sources.

2311	Accrued Rent
2312	Accrued Interest
2313	Accrued Insurance
2314	Accrued Income Taxes
2315	Accrued Property Taxes
2316	Accrued Sales/Excise Taxes
2317-2329	Other Accrued Liabilities

2330—Advances from and Settlements Due to Third-Party Agencies

2331	Advances from Medicare
2332	Advances from Medicaid
2333-2334	Advances from Other Third-Party Agencies. Amounts owed to third-party agencies for current financing and other advances that are due and payable within one year.
2335	Reimbursement Settlements Due to Medicare
2336	Reimbursement Settlements Due to Medicaid
2337-2339	Reimbursement Settlements Due to Other Third-Party Agencies. Amounts owed to third-party agencies arising from reimbursement settlements.

2340—Patient Deposits Amounts paid by patients in advance of specific services. This account is not to be used for payments received under a capitation plan.

2350—Estimated Contract Claims Payable Liability account used to record an estimation of the amounts owed to providers outside the group for medical services to prepaid patients of the group for which invoices have not been received. These are frequently referred to as "incurred but not reported" (IBNR) claims and are normally estimated using historical lag factors. When invoiced, the claims should be transferred to Account 2130—Contract Claims Payable.

2351	Accrued Referral Claims
2353	Accrued Hospitalization Claims

2360—Deferred Revenue—Capitation or Prepaid Plan Revenue received in one period from capitation or prepaid plans that is applicable to services to be rendered in some future period.

2370—Other Current Deferred Revenue Revenue received in one period that is applicable to services to be rendered in some future period. Any deferred revenue that is not earned within one year is treated as a long-term liability.

2380—Deferred Income Taxes—Current Portion Timing difference between tax on income reported in financial statements and tax on income reported in the tax return, when the timing difference is related to a current asset.

2390—Other Current Liabilities Current liabilities not recorded elsewhere.

2400 **Long-Term Liabilities**

Liabilities that will mature and require payment at some future time beyond one year. The current portion of any long-term liability should be included in Account 2150—Long-Term Debt—Current Portion, except those obligations to be refinanced or paid from a sinking fund.

2410—Long-Term Notes Payable Notes payable that mature more than one year from financial statement date.

2420—Mortgage Payable Long-term liability secured by a mortgage on real property that matures more than one year from financial statement date.

2430—Construction Loans Loans during construction stages that mature more than one year from financial statement date.

2440—Capital Lease Obligation—Long-Term Portion Present value of future lease payments, excluding interest and finance charges, that will be made beyond one year on leases that have been capitalized. Refer to Account 1560—Capital Leases—Buildings, for capitalization criteria.

2460—Deferred Third-Party Revenue Timing difference or difference in accounting methods between financial statements and third-party reimbursement accounting methods.

2461	Deferred Third-Party Revenue—Medicare
2462	Deferred Third-Party Revenue—Medicaid
2463	Deferred Third-Party Revenue—Other

2470—Deferred Compensation Liability for compensation to physicians and employees whose payment is being deferred until some future date.

2480—Deferred Income Taxes—Long-Term Portion Timing difference between tax on income reported in financial statements and tax on income reported in the tax return, when the timing difference is related to a noncurrent asset.

2490—Other Long-Term Liabilities Liabilities that will mature beyond one year and are not included above.

2500 **Partners' Equity**

Net assets of the partnership; that is, the excess of the partnership entity's assets over its liabilities. The balances in these accounts are the cumulative results of the partners' investments, past earnings and losses, and withdrawals.

2510—Contributed Capital Amounts invested by the partners. Subaccounts should be established for each partner.

2520—Undistributed Earnings Difference between revenues and expenses allocated to the partners as earned capital. Subaccounts should be established for each partner. (Accounts 2510 and 2520 are commonly combined into one account called Partners' Capital).

2530—Partners' Drawing Accounts Withdrawals made by a partner during an operating period. At the end of the period, this account is closed into Account 2520.

2590—Other Partnership Equity

2600 Stockholders' Equity

Net assets of the corporation; that is, the excess of the corporate entity's assets over its liabilities. The balances in these accounts are the cumulative result of the owners' investments and the equity originating from earnings retained by the corporation.

2610—Preferred Stock

2620—Common Stock

2630—Capital Contributed in Excess of Par Capital contributed by owners in excess of the par or stated value of the capital stock.

2640—Donated Capital Increase in owners' equity due to assets contributed to the corporation.

2660—Dividends Distribution to owners of retained earnings paid in cash, shares of stock, or property. This account is closed into Account 2670 at the end of the fiscal year.

2670—Retained Earnings—Unappropriated Net income (or loss) over the life of the corporation minus all distributions to owners and appropriations of retained earnings carried in Account 2680.

2680—Retained Earnings—Appropriated Restrictions placed on portions of earnings retained in the corporation. These restrictions may temporarily limit the amount of dividends available for distribution to owners. This account should be used to record creation of unfunded reserves required by state HMO laws or regulations.

2690—Treasury Stock Capital stock repurchased by the corporation that has not been retired. Treasury stock is usually carried at acquisition cost.

2700 Not-for-Profit Equity

Excess of the not-for-profit entity's assets over its liabilities. The balances in these accounts are the cumulative results of original investments, grants, gifts, donations, and revenues and expenditures.

2710—Unrestricted Fund Balance Unrestricted equity of the not-for-profit entity.
2720—Restricted Fund Balance Restricted equity of a not-for-profit entity. It offsets assets restricted by gift, law, or board of directors' designation.
2730-2750—Other Fund Balances Equity of other designated funds such as plant and equipment fund or endowment fund.
2760-2780—Reserves Reserves created through budgetary accounting, such as reserves for encumbrances, reserves for inventory, and appropriations of unrestricted fund balance created by board of directors' action, including unfunded reserves required by state HMO laws or regulations.

2800 **Revenue and Expense Summary**
A summary account for use in the closing of revenue and expense accounts when financial statements are prepared.

INCOME STATEMENT ACCOUNTS

3000 REVENUES

There are different measures of fee-for-service revenues, depending upon whether the group identifies gross charges, adjustments, and allowances; whether the group uses the cash or accrual basis of accounting; and whether the prepaid plan pays discounted fee-for-service or capitation.

The major changes from the 1979 CRAHCA Chart of Accounts for Medical Groups are in revenue accounts. Account 3300, previously called Net Revenue—Fee-for-Service, was not used by medical groups and has been changed to Gross Charges—Fee-for-Service for Prepaid Practice. Account 3500, previously a part of 3500-3700 Gross Charges—Contract, is now Cash Collected from Prepaid Plan—Discounted Fee-for-Service, providing separate accounts for fee-for-service revenues and prepaid revenues when the group is reimbursed on a fee-for-service basis and uses cash basis accounting. Accounts 3600-3700 will continue to be used for internal analysis by department and for the prepaid plan as a whole.

3100 **Gross Charges—Fee-for-Service**
Full dollar value, at the group's established rates, of services provided to patients who are not on a prepayment or capitation plan. Gross charges include the value of charity and free services as well as services for which payment is expected from patients or third-party reimbursing agencies.

Fee-for-service revenue accounts (3100 and 3200) and adjustment accounts (4100-4400) may be detailed further. Suggested breakdowns, using Account 3100 as an example, are as follows:

Pay Type

3110	Private Pay
3120	Blue Cross/Blue Shield
3130	Commercial Insurance
3140	Medicare
3150	Medicaid
3160	Workers' Compensation
3170	Other State Agencies
3180-3190	Other Pay Types

Location

3110	Group Practice
3120	Hospital
3130	Patient Residence
3140	Nursing Home
3150	Ambulance
3160	Urgent Care Facility
3170	Ambulatory Surgery Unit
3180-3190	Other Patient Locations

It is possible to combine the two breakdowns by assigning pay type to the third digit and location to the fourth. For example, gross charges for private pay at the clinic would be Account 3111, and adjusted gross charges for Medicare patients in a nursing home would be Account 3244.

3200 **Adjusted Gross Charges—Fee-for-Service**

Billings to patients for whom services are provided by the group and who are not on a prepayment or capitation plan. Adjusted gross charges represent the amount the group bills to patients and expects to collect. This account is equivalent to gross charges (Account 3100) less adjustments (Accounts 4100-4400). If gross charges and adjustments are used, this account is not necessary. However, if the group chooses to recognize adjusted gross charges (rather than gross charges) as revenues, the gross charges account (3100) and the adjustments accounts (4100-4400) are not used.

3300 **Gross Charges—Fee-for-Service for Prepaid Practice**
Billings to HMOs or prepaid plans for services provided to prepaid patients on a fee-for-service or discounted fee-for-service basis. If this account is used, Account 4200 will adjust gross charges to reflect appropriate discounts and Account 3500 is not used.

The fourth digit may be used to identify the gross charges for a particular prepaid plan or employer contract.

3400 **Cash Collected from Patients—Fee-for-Service**
Account used by any medical group recording revenues on the basis of cash collected from fee-for-service patients. If Account 3400 is used, Accounts 3100 and 3200 and related adjustments and allowances are not used.

3500 **Cash Collected from Prepaid Plan—Discounted Fee-for-Service**
Account used by any medical group recording discounted fee-for-service revenues collected from a prepaid plan on the cash basis of accounting. If Account 3500 is used, Account 3300 and related adjustments and allowances are not used.

The fourth digit may be used to identify the cash collected from a particular prepaid plan or employer contract.

3600-3700 **Gross Charges—Prepaid Contract**
Full dollar value, measured in fee-for-service equivalent gross charges, of services provided to prepaid patients assigned to the group. These accounts are used to evaluate departmental performance and are offset by Account 4500—Prepaid Contract Adjustments—Inside Services. Account 4500 is debited when these accounts are credited. This procedure balances contract gross charges when determining group income.

3800 **Prepaid Contract Revenues**
Capitation payments or premiums paid to the group. This account can be broken down by individual contract plan. Between the digits in the basic field and the responsibility center and provider fields, there is considerable flexibility on the quantity and type of information captured.

The third digit may be used to identify the type of prepaid revenues:

10-30	Capitation or premium revenues
40	Risk sharing—hospitalization
50	Risk sharing—outside referrals
60	Copayments
70	Coordination of benefits
80	Reinsurance recoveries
90	Other

The fourth digit may be used to identify the revenue from a particular prepaid plan.

3900 Other Revenues
Revenues from activities other than those of the group, such as an adjacent parking lot considered necessary to operations.

4000 ADJUSTMENTS AND ALLOWANCES TO GROSS CHARGES

Adjustments are the differences between the full dollar value of the group's services and the amounts actually billed to patients or third-party agencies. Adjustments include charitable adjustments, contractual adjustments, courtesy adjustments, employee discounts, etc. Allowances are the differences between adjusted gross charges and net revenues. Allowances include write-offs for bad debts and settlements. Most adjustments and allowances apply only to fee-for-service gross charges.

4100-4500 Adjustments
Adjustments to fee-for-service gross charges that represent the value of services performed for which payment is not expected.

4100 Charity Adjustments
Differences between the full dollar value of services provided (gross charges) to charity patients and the amount (if any) to be received in payment for these services. These debits and the corresponding credits to the appropriate accounts receivable account should be recorded at the same time the gross charges are recorded. Charity patients should be identified at the time service is provided, and any write-offs for charitable services should not be made to Account 4600, Provision for Bad Debts.

4200 **Contractual Adjustments**
Differences between the gross charges for services rendered and the contractually agreed-upon reimbursement for such services. This account also includes any differences between gross charges and reimbursable charges as determined by third-party reimbursing agencies (either indemnity insurers or HMOs reimbursing on a discounted fee-for-service basis). This account can be broken down using the revenue type categories described following Account 3800.

4300 **Courtesy Adjustments**
Differences between the gross charges for services rendered and the amounts actually charged for such services. This account is used for "policy adjustments," such as discounts to clergy and nongroup physicians, and may also be debited for adjustments made at the specific request of group physicians on behalf of patients who would not otherwise qualify for an adjustment.

4400 **Employee Discounts**
Differences between the gross charges for services rendered to employees and their immediate families and the amounts (if any) to be received in payment for these services. As with charity patients, the entry to this account should be made at the time of service.

4500 **Prepaid Contract Adjustments—Inside Services**
Contra-revenue account to Accounts 3600-3700, Gross Charges—Contract; this account is debited whenever Accounts 3600-3700 are credited and always has an equal contra value to Accounts 3600-3700. Accounts 3600-3700 may be used as performance measures in internal reports, Account 4500 may be used to evaluate prepaid contracts, and Account 3800 may be used as the measure of capitation revenue in the income statement.

4600-4800 **Allowances and Write-offs**
Differences between the amount the group expects to collect for fee-for-service services (for example, adjusted gross charges) and the amount actually collected. Write-offs include bad debts, settlements made with certain patients or agencies, and accounts assigned to collection agencies.

4600 **Provision for Bad Debts**
Periodic estimate of uncollectible accounts receivable and notes receivable. An aging schedule of accounts receivable may be

used to estimate the amount of uncollectible accounts. Other methods may be used, but a consistent and justifiable method of estimating the periodic charge to provision for bad debts (and the corresponding credit to Account 1230—Allowance for Uncollectible Receivables) should be applied systematically. Account 1230 is debited when specific accounts are deemed uncollectible. Most groups usually recognize bad debts only for private pay patients, for example, Account 4601. Settlements with third-party agencies should be recorded in Account 4700.

4601	Provision for Bad Debts—Private Pay
4602-4609	Provision for Bad Debts—Other Pay Types

4700 **Settlements**

Differences between adjusted gross charges and the amounts actually collected as settlements for particular accounts. Settlements may be made with individual patients or with third-party reimbursing agencies. These accounts should be classified using the pay type categories described earlier. Settlements with individual private pay patients should be recorded in Account 4710. Settlements with third-party reimbursing agencies should be recorded in their respective accounts. Any year-end-cost reimbursement settlement involving a prepayment to a third-party agency is charged to this account (4700), and a corresponding credit is recorded in the appropriate accounts payable. If a group receives more than its established rates or its anticipated adjusted gross charges from a third-party reimbursing agency, the difference should be credited to the settlements accounts and debited to the appropriate accounts receivable.

4800 **Collection Agency Write-offs**

Any accounts turned over to a collection agency. The corresponding accounts receivable should be credited. If the group wants to identify separately private pay accounts turned over to collection agencies, Account 4810 would be debited. These accounts should be credited as cash is received from collection agencies.

4900 **Provision for Cash Basis Conversion**

Used to convert revenues recorded on the accrual basis to collections recorded on the cash basis. This adjustment is optional and is provided for the group that may wish to compute revenues on both the cash and accrual bases. This account is used in conjunction with Account 1250—Allowance for Conversion to Cash Basis.

5000-7000 OPERATING EXPENSES

On the accrual basis, expenses are resources consumed in the process of generating revenue, regardless of when payment for the resources occurs. Operating expenses are expired costs incurred in the process of providing medical services to group patients and exclude all costs pertaining to nonoperating activities such as general investments, endowments, etc.

A change in expense classification from the 1979 CRAHCA Chart of Accounts must be noted. Account 7100, Purchased Services—Medical and Professional, has been separated into Account 7100, Purchased Services—Nonprepaid Professional and Medical, and Account 7200, Purchased Services—Prepaid Professional and Medical. The old Account 7200, Purchased Services—Electronic Data Processing, is now included in Account 7300, General and Administrative Expenses—Purchased Services, as Account 7370—Electronic Data Processing Services.

5000 HUMAN RESOURCE EXPENSES

All forms of personal compensation, including salaries regularly paid or stipulated to be paid (before deductions), to individuals for services performed while on the payroll of the medical group. For the purpose of comparisons with peer medical groups or comparative data services, salaries also may include the fair market value of services donated to the group by persons performing in an employee capacity. The credit for the donated services should be made to Account 2640—Donated Capital. Reimbursement of independent contractors, such as consulting physicians or an outside laboratory, should be excluded from human resource expenses and recorded in Accounts 7110-7190—Purchased Services—Professional and Medical, for services provided to nonprepaid patients of the group and in Accounts 7210-7290—Purchased Services—Prepaid Professional and Medical, for services provided to prepaid patients of the group.

5100 **Physician Salaries, Distributions, and Bonuses**
All payments to physician-owners and physician-employees, including salaries, bonuses, and other distributions to physicians. **5110-5120—Physician Salaries—Owner/Stockholder** Salaries paid to physician-owners. A separate account (5130) can be used to record bonuses paid in addition to regular salaries; however, if the group desires to combine all physician distributions, this

account (5110) should be used.

5130—Physician Distributions and Bonuses—Owner/Stockholder Payments other than salaries to physician-owners.

5140—Physician-Employee Salaries Salaries and bonuses of all physicians employed by the group to provide regular medical services to patients.

5150—Physician-Employee Bonuses Payments other than salaries to employed physicians.

5160—Physician Administrative Salaries Salaries or fees paid to physicians for services in an administrative capacity, such as medical director, corporate officer, or member of the board or executive committee.

5200 **Physician Benefits**

Benefits provided to physician-owners by the group, including payroll-related taxes, insurance, and pensions. Groups not wishing the detailed breakdown provided by the fourth digit may use Accounts 5210, 5220, and 5230 for tax, insurance, and pension costs, respectively.

5210—Payroll Taxes

5211	Payroll Taxes—FICA
5212	Payroll Taxes—Federal Unemployment
5213	Payroll Taxes—State Withholding
5214	Payroll Taxes—State Unemployment
5215	Payroll Taxes—State Workers' Compensation
5216-5219	Payroll Taxes—Other

5220—Insurance Insurance premiums paid by the group for the benefit of an individual physician excluding professional liability insurance, which is recorded in Account 7510.

5221	Insurance—Health
5222	Insurance—Dental
5223	Insurance—Life
5224	Insurance—Disability
5225-5229	Insurance—Other

5230—Pension and Retirement Benefits

5240—Physician Development Costs paid by group for physicians' continuing education, including costs of study materials.

5250—Dues, Memberships, and License Fees Costs paid by the group for physicians' dues and memberships in professional organizations, state and local license fees, etc.
5260—Meetings and Travel Costs paid by the group for physicians' meetings and travel.
5270—Medical and Dental Services Medical and dental services provided to physicians and paid for or reimbursed by the group. Accounts 7110-7190, Purchased Services—Nonprepaid Professional and Medical, should not be used for these services. Any free medical and dental services provided within the group to physicians should be treated as an adjustment to revenue and debited to Account 4400, Employee Discounts.
5280—Automobile Lease and operating costs of an automobile acquired for the exclusive use of a physician.
5290—Other Physician Benefits Physician benefits not included elsewhere.

5300 **Physician Extender Salaries**
Salaries and bonuses for all audiologists, nurse practitioners, optometrists, physician assistants, podiatrists, psychologists, social workers, and other individuals in related positions who can provide medical care and bill for services without continuous supervision by a physician.

5400 **Ancillary Department Salaries**
Salaries and bonuses of all employees in ancillary departments. This account should be used for ancillary department salaries if the responsibility center field is used. The accounts described below are for the group not using the responsibility field and therefore using only the basic four-digit field.

Suggested breakdown may include:

5401	Professional Technicians—Ancillary
5403	Nurses—Ancillary
5404	Medical Receptionists—Ancillary
5405	Medical Records Personnel—Ancillary
5406-5409	Other Employees—Ancillary

5410—Ancillary Department Salaries—Laboratory Salaries and bonuses of all employees in the laboratory.

Suggested breakdown may include:

5411	Professional Technicians—Laboratory

5413 Nurses—Laboratory
5414 Medical Receptionists—Laboratory
5415 Medical Records Personnel—Laboratory
5416-5419 Other Employees—Laboratory

5420—Ancillary Department Salaries—Radiology Salaries and bonuses of all employees in the radiology department.

Suggested breakdown may include:
5421 Professional Technicians—Radiology
5423 Nurses—Radiology
5424 Medical Receptionists—Radiology
5425 Medical Records Personnel—Radiology
5426-5429 Other Employees—Radiology

5430—Ancillary Department Salaries—Physical Therapy Salaries and bonuses of all employees in the physical therapy department.

Suggested breakdown may include:
5431 Professional Technicians—Physical Therapy
5433 Nurses—Physical Therapy
5434 Medical Receptionists—Physical Therapy
5435 Medical Records Personnel—Physical Therapy
5436-5439 Other Employees—Physical Therapy

5450-5490—Other Ancillary Department Salaries Salaries and bonuses of all employees in any other ancillary departments that the group may operate.

5500 **Medical Support Salaries**

Salaries and bonuses of all medical support personnel employed by the group who provide services to patients and maintain medical records. RNs, LPNs, receptionists, medical records personnel, medical librarians, and medical secretaries are included in this account. None of these personnel has full responsibility for treating and/or billing patients. Salaries of ancillary department personnel should be recorded in Account 5400.

5510—Registered Nurses' Salaries
5520—Other Nurses' Salaries—Aides, LPNs, etc.
5530—Medical Receptionist Salaries

5540—Medical Secretary/Transcription Salaries
5550—Medical Records Salaries
5560—Patient Services Salaries Salaries of employees of the group who provide assistance to patients, such as dietitians or lay counselors.
5570-5590—Other Medical Support Salaries

5600 **Administrative Salaries**
Salaries and bonuses of all administrative and business office personnel not responsible for any of the functions or services listed above. This account is charged for salaries of all accounting, data processing, credit and collections, and cashiering personnel, as well as salaries for any other administrative functions. Salaries of marketing personnel can be reported here or in Account 5800, Other Salaries.
5610—Medical Group Administrator and Staff Salaries
5620—Administrative Secretarial Salaries
5630—Business Office Salaries Salaries of business office employees, including insurance, billing, and credit employees.
5640—Accounting and Bookkeeping Salaries
5650—Data Processing Salaries
5660—Purchasing Salaries
5670—Personnel Salaries
5680-5690—Other Administrative Salaries

5700 **Housekeeping, Maintenance, and Security Salaries**
Salaries and bonuses for all housekeeping, maintenance, and security personnel employed by the group. Housekeeping is responsible for all care and cleaning of the interior of facilities. Maintenance includes all exterior care and cleaning as well as renovation and repair of all furniture, fixtures, and equipment (for example, painting, elevator repair, vehicle maintenance, groundskeeping, minor construction projects). Security is responsible for the protection of personnel and facilities.

5800 **Other Salaries**
Salaries and bonuses of all employees not covered by any of the above classifications. If the group has established a marketing department, this account may be used for marketing salaries.

5900 **Nonphysician Employee Benefits**
Benefits provided to nonphysician employees by the group, including payroll-related taxes, insurance plans, pension and retirement plans, education, meetings, travel, and medical and dental services.
5910—Payroll Taxes

5911	Payroll Taxes—FICA
5912	Payroll Taxes—Federal Unemployment
5913	Payroll Taxes—State Withholding
5914	Payroll Taxes—State Unemployment
5915	Payroll Taxes—State Workers' Compensation
5916-5919	Payroll Taxes—Other

5920—Insurance

5921	Insurance—Health
5922	Insurance—Dental
5923	Insurance—Life
5924	Insurance—Disability
5925-5929	Insurance—Other

5930—Pension and Retirement Benefits

5940—Professional Development Costs paid by the group for nonphysician employees' continuing education, including costs of study materials.

5950—Meetings and Travel Costs paid by the group for nonphysician employees' meetings and travel.

5960—Medical and Dental Services Medical and dental services provided to employees and paid for or reimbursed by the group. Accounts 7110-7190, Purchased Services—Nonprepaid Professional and Medical, should not be used for these services. Any free medical and dental services provided by the group to employees should be treated as an adjustment to revenue and debited to Account 4400, Employee Discounts.

5970—Bonuses Bonuses to nonphysician employees not includable in taxable compensation, such as Christmas gifts, certificates, or money. (Tax code limits bonus if nontaxable to employees.)

5980-5990—Other Employee Benefits Employee benefits not included elsewhere.

6000 PHYSICAL RESOURCE EXPENSES

Physical resource expenses are current expenses relating to the building, utilities, furniture, fixtures, equipment, and supplies.

6100 **Supplies Expense**

Supplies and minor equipment purchased for day-to-day use in the group practice. The group administrator should decide the degree of detail required in the supply accounts. This account does not include ancillary department supplies, which should be recorded in Account 6200.

6110—Drugs and Medications Pharmaceutical supplies used in the provision of medical services. This account does not include drugs and medications sold to patients.

6120-6130—Medical Supplies Medical supplies and materials used in patient care departments. Tracing the costs of these supplies to the different departments is done by using the responsibility field.

6140—Administrative Supplies Supplies, materials, and administrative forms used in the business office and other administrative departments.

6150—Medical Forms Forms and other documents used in maintaining patients' medical records.

6160—Housekeeping/Maintenance Supplies Supplies, materials, and minor equipment used in the housekeeping and maintenance of the facility.

6170—Linen Supplies Cloths and other fabric supplies used in the group practice.

6180—Cost of Goods Sold Cost of goods sold to patients. This account is used in those areas where items are sold to patients on a retail basis. Examples would include crutches or bandages sold by departments providing medical care, but not goods sold by ancillary departments.

6190—Other Supplies

6200 **Ancillary Department Supplies Expense**

Supplies and minor equipment that relate directly to an ancillary department. Cost of supplies and products sold to patients should be included in Account 6300. Groups using the responsibility center field should use Account 6200. Groups using only the basic four-digit field should use the ancillary department supply accounts below.

6210-6220—Laboratory Supplies Supplies and minor equipment that relate directly to the laboratory.

6230—Radiology Supplies Supplies and minor equipment that relate directly to the radiology department.

6240—Physical Therapy Supplies Supplies and minor equipment that relate directly to the physical therapy department.

6250—Optical Supplies Supplies and minor equipment that relate directly to the optical department. Frames, lenses, and other goods sold to patients should be included in Account 6350.

6260-6290—Other Ancillary Department Supplies Supplies and minor equipment that relate directly to any other ancillary departments in the group practice.

6300 **Cost of Goods Sold—Ancillary Departments**
Cost of goods sold to patients by ancillary departments. The group using the responsibility center field should use only Account 6300. Ancillary department cost of goods sold accounts described below are for groups using only the basic four-digit field.

6310-6320—Cost of Goods Sold—Laboratory Purchase price of goods sold to patients by the laboratory.

6330—Cost of Goods Sold—Radiology Purchase price of goods sold to patients by the radiology department.

6340—Cost of Goods Sold—Physical Therapy Purchase price of goods sold to patients by the physical therapy department.

6350—Cost of Goods Sold—Optical Purchase price of goods sold to patients (frames, lenses, contact lenses, etc.) by the optical department.

6360-6390—Cost of Goods Sold—Other Ancillary Departments Purchase price of goods sold to patients by other ancillary departments.

6400 **Occupancy and Use Expenses—Buildings and Grounds**
Expenses related to the occupancy and use of land and buildings. In the event that another legal entity owns the land or buildings, any rental fees, commissions, or charges paid to the other entity are charged to this account. For the purpose of peer comparison (for example, a comparative data or cost survey), a fair market rental value may be charged to this account even if no rent is otherwise charged to the group by the owning entity.

6410—Building Rent/Lease Rent for building (building and land if not identified separately) used for operations of the group. Facilities leased for nonoperating purposes should not be included in this account.

6420-6430—Land Rent/Lease Rent for parking lots maintained adjacent to group facilities considered to be part of operations and the land-use expenses related to such parking lots. Land rented or leased for nonoperating purposes should not be charged to this account.

6440—Property Taxes—Land and Buildings City, county, and state taxes on real property (the land and building) of the medical group. Taxes related to personal property should be accumulated in Account 6810. Groups that combine real and personal property taxes into one account should use this account (6440) and rename it Property Taxes—Land, Buildings, and Equipment.

6450—Insurance—Land and Buildings Fire and other casualty insurance related to land and buildings. Insurance costs related to furniture, fixtures, and equipment are accumulated in Account 6820. Groups wishing to combine insurance covering casualty and theft should use this account (6450) and rename it Insurance—Land, Buildings, and Equipment.

6460—Maintenance and Repairs—Buildings Repairs and maintenance expenses for buildings. This account should be used if the group wants to include maintenance of buildings and grounds in a single account.

6470—Maintenance and Repairs—Grounds and Parking Facilities Cost of maintenance and upkeep of grounds and parking lots. This account is used if the group wishes to record maintenance of grounds and parking facilities in a separate account.

6480—Utilities Cost of utilities used in group practice operations.

6481	Water
6482	Electricity
6483	Gas
6484	Fuel Oil
6485	Steam
6486	Waste Disposal
6487-6489	Other Utilities

6490—Other Occupancy and Use Expenses—Buildings and Grounds

6500 **Occupancy and Use Expenses—Building Depreciation** Accounts used to record building depreciation, leasehold improvements, and land improvements. These accounts follow the same numbering sequence as the related asset accounts.

6530—Amortization—Land Improvements Systematic periodic amortization of the costs of the land improvements included in asset Account 1530.

6540—Depreciation—Buildings Systematic periodic allocation of the purchase cost of buildings included in asset Account 1540 over their useful life. Entries to this account should be made routinely and systematically using a generally accepted method of calculating the periodic depreciation expense.

6560—Amortization—Capital Leases—Buildings Systematic periodic amortization of the initial cost of buildings acquired under capital leases recorded in Account 1560. The initial cost of a depreciable asset acquired under a capital lease should be amortized to its residual value over the term of the lease or, if the lease transfers title, over the life of the asset. This cost may be included in Account 6540.

6570—Amortization—Leasehold Improvements Systematic periodic amortization of the cost of leasehold improvements included in asset Account 1570.

6580-6590—Depreciation—Other Real Property Systematic periodic allocation of the purchase cost of depreciable assets included in Account 1590 over the useful life of the asset.

6600 Occupancy and Use Expenses—Rent/Lease—Furniture, Fixtures, and Equipment

Rent/lease expenses of furniture, fixtures, and equipment acquired under an operating lease and used by the group. If the group prefers to combine all equipment rent/lease into one account, this account is used.

6610—Rent/Lease—Furniture, Fixtures, and Equipment—Medical Group Rent/lease expenses of furniture, fixtures, and equipment used by the medical group for the direct provision of services to patients, including rent/lease of reception room furniture and fixtures.

6620-6640—Rent/Lease—Furniture, Fixtures, and Equipment— Ancillary Departments Rent/lease expenses of furniture, fixtures, and equipment used in ancillary departments. Groups using only the basic four-digit field may use the following accounts for the various ancillary departments.

6620—Rent/Lease—Furniture, Fixtures, and Equipment—Laboratory

6630—Rent/Lease—Furniture, Fixtures, and Equipment—Radiology

6640—Rent/Lease—Furniture, Fixtures, and Equipment—Other Ancillary Departments

---

Groups wishing to accumulate rent/lease expenses for furniture, fixtures, and equipment in additional ancillary departments must use the fourth digit. For example:

6641 Rent/Lease—Furniture, Fixtures, and Equipment —Physical Therapy

6642 Rent/Lease—Furniture, Fixtures, and Equipment —Optical

6650—Rent/Lease—Furniture, Fixtures, and Equipment—Office

6660—Rent/Lease—Furniture, Fixtures, and Equipment—Data Processing
6670—Rent/Lease—Furniture, Fixtures, and Equipment—Transportation
6680—Rent/Lease—Furniture, Fixtures, and Equipment—Maintenance
6690—Rent/Lease—Furniture, Fixtures, and Equipment—Other

6700 **Occupancy and Use Expenses—Depreciation—Furniture, Fixtures, and Equipment**
Depreciation of furniture, fixtures, and equipment owned and used by the group. If the group prefers to combine all equipment depreciation into one account, this account is used. Amortization of the cost of equipment acquired under a capital lease is included in this series of accounts.
6710—Depreciation—Furniture, Fixtures, and Equipment—Medical Group Depreciation of furniture, fixtures and equipment used by the group for the direct provision of services to patients, including depreciation of reception room furniture and fixtures. These assets are included in asset Account 1710.
6720-6740—Depreciation—Furniture, Fixtures, and Equipment—Ancillary Departments Depreciation of furniture, fixtures, and equipment used in ancillary departments. These assets are included in asset Accounts 1720-1740. Groups using the responsibility center field should use Account 6720 to record depreciation of ancillary department furniture, fixtures, and equipment, while groups using only the basic four-digit field should use Accounts 6720-6740.
6720—Depreciation—Furniture, Fixtures, and Equipment—Laboratory
6730—Depreciation—Furniture, Fixtures, and Equipment—Radiology
6740—Depreciation—Furniture, Fixtures, and Equipment—Other Ancillary Departments

---

Groups wishing to accumulate depreciation of furniture, fixtures, and equipment in additional ancillary departments must use the fourth digit. For example:

6741	Depreciation—Furniture, Fixtures, and Equipment—Physical Therapy
6742	Depreciation—Furniture, Fixtures, and Equipment—Optical

6750—Depreciation—Furniture, Fixtures, and Equipment—Office Depreciation of office furniture, fixtures, and equipment on assets included in asset Account 1750.

6760—Depreciation—Furniture, Fixtures, and Equipment—Data Processing Depreciation of data processing equipment on assets included in asset Account 1760.

6770—Depreciation—Furniture, Fixtures, and Equipment—Transportation Depreciation of transportation equipment on assets included in asset Account 1770.

6780—Depreciation—Furniture, Fixtures, and Equipment—Maintenance Depreciation of maintenance equipment on assets included in asset Account 1780.

6790—Depreciation—Furniture, Fixtures, and Equipment—Other Depreciation of other furniture, fixtures, and equipment on assets included in asset Account 1790.

6800 Occupancy and Use Expenses—Other Furniture, Fixtures, and Equipment Expenses

6810—Property Taxes—Furniture, Fixtures, and Equipment City, county, and state taxes on personal property (furniture, fixtures, and equipment) of the group. Groups wishing to combine all property taxes into one account should use Account 6440, retitling it Property Taxes—Land, Buildings, and Equipment.

6820—Insurance—Furniture, Fixtures, and Equipment Fire and casualty insurance related to furniture, fixtures, and equipment. Groups wishing to combine all casualty insurance into one account should use Account 6450, retitling it Insurance—Land, Buildings, and Equipment.

6830—Maintenance and Repairs—Furniture, Fixtures, and Equipment—Medical Group Maintenance and repairs expenses for furniture, fixtures, and equipment paid to an outside contractor. Only parts, materials, and other repair costs that are not appropriately identified elsewhere (as are maintenance salaries, Account 5700) should be included for maintenance and repairs performed by group employees.

6840-6880—Maintenance and Repairs—Furniture, Fixtures, and Equipment—Ancillary Departments Maintenance and repairs expenses for furniture, fixtures, and equipment used in ancillary departments. Groups using the responsibility center field should use Account 6840 to record maintenance and repairs of ancillary department furniture, fixtures, and equipment, while groups using only the four-digit basic field should use Accounts 6840-6880 to record expenses for particular ancillary departments.

6840—Maintenance and Repairs—Furniture, Fixtures, and Equipment—Laboratory

6850—Maintenance and Repairs—Furniture, Fixtures, and Equipment—Radiology
6860—Maintenance and Repairs—Furniture, Fixtures, and Equipment—Physical Therapy
6870—Maintenance and Repairs—Furniture, Fixtures, and Equipment—Optical
6880—Maintenance and Repairs—Furniture, Fixtures, and Equipment—Other Ancillary Departments
6890—Other Furniture, Fixtures, and Equipment Expenses

6900 **Other Occupancy and Use Expenses**
Occupancy and use expenses not included elsewhere.

7000 PURCHASED SERVICES AND GENERAL AND ADMINISTRATIVE EXPENSES

7100 **Purchased Services—Nonprepaid Professional and Medical**
Fees and other charges paid to health care providers and organizations outside the group (such as referrals and hospitalization) for services provided to patients of the group.
7110—Purchased Services—Physicians Fees paid to physicians not regularly employed by the group, including fees for consulting, diagnosing, prescribing, and providing treatment for patients.
7120—Purchased Services—Nonphysician Professionals Fees paid to therapists, physician extenders, and other medical specialists not regularly employed by the group for services provided to patients.
7130—Purchased Services—Laboratory Fees paid to outside laboratories for services provided to patients.
7140—Purchased Services—Radiology Fees paid to outside radiology units for services provided to patients.
7150-7190—Purchased Services—Other Nonprepaid Professional and Medical Fees and charges paid to other health care providers outside the group for services provided to patients.

7200 **Purchased Services—Prepaid Professional and Medical**
Fees and other charges paid to health care providers and organizations outside the group (such as referrals to specialists and hospitalizations) for services provided to prepaid patients of the group where the group is responsible for referrals under a prepaid contract.
7210—Purchased Services—Prepaid Practice—Physicians Fees paid to outside physicians for services provided to prepaid patients of the group.

7220—Purchased Services—Prepaid Practice—Nonphysician Professionals Fees paid to outside therapists, physician extenders, and other medical specialists for services provided to prepaid patients of the group.

7230—Purchased Services—Prepaid Practice—Laboratory Fees paid to outside laboratories for services provided to prepaid patients of the group.

7240—Purchased Services—Prepaid Practice—Radiology Fees paid to outside radiology units for services provided to prepaid patients of the group.

7250—Purchased Services—Prepaid Practice—Hospital Inpatient Fees paid to hospitals for inpatient services provided to prepaid patients of the group.

7260—Purchased Services—Prepaid Practice—Hospital Emergency Room Fees paid to hospitals for emergency room services provided to prepaid patients of the group.

7270—Purchased Services—Prepaid Practice—Ambulance Fees paid to ambulance companies for services provided to prepaid patients of the group.

7280—Purchased Services—Prepaid Practice—Out-of-Area Emergency Care Fees and other charges paid for emergency care rendered outside the defined service area to prepaid patients of the group.

7290—Purchased Services—Prepaid Practice—Other Professional and Medical Fees and charges paid to other health care providers outside the group for services to prepaid patients of the group.

7300 **General and Administrative Expenses—Purchased Services** Costs of all services of a general and administrative nature purchased from outside vendors.

7310—Accounting Services Fees for accounting services provided by outside accountants, other than an audit by a certified public accountant (CPA). If the group wishes to combine all accounting services into one account, this account should be used.

7320—Accounting Audits Fees for audits by a CPA.

7330—Legal Services Fees for legal services paid to attorneys who are not employees of the group.

7340—Management Consultants Fees paid to management consultants who are not employees of the group.

7350—Collection Services Collection agency fees, commissions, or discounts. This account is used for expenses relating to independent collection agencies that are neither owned nor controlled by the group.

7360—Clerical Services Fees paid to independent agencies that provide part-time or temporary clerical assistance.

7370—Electronic Data Processing Cost of EDP services purchased from outside service bureaus.
7380—Actuarial Services Cost of actuarial services purchased from outside actuaries or consultants.
7390—Other General and Administrative Purchased Services

7400 **General and Administrative Expenses—Employee-related** Expenses for recruiting, entertaining, educating, and, in general, improving relations with employees when the benefits are for the group as a whole rather than for specific employees. Employee benefits such as insurance and professional development should be included in Account 5200, Physician Benefits, or Account 5900, Nonphysician Employee Benefits.
7410—Recruitment Costs associated with recruiting and hiring physicians, administrators, and other personnel; includes the costs of advertising, screening, testing, entertainment, and travel for recruiting purposes.
7420—Employee Development and Training Costs of attendance at meetings, training programs, and other employee development programs that benefit the group as a whole.
7430—Employee Relations Costs of employee coffee room, employee picnics, dinners, and other entertainment.
7440—Cafeteria Amount of loss from operating cafeteria for the group's employees.
7450—Uniforms and Laundry Costs of employee uniforms and laundry paid by the group.
7460-7490—Other General and Administrative Employee-related Expenses

7500 **General and Administrative Expenses—Liability Insurance** Premiums for liability insurance.
7510—Professional Liability Insurance Premiums for coverage of malpractice claims.
7520—General Liability
7530—Reinsurance Premiums for reinsurance coverage of catastrophic claims, emergency care outside the area, and insolvency.

7600-7700 **Other General and Administrative Expenses** General and administrative expenses not included in other expense categories.
7610—Telephone and Other Communications Costs of all telephone and other communication services or equipment purchased or leased by the group. (Excludes directory listing in Account 7620.)

7620—Professional Listings and Promotion Costs of listings in directories and promotion of the group physicians.
7630—Postage and Freight Costs of all postage, UPS, air freight, and other charges for shipping and mailing.
7640—Printing Costs of printing services used by the group, excluding forms. Printing of forms should be included in Accounts 6140 and 6150.

7641-7649 The fourth digit may be used to identify the type of printing, such as administrative, marketing, etc.

7650—Books and Subscriptions Costs of books and subscriptions not included in Account 5250, as well as subscriptions for waiting room periodicals. If a technical library is maintained, technical books and subscriptions not acquired for a specific employee's use should be included in Account 7670.
7660—Patient Education Costs of patient education, excluding salaries, dealing with preventive medicine and better use of the group's facilities. Use this account only if the patient is not charged for the service.
7670—Library Costs of operating a technical library, including technical books and subscriptions not acquired for a specific employee.
7680—Taxes—Excise and Other Business Taxes Sales, excise, and other taxes not included elsewhere. This account also includes business, occupation, use, and corporate franchise taxes paid by the group.
7690—Business Transportation Costs of group-related travel including trips to satellite clinics, errands, etc.
7710—Marketing Expenses Costs of marketing services and advertising media used to promote the health care services provided by the group.
7720-7790—Other General and Administrative Expenses

7800 Interest Expenses
Interest on any indebtedness incurred for the general operations of the group. This account excludes interest paid to a related entity for occupancy and/or use of group property (see Account 6410).

8000 NONOPERATING REVENUES AND EXPENSES, INCOME TAXES, AND EXTRAORDINARY ITEMS

Nonoperating revenues and expenses are revenues and expenses not directly related to the operations of the group. Extraordinary gains and losses result from transactions of an unusual nature that are not reasonably expected to recur in the future. Extraordinary items are shown net of the related income tax consequences.

8100 **Nonoperating Revenues**

Revenues not directly related to patient care or the provision of medical services. The following accounts are examples of nonoperating revenues.

8110—Interest Income Interest earned on marketable securities, savings accounts, and other short-term investments.

8111-8119 The fourth digit may be used to categorize interest earned by specific investments or to account for interest earned by investment of specific revenues such as capitation payments.

8120—Income from Long-Term Investments Income from securities and other long-term investments not currently used in the group's operations.

8130—Property Rentals Rent/lease revenue received from property owned by the group but not used in group operations.

These accounts are not intended to be definitive but only to show the general nature of nonoperating revenues. The nature of nonoperating revenues will vary greatly from group to group. Each group should determine the accounts that will best serve its own needs.

8200 **Nonoperating Expenses**

Expenses not directly related to patient care or the provision of medical services. For example, expenses relating to investment property management and brokerage fees are included in this account.

8210—Interest Expenses—Nonoperating Interest incurred on borrowings not related to group operations.

8300 **Income Taxes**

Taxes paid on the group's income.

8400 **Extraordinary Gains**

Gains, net of income taxes, from transactions that are of an unusual nature and not reasonably expected to recur in the foreseeable future.

8500 **Extraordinary Losses**
Losses, net of income taxes, from transactions that are of an unusual nature and not reasonably expected to recur in the foreseeable future.

Chapter 4

Principles of Accounting Underlying General Purpose Financial Statements

This chapter describes principles of accounting governing development of general purpose financial statements for medical groups, regardless of the proportion of their practice represented by the provision of services on a prepaid basis. The conceptual framework of financial statements is explained, together with certain assumptions underlying statement preparation. A part of the chapter is devoted to discussion of cash and accrual bases of accounting. These methods are illustrated by condensed general purpose financial statements. Also included are measurement principles that guide the accountant in recording transactions involving financial assets and liabilities.

Over a period of many years the accounting profession has developed reporting standards for financial reporting to external users of financial statements. The principal external users of financial statements include: financing institutions, the Internal Revenue Service, state and federal regulatory authorities, third-party payers, and HMOs with which the medical group contracts. A complete system of financial reporting, however, includes financial reports to the administrator and physician-owners of the group and financial reports to the managers of responsibility centers, as well as financial statements to external users. Financial reporting for internal users is not bound by the generally accepted accounting principles that guide external financial reporting. Instead, internal financial reporting must be relevant to the specific needs of management. A full discussion of reporting for management needs is presented in Part III, *Financial Planning and Control*.

The accounting profession has developed standards for measuring transactions as a result of two very different occurrences: first, the evolution of accepted practice, and second, authoritative pronouncements by rule-making bodies. Over generations of economic activity, financial statements have evolved that provide useful financial information. However, because of variations among industries, differences in accounting measurements of assets, liabilities, revenues, and expenses have occurred. Because of the diversity in accounting practices, the accounting profession has issued accounting standards through its committees and boards (now the Financial Accounting Standards Board or FASB). Through the rule-making process, a body of generally accepted accounting principles (GAAP) has been developed. The role of the CPA as an auditor is to attest that the financial statements of an entity present fairly the financial position and results of operations in conformity with this body of generally accepted accounting principles. The major weakness of the rule-making process has been that the rule-making boards have been preoccupied with specific problems and only now are developing a broad framework of objectives for external financial statements.

In this text, when a statement is made such as "accounting authorities require," it means that generally accepted accounting principles have been established that either require a specific accounting method or provide a choice from among several accepted methods.

Conceptual Framework for Financial Reporting

In an attempt to develop a conceptual framework (or constitutional document) for financial reporting, the FASB recently developed a statement of objectives of financial reporting. Financial reporting means the general purpose financial statements, and other information that relates directly to the financial statements, that are prepared for external users who do not have the authority to prescribe financial information they want. These users must instead rely upon the information management communicates to them.

The objectives of financial reporting developed by the FASB stress that information provided to external users should be useful in making investment, credit, and similar decisions. Further, financial reports should assist the user in assessing future cash flows and analyzing past performance, as well as presenting financial position and changes therein.

A second statement issued by the FASB outlines the qualitative characteristics of accounting information. Decision usefulness is identified as the most important qualitative characteristic. To be useful, accounting information must be both relevant and reliable. Relevant information has the capacity to influence a decision by a user. It may have predictive value when used to evaluate future events or feedback value that confirms or corrects expectations. In any case, the information must be timely enough to have the potential of influencing the decision. According to the FASB, reliable accounting information must be neutral, possess representational faithfulness, and be verifiable. In brief, this means that if accounting information is to be reliable, it must be free from error and bias, represent what it purports to represent, and be verifiable by different accountants using the same objective data and measurement techniques.

Secondary qualities identified by the FASB as supporting both relevance and reliability are comparability and consistency. Financial statements of the organization should be comparable over time and, to a lesser extent, be comparable with similar organizations.

The FASB has issued other statements that are components of the conceptual framework, and it promises to issue still others in the near future. Among these other components are statements dealing with the definition of accounting elements (assets, liabilities, revenues, expenses, etc.), their measurement, and the criteria for their recognition in accounting records. When the conceptual framework is complete, it should serve as a general constitution to be used by the FASB to evaluate financial accounting standards already issued and to evaluate alternative proposed standards in the future. In any event, it has emphasized that accounting information should have decision usefulness based on the criteria of relevance and reliability.

Assumptions Underlying Financial Statements

The form and content of financial statements are influenced by the business environment in which a medical group operates. Four assumptions are examined below: entity, continuity of life, objective measurement of transactions, and measurement in monetary units.

Entity

Financial statements should reflect the economic activities of individual business enterprises. Accordingly, the entity (a specific area of interest defined by the owners or managers for which separate accounting records are maintained) establishes the boundaries to be observed in financial statements. A medical group operates as a separate financial unit, independent of the persons owning, managing, or working for it. A number of entities can be identified for a particular medical group. One entity is the legal organization owning and operating the practice (the professional corporation or partnership); another may be a part of the practice for which responsibility has been defined (a medical specialty or an ancillary department); and yet another possibility is a combination of legal entities representing the larger economic entity (consolidation of the practice corporation and the HMO corporation). Financial statements may be prepared for each type of entity.

A practice operating more than one entity may use the same chart of accounts by using the entity field of the coding structure to identify each entity. Using uniform accounts for all entities allows financial statements to be combined into a set of financial statements for the practice as a whole.

Continuity of Life

It is assumed that the practice will continue as an organization for an indefinite period of time. This assumption is the basis for ignoring liquidation values and fluctuations in market values of most assets and liabilities. Assuming a long life for a practice, however, poses problems in evaluating performance over a short period of time (month, quarter, year). To measure net income, revenues and expenses must be matched with applicable time periods. This matching requires systematic allocations of expenses to time periods. Depreciation expense, for example, is estimated annually (or monthly) because depreciable assets benefit a number of periods.

Objective Measurement of Transactions

Business activity involves an exchange of goods or services at a specified price. The normal accounting procedure is to record these transactions at their cost, which is measured by the value of the resource given in exchange. Measurement of these exchanges must be objective and verifiable. Accounting records, therefore, must be supported by documentation arising out of exchange transactions.

Measurement in Monetary Units

The accounting system measures and reports the results of transactions and events in dollars that represent the value of equipment and supplies at the time of their acquisition. In this way, assets, liabilities, revenues, and expenses may be measured and presented in the financial statements. Currently, number of dollars is used in measuring transactions regardless of changes in the purchasing power of the dollar. For example, the cost of an asset acquired in a year when the price level was 110 is added to the cost of an asset acquired when the price level was 150. As the dollar's purchasing power changes, its usefulness as the unit of measure is affected. Although an adjustment could be made to reflect these changes in purchasing power, the accounting profession has not, as yet, decided upon a satisfactory treatment of price level adjustments.

Accounting Principles for Medical Groups with a Prepaid Component

One of the major objectives of financial statements is relevancy—information must be relevant to the users. The choice of accounting principles, in particular the use of cash or accrual basis accounting, should be made on the basis of relevancy. Most physicians and fee-for-service medical groups operate in an environment in which external needs for financial information are limited or nonexistent. Decisions tend to be made on the basis of medical desirability, with limited financial information available to decision makers. Traditionally, fee-for-service groups have used cash basis accounting because it is simple and easily understood; it provides a tax advantage; it is conservative; and the financial statements are limited to internal use (or accepted by the bank). As a group grows and financial control and decision making become more complex, cash basis financial statements will not meet the group's needs.

As the medical group enters prepaid practice, the nature of the practice, the risks involved, and the information needs change. The amount and nature of the risks depend upon the type of contract. There are at least four contractual arrangements under which a medical group may offer prepaid care:

(1) Discounted fee-for-service (generally with an IPA-model HMO)

(2) Discounted fee-for-service, with a shared risk pool

(3) Capitation for provision of prepaid care

(4) Development of a captive HMO.

Providing prepaid care on a discounted fee-for-service basis is essentially no different than fee-for-service practice. The group incurs no additional risk. In fact, the risk of collection is exchanged for a reduced fee. The group may be asked to inform the HMO of referrals and hospitalization or may be required to seek preauthorization for referrals and hospitalization. The accounting issues, however, are no different than in the fee-for-service practice.

The HMO that contracts on a discounted fee-for-service basis many times will ask the group to share the risk (and benefits) of hospitalization and/or referrals. When the group participates in a shared risk pool, there is a need for nonfinancial measures of utilization. The group must be able to compare utilization of medical services by the prepaid patients with the norms established by the HMO. Accounting measurements and financial statements, however, may remain the same as in the fee-for-service practice.

When a medical group accepts a capitation contract for prepaid care, the nature of the risks changes and new financial controls are necessary. The group is paid in advance of performing service and is therefore responsible for all services needed by the prepaid patients. The group must have nonfinancial controls to track and evaluate the patients' utilization of health care services. Cash basis accounting will not meet the accounting needs of the group. It is critical that the group match the revenues received from the prepaid patients with the costs incurred in serving those patients. A number of matching problems arises with prepaid care. On the revenue side, the capitation payment may be received in the month preceding the delivery of service. On the expense side, incurred but not reported claims for referrals and hospitalization will be paid in a later period. If the group uses the cash basis of accounting, serious mismatches of revenues and expenses may lead the group into assuming its performance was more favorable than it actually was. Proper measurement of group performance requires the use of accrual accounting.

If the group develops its own HMO, the entire risk for prepayment falls upon the group. In addition to delivering health care, the group also assumes the administration and marketing of the plan. Generally, a captive HMO is organized as a separate entity, perhaps with different ownership. The group has the same accounting needs as the capitated group discussed earlier. Both the group and the HMO need accrual basis accounting to measure operating performance and financial position.

Depending upon the extent of the prepaid practice, the entities involved, and the laws of the state in which the group practices, there may be a need for a periodic report to the state insurance commissioner's office. Similarly, if the medical group successfully obtains federal qualification as an HMO, it will have reporting requirements to the Office of Health Maintenance Organizations of the U.S. Department of Health and Human Services. The reporting requirements require the use of accrual accounting.

In this text the accrual method of accounting is stressed because of the increased information needs of groups with prepaid components and because of the requirements of external users of the statements. This expressed support for the accrual basis of accounting should not be construed to mean that cash flow is not important to the medical group. In fact, knowledge of cash flow is crucial and should be included within every set of financial statements.

Cash Basis Accounting

Cash basis accounting recognizes revenues when cash is received and expenses when cash is paid out. Receivables, payables, accruals, and deferrals arising from operations are ignored. On a pure cash basis, long-lived (fixed) assets are expensed when acquired, leaving cash and investments as the only assets and loans and payroll withholdings as the only liabilities.

In practice, a modified cash basis is used by medical groups primarily because tax laws require recording of long-lived assets and expensing their costs through depreciation and recognition of inventories of goods intended for resale. Purchase of buildings and equipment, leasehold improvements, and payment of insurance premiums applicable to more than one accounting period are normally recorded as assets under the modified cash basis. Costs for these assets are allocated to accounting periods in a systematic and rational manner over the length of time the group benefits from the assets. In this text, the term cash basis refers to any form of cash basis accounting.

Cash Basis Financial Statements

The cash basis of accounting does not provide a full picture of the group's financial position inasmuch as several of the assets and liabilities affecting financial position are not recorded. The accounting profession recommends that the titles, "statement of financial position" (balance sheet) and "income statement" be used only for accrual basis financial statements. Groups on the cash basis of accounting should use the titles, "statement of assets and liabilities" rather than "statement of financial position" and "statement of revenues collected and expenses" rather than "income statement."

Statement of Assets and Liabilities

The statement of assets and liabilities format is based upon the accounting equation:

Assets − Liabilities = Owners' Equity

In this statement, liabilities are deducted from assets, resulting in a difference representing owners' equity.

STATEMENT OF ASSETS AND LIABILITIES
(Cash Basis)

Assets	$100,000
Liabilities	80,000
Owners' Equity	$ 20,000

At a minimum, assets in this statement consist of cash and investments. Additional asset accounts are included depending upon accrual basis concepts used. Generally, long-lived assets such as land, buildings, and equipment are recorded. Prepayments of expenses for a period of less than one year, or expenses such as professional liability insurance and leasehold costs, are often included for financial reporting but not for tax reporting. On cash basis financial statements, liabilities represent the amounts owed for borrowed money and for payroll withholdings. Receivables and advances from patients and payables to suppliers are not included in the cash basis statement of assets and liabilities.

This statement is adequate for fee-for-service groups having relatively stable cash flows and minimal reporting needs. It may pose some limitations, however, in meeting the needs of groups with complex activities when used to provide information for performance analysis. A major problem of cash basis accounting is that a good deal of information that affects the group's financial position is not recorded on the books and presented in the financial statements. In a number of instances, cash basis accounting is conservative in recognizing the value of the group's assets. On the other hand, cash basis accounting overstates the financial position of groups providing significant prepaid health care services. This conservatism in a group without a prepaid component results in understating both assets and liabilities and, as a result, its financial position. Because material data concerning the group's financial position often are never disclosed, the statement of assets and liabilities may have limited worth for a group that provides services solely on a fee-for-service basis. For medical groups offering significant prepaid health care services, the statement of assets and liabilities is seriously misleading, because cash is received before service is performed and claims for referrals and hospitalization are not reported as liabilities.

Statement of Revenues Collected and Expenses

Groups on the cash basis present net income by deducting cash expenses and depreciation from cash collections from patients. The amount of revenues and expenses included in the statement depends upon the extent to which accrual concepts are used. As a group grows and its operations become more complex, use of accrual methods tends to increase until patient receivables may be the only account not handled on the accrual basis. The format generally used is as follows:

STATEMENT OF REVENUES COLLECTED AND EXPENSES
(Cash Basis)

Revenues:		
Collections from patients		$750,000
Expenses:		
Cash operating expenses	$360,000	
Depreciation expense	40,000	$400,000
Excess of revenues over expenses		$350,000
Distributions to physicians		350,000
Excess of revenues over expenses and distributions to physicians		$ 0

The use of the cash basis is potentially seriously misleading for a group that has a significant portion of its revenues attributable to prepaid health care contracts. As an example, consider the following situation where 40 percent of total revenues are attributable to prepaid contracts, the group is in its first year of providing prepaid services, and 50 percent of the needed services are purchased outside the medical group. If it is assumed that the group continues to operate as it did before accepting prepaid patients, the following operating statement would result.

GROUP WITH PREPAID COMPONENT
STATEMENT OF REVENUES COLLECTED AND EXPENSES
(Cash Basis)

Revenues:		
Fee-for-service collections		$1,500,000
Premiums on prepaid contracts		1,000,000
		$2,500,000
Expenses:		
Cash operating expenses	$960,000	
Services purchased outside the group	395,000	
Depreciation expense	80,000	$1,435,000
Excess of revenues over expenses		$1,065,000
Distributions to physicians		1,065,000
Excess of revenues over expenses and distributions to physicians		$ 0

The operating statement does not reflect unpaid claims at the end of the year amounting to $105,000. Since this is the first year of the prepaid contract, the category of services purchased outside the group does not include a full year's expenses, which would be $1,540,000 (1,435,000 + 105,000). Correspondingly, only $960,000 should have been distributed to physicians rather than the $1,065,000 indicated as available for distribution to physicians.

Cash basis financial statements may vary widely depending upon the extent of accrual concepts used.

Accrual Basis of Accounting

Accrual basis accounting records revenues as earned when services are performed rather than when cash is received. Expenses are recorded in the period during which they are incurred, that is, when the asset or service is used, regardless of when cash is paid. In our earlier illustration, the $105,000 incurred but not reported claims would be recognized as an expense of the first year of operations. Expenditures for goods and services that will be used to produce revenues in the future are reported as assets and considered as expenses in future periods. Net income is measured by matching current revenues with their associated costs for the accounting period. In addition to the assets and liabilities of the cash basis statement, the statement of financial position includes receivables from patients, prepayments and deferrals of expenses, accruals of expenses and revenues, and payables to suppliers.

The following summary of guidelines for recording transactions under the accrual basis was developed by the accounting profession:

(1) Assets and liabilities should be recorded at their initial cost, that is, the value of the consideration given. An expenditure (other than to repay a lender or to make a distribution to owners) should be regarded as an asset—an unexpired cost. When an asset is used or consumed, it is an expense—an expired cost.

(2) Revenues from the provision of health care services should be recognized when the group performs the services and is, in the case of fee-for-service patients, entitled to collect from the patients. For prepaid health care contracts, collection typically is made in advance of the provision of services.

Revenues are recognized when the services are performed or the contract period has elapsed. Generally, revenues should be recognized when services are performed regardless of when cash is collected; however, if the uncertainty of cash collection from patients served is so great that there is no reasonable basis for its estimation, recognition of revenues should be delayed until cash is collected.

(3) Recognition of expenses (the assets or costs that are used in providing a service) depends upon the nature of the expense.

- Costs directly related to specific revenues, such as drugs in the pharmacy inventory, should be carried as assets (unexpired costs) until the items are sold or consumed, then treated as expenses (expired costs).

- For a long-lived asset, there is no direct relationship between the cost of the asset and the revenues generated by the asset. For example, there is no direct relationship between cost of a piece of laboratory equipment and revenue from a test performed for a particular patient. A systematic and rational plan of allocating cost of the asset to specific time periods over its useful life must be established. This process is called depreciation or amortization. The term depreciation is used for tangible, long-lived assets, while the term amortization is employed for other long-lived assets such as prepaid insurance or goodwill.

- Costs that do not have a direct relationship to particular revenues or do not relate to long-lived assets should be considered expenses (expired costs) during the period the costs are incurred. These costs usually relate to the passage of time.

Exhibit 4-1 illustrates some measurement principles for the accrual process by presenting transactions relating to revenues and expenses.

EXHIBIT 4-1
GUIDELINES FOR THE ACCRUAL BASIS OF ACCOUNTING

Transactions in Previous Months	Transactions during Current Month (March)	Transactions in Subsequent Months
Revenue Transactions:		
	Capitation revenue is recognized when the period for which coverage was paid has elapsed (e. g., at the end of the month for which coverage was provided).	
Capitation payment received in February for for coverage in March. Until the service is provided, the payment is a liability.	Revenue is recognized in March when service to the patient is performed. Receivables are established for FFS services provided in March but not collected until later.	Collections in April or later for FFS services performed in March are treated as collections of assets.
	Allowances are estimated for receivables that will become uncollectible in later months.	
Expense Transactions:		
	Expenditures, except to repay lenders or make distributions to owners, are regarded as assets when made; then expensed as the resources are consumed. Expenses are recognized in March by applying three measurements to determine when the assets (unexpired costs) are used to generate revenue and become expenses (expired costs).	
Lenses and frames in the optical department acquired in February and earlier. The costs are carried as assets (unexpired costs).	1. When there is a direct cause and effect relationship between a specific cost and a specific revenue, the expense is recognized in the month the revenue is recognized, e.g., lenses and frames purchased by the optical department in February are carried in inventory until sold to patients in March, then their cost is expensed as cost of goods sold.	

Transactions in Previous Months	Transactions during Current Month (March)	Transactions in Subsequent Months
	Liabilities are established for unpaid unpaid March expenses. It is necessary to estimate the claims, if any, that are unpaid for referrals and hospitalization.	Payments in April or later for March expenses are treated as payments of liabilities.
Long-lived assets, buildings and equipment, acquired and paid for in February and earlier. Professional liability insurance paid at the beginning of the year.	2. Cost of a long-lived asset that benefits several periods but has no direct relationship to revenue in a period is expensed through depreciation or amortization; e.g., equipment having a five-year life is depreciated at the rate of one-sixtieth per month (5 years × 12 months).	
	3. Some goods and services acquired during March that have no direct relationship to revenue or benefit to future periods are expensed in March; e.g., March rent, salaries, and marketing expenses for the prepaid component are paid in March and expensed in March.	
	Net income (loss) is the difference between revenue and expenses recognized in March.	

Concerns in the Use of the Accrual Basis

It must be understood by everyone in the medical group that the income statement and departmental operating statements (whether prepared on the cash or accrual basis) should present the clearest picture possible of performance. The measurement of performance identifies the amount of resources generated and resources consumed in the provision of services to patients. The statement of financial position should present the clearest picture possible of financial position at a given time. Proper cash management requires a statement of changes in financial position that presents a full picture of cash flows and discloses the amount of cash available for distribution to physicians.

Groups often continue to use the cash basis of accounting when, in fact, the measurement of performance would dictate the use of accrual accounting. These groups express three major concerns in the use of accrual basis accounting: first, measurement of income for tax purposes; second, measurement of income for distribution to physicians; and third, measurement of financial position for buy-in, buy-out by physicians.

Occasionally, medical group administrators are concerned that the use of accrual basis accounting on the books and in the financial statements will require the use of accrual basis accounting for income tax purposes. This is not necessarily true. Accounting policies for tax reporting may be different from accounting policies for financial reporting. The group may continue to recognize income in the tax return on the basis of cash transactions and yet recognize income in the income statement for management and lenders on the accrual basis. The Internal Revenue Service requires only that the taxpayer's accounting records clearly show the amounts used in the tax return. Proper cash management requires the accumulation of cash transactions regardless of the method of income measurement selected.

One of the perceived major drawbacks of medical groups' using accrual basis accounting is in the measurement of income available for distribution to physicians. The amount of cash to be distributed to a particular physician depends upon the distribution formula and the amount of cash available. In the vast majority of fee-for-service medical groups, the statement of revenues collected and expenses (cash basis income statement) is used as the measure of income available for distribution to physicians. It is understandable to physicians and if, in some instances, cash must be retained for equipment purchases or debt retirement, these facts can be easily explained. The accrual basis income statement is intended to report performance. It was never intended to measure the amount of cash available for distribution to physicians or for any other cash distributions.

Because of asset acquisition, debt transactions, and investments, income before distribution to physicians may be more than, equal to, or less than the amount of cash available, whether accounted for on a cash or accrual basis.

It may be difficult to explain to physicians why income is high but cash available for distribution is low. On the other hand, the statement of changes in financial position, the third statement on either the cash or accrual basis, is intended to explain all sources and uses of cash.

Management of cash is a major concern of medical group administrators on either the cash or accrual basis of accounting. The distribution formula must specify how to determine the amount of cash available to physicians (the sum of the pie) and how much is to be distributed to each physician (the size of the individual slices).

The third concern in the use of accrual basis accounting involves the measurement of financial position for buy-in and buy-out by physicians. Buy-in and buy-out agreements involve many considerations beyond what is shown in the statement of financial position. Regardless of what is presented in the financial statements, tax considerations and the ability of the new physician to make the required investment will dominate the buy-in, buy-out agreement. The buy-in, buy-out agreement should include whatever the medical group wants it to reflect. Omitting or including receivables and payables in the formal financial statements should have no impact on what is designated in the buy-in, buy-out agreement, which logically must take receivables and payables into consideration.

The confusion and concern over financial statements arise because the same statements are asked to serve many objectives. Evaluation of performance and financial position, determination of income available for taxes, determination of cash available for distribution to physicians, and determination of financial position for buy-in and buy-out by physicians require different information. The goals and objectives of the medical group should clearly indicate the information needs for each purpose and how they are to be achieved.

Accounting Procedures for Prepayment

The emphasis in the chapter thus far has been to describe generally accepted accounting principles and how these principles relate to medical groups. The purpose of the balance of this chapter is to explain the accounting procedures for prepayment plans.

In the typical prepayment plan, the member makes a predetermined, fixed, periodic prepayment to cover the cost of an agreed-upon package of health care services. Over the contracted time period, the medical group provides services through its employees and facilities, as well as through specialists, hospitals, and other health care organizations.

There is a dramatic difference between planning and controlling revenue and costs in fee-for-service reimbursement and doing so in a prepayment plan.

Under fee-for-service reimbursement, costs are reasonably well known and also subject to greater control. However, revenues are uncertain, both in the amount of services to be provided and in the timing and amount of cash collected. In a prepayment plan, knowledge of revenues and costs is reversed. Revenues are certain both in amount and timing and, once contracted for, are not likely to change for some given period of time. Expenses, particularly outside costs (such as those for specialists and hospital care), are uncertain and to some extent under the control of others. It is imperative, therefore, that good forecasts of expenses serve as a basis for establishing the prepayment schedules and that control over costs is carefully exercised.

Three levels of financial performance evaluation should be made by groups with prepayment plans: first, financial evaluation of the entire group; second, financial evaluation of the specialties and departments; and finally, financial evaluation of the contracts with prepaid plans or HMOs. The income statement for the group as a whole provides a comparison of contract revenues from the plan (and gross charges to fee-for-service patients) with operating expenses of the group.

Evaluation of financial performance of a particular specialty or ancillary department should involve a comparison of the direct costs incurred with the value of services provided. This is particularly true if the group offers both prepayment and fee-for-service, because the physician or other health care provider does not control the mix of patients. It should not matter to the health care provider whether the patient is a member of a prepayment plan or paying a fee for the service received. The health care provider should be concerned with the relationship of direct costs to service provided. The group may wish to allocate indirect costs to individual departments to achieve a more complete picture of profit or loss by department.

For a particular contract (such as a prepayment contract with an HMO, an employer, or a labor union), the amount prepaid on the contract should be compared with the value of services provided. It is difficult to allocate the cost of health care services provided within the group to particular prepaid contracts, and it must be done on an arbitrary basis. However, some measure of service provided is necessary to decide if the contract is financially feasible and, if so, the amount that should be negotiated as the contract premium. The fee-for-service equivalent of service provided is generally used as the measure of the "cost" of service provided on a contract.

The operations of a prepayment plan may be illustrated through a series of accounting entries and reports using the following transactions.

	Data for Entire Group	Data for a Medical Specialty
Prepayment for month	$100,000	—
Value of services provided to patients enrolled in the prepayment plan (measured by gross charges for the services provided)	$80,000	$35,000
Cost of professional and medical services purchased outside the group for patients in the prepayment plan	$30,000	—
Operating expenses of the group including distributions to physicians	$75,000	$31,000

In this example, only the prepayment plan is illustrated. Any fee-for-service transactions would be recorded in accordance with procedures illustrated earlier in this volume.

1. Entry to record the collection of the contractual prepayment for the month:

Account		Debit	Credit
1110	Cash	$100,000	
3800	Prepaid contract revenues		$100,000

Amount to be prepaid is based upon the contracted prepayment schedule and the number of patients enrolled in the plan.

If prepayment is received in a period before service is provided, the credit is made to Account 2360—Deferred Revenues—Capitation or Prepaid Plans. Then, in the month of service the revenues are recognized by a debit to Account 2360 and a credit to Account 3800.

2. Entry to record the fee-for-service equivalent for services performed by the group's health care providers (physicians, physician extenders, and ancillary departments):

Account		Debit	Credit
4500	Prepaid contract adjustments —inside service	$80,000	

3600-10	Gross charges—prepaid contract (for a medical specialty)	$35,000
3600-(20-90)	Gross charges—prepaid contract (for all other specialties)	$45,000

In this particular medical department, $35,000 of services were provided. Other departments would be similarly identified.

In the income statement, only Prepaid Contract Revenues (Account 3800) from Entry 1 appears as the revenues to be matched with operating costs.

In departmental reports, Gross Charges—Prepaid Contract (Account 3600-10) is used by the particular specialty or department to evaluate performance.

To evaluate the the group's performance on a particular contract, the sum of gross charges on the contract (Account 4500) and the costs of purchased services on the contract (Account 7200) in Entry 4 are compared with contract revenues (Account 3800).

3. Entry to record operating expenses of the group, including distributions to physicians:

Account		Debit	Credit
5000-7000-10	Operating expenses	$31,000	
5000-7000-(20-90)	Operating expenses	$44,000	
1110	Cash		$75,000

Direct operating expenses are identified for a particular specialty. Other operating expenses could be identified with specific responsibility centers.

4. Entry to record payment for outside professional and medical services used by patients enrolled in the prepayment plan:

Account		Debit	Credit
7200-(20-90)	Purchased services—prepaid professional and medical	$30,000	
1110	Cash		$30,000

This is the normal entry that would be used by any group purchasing professional and medical services outside the group. It is possible to identify the purchased service with particular specialties or ancillary departments. To the extent the physicians in a particular specialty have control over whether a member of a prepayment plan uses outside services, the costs should be identified with that particular specialty.

Income Statement
In the income statement, contract revenues are compared with operating expenses incurred to provide services. Gross Charges—Prepaid Contract (Account 3600) and Prepaid Contract Adjustments—Inside Services (Account 4500) could be presented and netted in the income statement.

INCOME STATEMENT

Revenues:		
3800	Prepaid contract revenues	$100,000
Operating expenses:		
5000-7000	Operating expenses (all inside expenses of the group including distributions to physicians)	$ 75,000
7200	Purchased services—prepaid professional and medical	30,000
	Total operating expenses	$105,000
	Operating loss	$ (5,000)

During the month, the group sustained an operating loss of $5,000.

Report for Specialties and Departments
Reports for particular specialties and departments should relate gross charges for services performed to their direct costs. Indirect costs could be allocated to the revenue-producing specialties and departments. For purposes of control, however, the direct costs and allocated costs should not be merged. The statement should show contribution of the department to common costs and income. Allocated costs clearly identified could appear as a subtraction from the controllable contribution to common costs and income.

DEPARTMENT REPORT

Revenues:		
3600-10	Gross charges—prepaid contract	$35,000
Direct costs:		
5000-7000-10	Operating expenses	31,000
	Contribution to common costs and income	$ 4,000

During the month, the specialty in this illustration provided $35,000 of services and incurred operating expenses of $31,000 (including physician compensation), generating a contribution of $4,000 to cover common costs.

Report for Prepaid Contracts

Each month the group's performance on prepaid contracts should be assessed by comparing the contract revenues received with the value of services provided on the contracts and the amount of professional and medical services purchased for the contracts. Performance on individual contracts also should be examined.

PREPAID CONTRACTS REPORT

Revenues:		
3800	Prepaid contract revenues	$100,000
Services provided:		
4500	Prepaid contract adjustments—inside services	$ 80,000
7200	Purchased services—prepaid professional and medical	30,000
	Total services provided	$110,000
	Excess (deficiency) of value of services provided over contract revenues	$ (10,000)

During the month, the group provided $10,000 more in services than it received in contract revenues. There will be variations between the amount of contract revenues received and the value of services provided in particular months; however, a cumulative difference over the years should be small. A similar evaluation should be made for each contract.

Gross Charges as an Indicator of Value

It has been assumed thus far that gross charges is an indicator of the value of services that can be applied by the medical group in all instances. It is an assumption that simplifies the discussion and, in certain instances, is reflective of reality.

To the extent that gross charges, plus the cost of care purchased outside the group, approximates the portion of the premium charged to the member of the plan that is paid to the group as the capitation payment, it is appropriate to use gross charges as an indicator of the value of services rendered to the prepaid patient. There are, however, two reasons why gross charges may not always be a good measure of value in the prepaid setting. First, the prepaid patient tends to use health care differently than the fee-for-service patient. Therefore, fee-for-service gross charges in the medical group may not be representative of the services that will be used by the prepaid patient. Second, the prepaid capitation has no contractual or charity adjustments and no bad debts, while the fee-for-service gross charges includes these adjustments and allowances.

There is little that the group can do to compensate for the first problem—different utilization. Over time the group will develop data on prepaid utilization and may then revise "outside service" gross charges. The second problem—adjustments and allowances—can be compensated for easily by using discounted fee-for-service gross charges. Another distinction in the use of gross charges is the tendency of some groups to constantly adjust their gross charges upward so that third-party reimbursers will correspondingly adjust reimbursement levels upward.

Summary

As a group enters into prepaid contracts, the need for more accurate and reliable measures of financial position and results of operations is critical. Therefore, the group must consider generally accepted accounting principles and, specifically, accrual accounting. This chapter introduced the conceptual framework of accounting, assumptions underlying financial statements, and generally accepted accounting principles.

The chapter discussed accounting principles as they apply to medical groups and related the financial risks of prepaid practice to the need for accounting information. A brief comparison of the cash and accrual bases of accounting was presented, with a strong recommendation for the adoption of accrual measurements for evaluation of performance in prepaid groups.

The chapter closed with some illustrations of accounting procedures for prepayment. Examples of data for evaluating the group's overall performance, the performance of individual departments and specialties, and for evaluation of prepaid contracts were presented. Also, some problems in the use of fee-for-service gross charges as a measure of the value of services provided on a prepaid contract were briefly discussed.

Chapter 5

Statement of Financial Position

In the first section of this chapter, assets, liabilities, and owners' equity are defined because they make up the equation that underlies the statement of financial position. Major classifications within the statement of financial position and the most common accounts used by medical groups are presented, with emphasis on the accounts having greater potential for being misunderstood. For example, owners' equity accounts receive more attention because they are influenced by both accounting and legal requirements. All of the account numbers, account titles, and classifications are drawn from the chart of accounts presented in Chapter 3. The last section of the chapter provides a format for the statement of financial position prepared on an accrual basis.

Financial Position Equation and Basic Definitions

The financial position equation, assets equal equities, underlies every financial position statement. Assets are resources of the entity, while equities are claims against these resources. Equities are divided into two major groups: liabilities, which represent amounts owed to outside creditors; and the residual (owners' equity). The condensed statement of financial position shown below, although not acceptable because of insufficient disclosure, illustrates the interrelationships of the major components of the entity's position.

Seaview Medical Group
Statement of Financial Position
June 30, 19X4

Assets	$800,000	Liabilities	$300,000
		Owners' equity	500,000
Total assets	$800,000	Total equity	$800,000

Assets (Accounts 1000 through 1999) are cash or other resources controlled by the entity that have the potential to increase future cash inflows or conserve future cash outflows.

Liabilities (Accounts 2000 through 2499) are debts or obligations arising from past transactions of the entity that will require a future outlay of cash or its equivalent in goods or services.

Owners' Equity (Accounts 2500 through 2799) is the excess of an entity's assets over its liabilities. The owners usually have no claim to cash payments other than those approved by the entity's governing board as a distribution of earnings or a return of amounts invested.

These definitions are based on the theory that the value of an entity, although measured imperfectly, is related to cash and future cash flows. Proper measurement of income for a period requires expansion of the definition of assets and liabilities to include amounts that will be carried forward as balances into the future, although they will not have an impact on cash. To the extent these amounts are recognized as assets and liabilities within the framework of generally accepted accounting principles, they must be so classified.

Statement of Financial Position Classifications

If the statement of financial position is to be useful in making a variety of decisions, assets and liabilities must be classified by type, and disclosures within the statement and in the footnotes must describe adequately the group's financial position. The most common subdivision is to separate assets and liabilities into short-term (or current) and long-term categories. Current assets and current liabilities from this classification provide an indication of liquidity of a medical group or other entity. The most widely used ratio to demonstrate liquidity is the current ratio (current assets divided by current liabilities).

In addition to recognizing the current portions of assets and liabilities, six other classifications commonly used within the statement of financial position are presented below along with their identifying account numbers from the CRAHCA Chart of Accounts. All eight of these classifications are described in this section, with selected accounts providing even greater detail within each class.

Assets

1100-1300	Current assets
1400	Investments and long-term receivables
1500-1800	Noncurrent tangible assets (fixed assets)
1900	Intangible and other assets

Liabilities

2100-2300	Current liabilities
2400	Long-term liabilities

Owners' Equity

2500	Partners' equity (partnerships)
	or
2600	Stockholders' equity (corporations)

1100-1300 Current Assets

Current assets include cash or other assets that will be converted into cash within one year through normal operations of the medical group. This definition excludes restricted cash and investments, which, although highly marketable, are not available to finance operations. Classifications of current assets and current liabilities are intended to show the group's liquidity at the date of the financial statement. Current liabilities often are subtracted from current assets to measure working capital. Changes in working capital give some indication of ability to pay debts and finance new opportunities. Examples of current assets in a medical group are:

1110	Cash—unrestricted
1170	Marketable securities and short-term investments
1210	Accounts receivable
1310	Supply inventories
1340	Ancillary department supplies
1380	Prepaid expenses (e.g., insurance)

Allowance for Uncollectible Receivables (Account 1230) is a contra-asset account that is created when Provision for Bad Debts (Account 4600) is reported on the income statement. This contra account (1230) is reduced when specific patient receivables prove to be uncollectible and are written off the books. In no way does the allowance account represent cash or other resources set aside to offset losses on bad accounts, an implication that may have been conveyed by the older terminology "reserve for bad debts." Medical groups using direct write-off would not use Account 1230.

1400 Investments and Long-Term Receivables

These investments are segregated from current assets because they are held for purposes other than conversion into cash to finance current operations. Their acquisition actually may use cash that would otherwise be available as a current asset. Examples of investments and long-term receivables include the following:

1410	Cash—restricted
1420	Long-term receivables
1430	Investments in securities

1440	Investments in an affiliate
1450	Property held for future use

Securities such as long-term bonds, deposit certificates, and preferred or common stock (Account 1430) may be accumulated in a fund to accomplish a special purpose, such as repayment of long-term debt or facilities expansion. The fund is built up over time so that there is no current drain on working capital when the long-term debt is paid or the facilities are acquired.

Another type of investment is that held to exercise control of, or to significantly influence a closely related entity (Account 1440). If 20 percent or more of the voting common stock of one corporation is owned by another, the investor is presumed to be able to influence the activities of the investee company significantly. These securities are carried as an investment and are accounted for under the "equity method," whereby the investor accrues a share (equal to its ownership percentage) of the investee's income or loss. Dividends are treated as a reduction of the investment rather than as income. If more than 50 percent of the voting stock is owned, the investor has control of the investee corporation and consolidated financial statements should be prepared that treat the investor and the investee as one economic entity. Further discussion of consolidated statements is beyond the scope of this volume.

A third type of investment (Account 1450) involves holding property that is not used currently in operations but that may be used in the future.

1500-1800 Noncurrent Tangible Assets
This classification includes tangible, long-lived assets used in group operations. The previous section classified property not used in group operations as investments. Examples of long-lived tangible assets used in a group are:

1510	Land
1530	Land improvements
1540	Buildings
1700	Furniture, fixtures, and equipment

For each asset or group of similar assets subject to depreciation (or in the case of leased property and equipment, subject to amortization), a contra account (1600-1699, 1800-1899) for accumulated depreciation is maintained. The difference between the cost of an asset recorded in the asset account and its related accumulated depreciation is that asset's book value. Accumulated depreciation is merely the amount equal to that portion of the asset's cost charged to operations as depreciation in the past. The caveat holds here as well as with other contra-asset accounts that the accumulated depreciation account has nothing to do with the replacement of the asset, as the older terminology, "reserve for depreciation," might imply.

When an individual asset is retired or sold, it is necessary to remove the balance in both the asset and accumulated depreciation accounts in order to accomplish removal of the asset's book value in question. The difference between book value and sale proceeds measures the gain or loss on the sale.

1900 Intangible and Other Assets
Long-lived intangible assets probably are few in number in a medical group; however, there are several possibilities:

1910	Organization costs
1920	Goodwill
1930	Relocation costs

Organization costs include legal, accounting, and state-imposed fees that are necessary incorporation costs. These sums usually are written off over the 60-month period following the organization date, because this minimum amortization period is allowed by the Internal Revenue Code. Purchased Goodwill (Account 1920) is the amount paid for a going concern in excess of the fair market value of all other acquired assets. According to generally accepted accounting principles, goodwill is to be written off in no more than 40 years. This treatment is at variance with income tax regulations prohibiting goodwill from being written off as an operating expense. Relocation costs are expenditures related to moving the group practice as a whole, or a material segment of it, to benefit the group's future operations. These costs may be capitalized and written off over a reasonable period, perhaps three to five years. The three intangible assets above cannot be sold separately from the entire medical group or major segments of it and therefore have no cash value. This fact explains why the accounting profession in general and credit grantors in particular traditionally put little weight on intangibles when they are considering assets as security for a loan.

2100-2300 Current Liabilities
Current liabilities are obligations arising from past transactions that must be paid within one year by using current assets or creating other current liabilities. The chart of accounts has identified three groups of current liabilities. The 2100 series includes accounts payable, notes payable, claims payable for the prepaid component, and other short-term liabilities. The 2200 series includes payroll liabilities and accruals, and the 2300 series includes other accruals, deferrals, and miscellaneous current liabilities. Examples of current liabilities are:

2110	Accounts payable
2130	Claims payable
2140	Notes and loans payable
2150	Long-term debt—current portion
2210	Payroll withholdings

2250	Accrued payroll liabilities
2252	Accrued vacation, holiday, and sick pay
2310	Accrued liabilities—nonpayroll
2340	Patient deposits
2350	Accrued contract claims payable
2360	Deferred revenue—capitation or prepaid plan
2380	Deferred income taxes—current portion

Three of the accounts above require further comment. Accrued Liabilities-Nonpayroll (Account 2310) are recorded in the accounting records by an end-of-the-period adjusting entry. In these instances, services have been received and used by the group in operations prior to the supplier's billing date, which falls in the next accounting period. The adjusting entry reflects use of these services as an expense in the income statement and shows an unpaid liability in the balance sheet. For example, claims for outside referrals and hospitalization of prepaid patients not yet invoiced to the group must be estimated and recorded as an expense of the period (Account 7200) and as a liability at the end of the period (Account 2350). Later, when the invoice is received, the claim should be transferred to Account 2130, Contract Claims Payable. An adjusting entry is also made to show the correct amount patients have paid in advance and to transfer any amounts earned to a revenue account in the income statement. Deferred Revenue—Capitation or Prepaid Plans (Account 2360) represents capitation payments received by the group in advance of the period for which the group is to provide care.

Long-Term Debt—Current Portion (Account 2150) is classified as a current liability if current assets are to be used to satisfy this debt. Regardless of its classification, the current portion of long-term debt should include only the principal that will be repaid plus the interest expense that has accrued as of the balance sheet date.

2400 Long-Term Liabilities

These obligations will not mature and therefore will not require use of current assets within a year of the balance sheet date. The current portion related to these debts was discussed under current liabilities. Disclosure should be made of the interest rate, repayment schedule, security covenants, and other material information in the notes to the financial statements. Illustrations of accounts classified as long-term liabilities are:

2410	Long-term notes payable
2420	Mortgage payable
2430	Construction loans
2440	Capital lease obligation—long-term portion
2480	Deferred income taxes—long-term portion

The last two accounts listed above require more explanation: capital leases because they are becoming increasingly common, and deferred income taxes because they are frequently misunderstood.

Noncancellable leases that meet one or more of the following criteria established by the Financial Accounting Standards Board must be recorded as a Capital Lease Obligation (Account 2440).

- Lease transfers ownership to the lessee during lease term.
- Lease contains a bargain purchase option.
- Lease term (including any bargain renewal options) is 75 percent or more of the estimated economic life of the property.
- Present value of the minimum lease payments (excluding executory costs, for example, maintenance, taxes, and insurance) equals or exceeds 90 percent of the fair value of the leased property.[1]

Accounting for a capital lease is very similar to accounting for the purchase of an asset on the installment plan. Fair value of the asset and payments required under the lease are used to determine the effective interest rate and initial present value of the capital lease liability. Once capitalized, the asset and lease liability are accounted for separately. The asset is depreciated, using an acceptable depreciation method over its economic useful life, and the lease liability is treated like any other installment liability.

Leases that are noncancellable but do not meet any of the four criteria above are discussed in the following chapter as operating leases. For all noncancellable leases, capital or operating, a general description of the leasing arrangements should be included in the notes to the financial statements. These include, but are not limited to, the following: basis for contingent rental payments, renewal or purchase options, escalation clauses, and financial restrictions. FASB Statement #13 should be consulted for additional disclosure requirements that apply specifically to capital leases.

Chapter 3 explains the contents of Account 2380, Deferred Income Taxes—Current Portion, as follows: "Timing differences between tax on income reported in financial statements and tax on income reported in the tax return, when the timing difference is related to a current asset." The explanation for Account 2480, Deferred Income Taxes—Long-term Portion, is identical except noncurrent is substituted for current. Medical groups subject to income taxes and, in fact, having taxable income would use a deferred income tax account

[1]FASB Statement #13, *Accounting for Leases*, November, 1976.

if they use accounting methods for a given revenue or expense item on the income statement that are different from those used on the tax return. An example of this would be using straight-line depreciation for an x-ray machine on the books and accelerated depreciation on the tax return. This situation results in a timing difference in depreciation expense, causing income taxes in the income statement to be different from actual income taxes on the tax return. When timing differences cause the income tax expense reported on the income statement to be larger than the actual amount determined on the tax return, the deferred income tax account is increased and vice versa.

2500 Partners' Equity

Partners' equity often is displayed on the balance sheet simply as total partners' capital. Contributed capital and undistributed earnings frequently are lumped together because the partnership agreement, rather than a state incorporation statute, governs any distributions to owners. General partners also have unlimited liability with respect to the debts of the partnership, so the record of contributed capital is not as important to creditors as it would be in a corporation. The chart of accounts separates the two as follows in order to promote a clear record for each individual partner.

2510	Contributed capital
2520	Undistributed earnings

The remainder of this section will concentrate on stockholders' equity for an incorporated medical group.

2600 Stockholders' Equity

Stockholders' equity in a corporate organization is divided into components of contributed capital and retained earnings. This section of the statement of financial position (balance sheet) often is confusing to the uninitiated reader because it contains an admixture of legal and accounting terminology that has not been standardized fully. Some examples are par value, stated value, capital contributed in excess of par, and restricted or appropriated retained earnings. One major objective here is to clarify these terms and to demonstrate the relationship between the retained earnings account and the income statement. Stockholders' equity accounts include the following:

2610	Preferred stock
2620	Common stock
2630	Capital contributed in excess of par
2640	Donated capital
2670	Retained earnings—unappropriated
2680	Retained earnings—appropriated
2690	Treasury stock

Contributed Capital. Investments by a stockholder directly in a corporation usually increase both assets and owners' equity. If the amount invested exceeds the par value (or stated value) indicated on the shares issued, the excess is recorded properly in Capital Contributed in Excess of Par (Account 2630). The par or stated value of the contributed capital is recorded in the capital stock account (2610 for preferred or 2620 for common) and represents the legal or stated capital that provides creditors with a financial cushion. Unless the laws of the state of incorporation provide otherwise, the stockholders' equity in total may not be reduced below this legal or stated capital benchmark by declaring dividends or reacquiring owners' shares. The par value of a share, then, is nothing more than the legal capital per share and, at the same time, the minimum consideration the corporation must receive to issue the share as fully paid. Once so issued, any holder's liability is limited to the amount invested.

Preferred Stock (Account 2610) has certain preferences and limitations written into the contract between the corporation and the preferred stockholders. Typical preferences include dividends up to some specified percent, if declared, and accumulation of dividends in arrears for years in which they were not distributed. Dividends in arrears are not a liability until declared, but they are disclosed in the notes to the financial statement and, generally, they must be declared and paid before any dividend can be declared on common stock. Another preference is a prior claim on assets over common stock if the corporation is liquidated.

Limitations in preferred stock contracts commonly include foregoing the right to vote for directors and to participate in dividends beyond a given percent or a set dollar amount per share.

With both common and preferred stock, the number of shares authorized, issued, and outstanding must be disclosed in the financial statement along with the number of shares reacquired but not cancelled. These reacquired shares are called Treasury Stock (Account 2690) and they are usually subtracted from total owners' equity. If they are reissued above their acquisition cost, the excess is added to an appropriate contributed capital account such as "Capital Contributed from Treasury Stock Transactions." This gain (or any other dealing in the corporation's own stock) must never be included in retained earnings. If the treasury shares are issued at less than cost, this difference may first be applied to reduce Capital Contributed in Excess of Par (Account 2630). If the difference is larger than this latter account, retained earnings will be reduced for the remainder in a manner similar to a dividend transaction.

The balance sheet also should disclose key preferences of the preferred stock and its limitations such as "seven percent, cumulative, and nonparticipating."

Retained Earnings. The definition of owners' equity provided in the first section of this chapter stressed its residual nature. Owners' equity is equal to assets minus liabilities or net assets. When net assets increase, owners' equity increases and vice versa. When net income is recorded, net assets obviously increase and the opposite is true in the case of a net loss. The retained earnings account (2670) is the component of owners' equity that accumulates net income or net loss. It is neither an asset nor a device to earmark assets; it is used to report the source of part of the medical group's net assets and, hence, owners' equity.

When a dividend is declared, retained earnings are decreased because net assets are decreased in the same amount as the increase in the current liability, "Dividends Payable." A stock dividend payable in the medical group's own stock, however, does not decrease net assets but decreases retained earnings by the same amount as the increase in contributed capital caused by the issuance of more shares of stock.

In unusual instances, transactions involving corrections of prior years' income may be reported directly in the retained earnings account. These changes, which also affect net asset components, necessarily cause the level of retained earnings on the balance sheet to change.

Retained earnings may be restricted by statute, creditor's contract, or action by the board of directors. State law may require the restriction of retained earnings equal to the cost of any treasury stock. Once the cost of treasury stock acquired is equal to the total retained earnings, no more treasury stock may be acquired or dividends declared because to do so would reduce total owners' equity and net assets below the legal capital. The board of directors also may "appropriate" retained earnings by shifting them to one or several retained earnings accounts, such as "Retained Earnings—Appropriated for Expansion." Again, this does nothing to the net assets and does not earmark any asset for a special project. The board that follows this tactic may better serve its purposes by a letter accompanying the financial statement and, if liquid assets are available, may actually establish a special asset fund.

Further misunderstandings are created when the older terminology, "earned surplus" is used for retained earnings and "capital surplus," is used to describe all contributed capital amounts in excess of legal capital. It is no surprise that the accounting profession has taken the stand that both the terms "surplus" and "reserve" (other than retained earnings appropriations) should be dropped from all account titles and captions in the balance sheet.

Donated Capital (Account 2640), on the other hand, is a legitimate description to use when assets have been contributed to the group as a gift. This account is a component of contributed capital because a gift of assets does not give rise to earnings retained as a result of successful operations. It is disclosed separately because no stock is issued in exchange for the assets received. If the donor has placed a restriction on the use of the capital then the restriction needs to be disclosed and a separate category of donated capital created until the restriction has expired.

A Comparison of the Statement of Financial Position and the Statement of Assets and Liabilities

Almost all of this chapter and the next are devoted to the development and understanding of external financial statements prepared on the accrual basis—the basis required by generally accepted accounting principles. The vast majority of fee-for-service medical groups, however, report on a modified or partial cash basis for income tax purposes as well as for external financial statements. This practice is convenient and well-accepted, but these statements may differ materially from those prepared on the accrual basis. The name of the cash basis statement that parallels the statement of financial position is statement of assets and liabilities.

To highlight the differences between the cash and accrual bases, a statement of financial position is presented and compared with a statement of assets and liabilities based on cash transactions in Exhibit 5-1. The accounts and classifications used are the financial position classifications and accounts introduced earlier in this chapter. It is assumed that both statements are prepared for the same entity and the same period of time.

When the two columns in Exhibit 5-1 for Seaview Medical Group are compared, it is readily apparent that the cash basis statement of assets and liabilities omits a significant number of assets and liabilities included in the accrual basis statement of financial position. Specifically, accounts receivable are omitted because the cash basis does not record revenue until cash is collected for services to patients. Supply inventories, prepaid expenses, goodwill, and relocation costs are omitted because the cash outlay for these items, made in the past, is treated immediately as an expense. Liabilities related to operations (accounts payable, claims payable, accrued liabilities, and deferred income taxes) are omitted because their related expenses are not recognized under the cash basis until they are actually paid in cash. Another liability, Deferred Revenue—Prepaid Plan (Account 2360), is omitted because the cash received from the prepaid plan for future services is treated upon its receipt as earned revenue.

Differences between assets and liabilities reported on the cash basis and those reported on the accrual basis necessarily give rise to differences in the owners' equity—specifically, retained earnings. Exhibit 5-2 reconciles retained earnings on the cash basis with retained earnings on the accrual basis by adding or subtracting differences in asset and liability reporting between the cash and accrual bases. Differences between the cash and accrual bases are generated

EXHIBIT 5-1
STATEMENT OF FINANCIAL POSITION COMPARED WITH STATEMENT OF ASSETS AND LIABILITIES

SEAVIEW MEDICAL GROUP
POSITION STATEMENT
December 31, 19X4

		Statement of Financial Position (Accrual Basis)	Statement of Assets and Liabilities (Cash Basis)
ASSETS			
Current assets:			
1110 Unrestricted cash		$ 74,300	$ 74,300
1170 Marketable securities		1,500	1,500
1210 Accounts receivable	$360,000		
1230 Uncollectible accounts	(20,000)	340,000	
1310 Supply inventories		32,000	
1380 Prepaid expenses		30,000	
Total current assets		$477,800	$ 75,800
Investments:			
1450 Property held for future use		$ 76,000	$ 76,000
Fixed assets:			
1510 Land		$100,000	$100,000
1700 Furniture, fixtures, and equipment		240,000	240,000
1800 Accumulated depreciation		(186,000)	(186,000)
Total fixed assets		$154,000	$154,000
Intangible assets:			
1910 Organization costs		$ 11,000	$ 11,000
1920 Goodwill		9,000	
1930 Relocation costs		15,000	
Total intangible assets		$ 35,000	$ 11,000
Total assets		$742,800	$316,800

EXHIBIT 5-1 (continued)

LIABILITIES AND OWNERS' EQUITY		
Liabilities		
Current liabilities:		
2110 Accounts payable	$ 40,000	
2130 Contract claims payable	30,000	
2150 Current portion of long-term debt	8,900	8,900
2160 Capital lease obligation	2,400	2,400
2210 Payroll withholding	9,000	9,000
2250 Accrued payroll liabilities	9,000	
2310 Accrued liabilities—nonpayroll	3,000	
2360 Deferred revenue—prepaid plan	30,000	
2380 Deferred income taxes	(6,000)	
Total current liabilities	$126,300	$ 20,300
Long-term liabilities:		
2420 Mortgage payable	$125,400	$125,400
2440 Capital lease obligation	21,100	21,100
2480 Deferred income taxes	0	
Total long-term liabilities	$146,500	$146,500
Total liabilities	$272,800	$166,800
Owners' equity		
Contributed capital:		
2620 Common stock	$ 60,000	$ 60,000
2630 Capital contributed in excess of par	5,000	5,000
2640 Donated capital	1,000	1,000
Total contributed capital	$ 66,000	$ 66,000
Retained Earnings:		
2670 Retained earnings—unappropriated	$404,000	$ 84,000
Total owners' equity	$470,000	$150,000
Total equities	$742,800	$316,800

by omitting patient receivables, short-term prepayments, and most payables related to operations from the statement of assets and liabilities. In terms of balance sheet classifications, current assets, current liabilities, and stockholders' equity are most affected. For a credit grantor, the cash basis may present a serious deficiency because analysis of liquidity depends on an accurate reporting of the two factors that determine working capital (current assets less current liabilities). Owners, present or prospective, who are interested in the book value of the shares of stock may be misled because retained earnings might be greater or less than they would be under the accrual system. For groups providing prepaid care, external reporting requirements vary from state to state, but federal regulatory agencies mandate the use of the accrual method.

EXHIBIT 5-2
RECONCILIATION OF RETAINED EARNINGS

SEAVIEW MEDICAL GROUP
RECONCILIATION OF RETAINED EARNINGS—CASH AND ACCRUAL
December 31, 19X4

Cash basis retained earnings			$ 84,000
Add:			
Accounts receivable not recorded on the cash basis		$340,000	
Assets on hand that were expensed when paid for in cash:			
Supply inventories	$32,000		
Prepaid expenses	30,000		
Goodwill	9,000		
Relocation costs	15,000	86,000	426,000
			$510,000
Less:			
Liabilities not recorded on cash basis:			
Accounts payable	$40,000		
Contract claims payable	30,000		
Accrued payroll liabilities	9,000		
Accrued liabilities—nonpayroll	3,000		
Deferred income taxes	(6,000)	$ 76,000	
Patient deposits treated on the cash basis as revenue		30,000	$106,000
Accrual basis retained earnings			$404,000

Why use the accrual approach in the statement of financial position if the net differences possibly would be slight in comparison to using the cash basis? At least three reasons stand out. First, the accrual approach provides much more information about the current asset and current liability components of working capital. Second, the reported working capital cannot be distorted by the timing of bill payments and collection efforts as it can be under the cash basis. Third, if audited statements are required, generally accepted accounting principles call for use of the accrual basis to allow the auditor to provide an unqualified opinion on the financial statements.

The accrual basis statement of financial position and the cash basis statement of assets and liabilities presented for Seaview Medical Group assume an incorporated medical group. What further differences between these two approaches would be introduced if the medical group was organized as a partnership? On the accrual basis, the partnership would report no income tax liability because the partners pay taxes on their respective shares. Any physician-owner bonus is accrued as a liability in a corporation, while in a partnership this amount is included in the undistributed earnings. On the cash basis, the differences between an incorporated medical group and a partnership are slight. The physician-owner bonus is included among the expenses in arriving at corporate net income; in a partnership, net income is added to undistributed earnings and the sum is then reduced by any physician-owner bonus.

Summary

This chapter presented the definitions of assets, liabilities, and owners' equity—the components of financial position. These definitions were followed by major classifications within the statement of financial position along with accounts used frequently by medical groups, with particular attention given to accounts commonly misunderstood. The final section of this chapter compared and explained the differences between the statement of financial position prepared on the accrual basis and the statement of assets and liabilities prepared on the cash basis. Receivables, short-term prepayments, and most payables related to operations are omitted in the statement of assets and liabilities. These individual components of current assets and current liabilities enter into the determination of working capital. In addition, because of offsetting omissions, inherent differences between the two approaches may be reduced with respect to classification totals such as working capital, net assets, and retained earnings. Analysis of financial liquidity requires that the individual components of working capital, as well as the totals, be known. This aspect of the comparison stresses the accrual basis of accounting for external reporting purposes.

Chapter 6

Income Statement

As recently as 50 years ago, major public corporations did not publish an income statement because they were afraid it would be too revealing. Today, income statements are routinely provided by public corporations to external users and made available to the interested public in general. Closely held entities such as medical groups organized as professional corporations only need to provide this information to those who either have a legal right to see it or have close business relationships warranting it.

The income statement provides data addressed to an issue of key importance: "What were the results of operations for a given time period?" It provides information on accomplishments, measured in revenue dollars and matched with related efforts, which are reflected by goods and services consumed (expenses). By comparing income statements for several periods, significant trends may be identified and projections made of the entity's future earning power.

This chapter will show how the income statement interrelates with the statement of financial position (balance sheet) and how the income statement is developed on the accrual basis; it will conclude with various income statement formats.

Interrelationship between the Income Statement and the Statement of Financial Position

At one time in the development of accounting, individual transactions were not recorded. At the end of a period of time, assets and liabilities were listed and income for the period was determined by the change in net assets (assets minus liabilities), adjusted for any withdrawals or contributions by the owners. This change in net assets represented the increase in owners' equity. Today, with each transaction recorded, an increase in net assets caused by operations is also recorded in a revenue account. Likewise, any decrease in net assets due to operations is recorded in an expense account. The difference between revenues and expenses is the net income and, also, the increase in owners' equity due to operations.

The following illustration shows the relationship between the statement of financial position prepared at the end of 19X3, the income statement for 19X4, and the new statement of financial position prepared at the end of 19X4. To simplify the illustration, only a few columns representing major categories are used and only revenue and expense transactions affecting operations have been included. Note that the columns present the basic equation in accounting:

Assets = Liabilities + Owners' Equity.

In the illustration, the net income is $10,000, the difference between revenues of $510,000 and expenses of $500,000. Net assets and retained earnings also are increased by the same amount. Revenue transactions brought in $495,000 of new assets, and existing liabilities were reduced by $15,000 because services were provided to patients who had paid in advance. Without regard to expenses, the revenue transactions created net assets of $510,000. Expenses, however, involved both consuming $470,000 of assets and increasing liabilities by $30,000, because goods and services were used for which payment had not yet been made. When these expense transactions, which caused net assets to decrease by $500,000, are matched with the revenue transactions, the overall impact on net assets is an increase of $10,000. As observed before, when net assets increase because of operations, the residual owners' equity also increases. The retained earnings component reflects this change. The income statement, then, explains the changes in the balance sheet's retained earnings account that are caused by business operations.

	Assets	=	Liabilities	+	Owners' Equity		
					Contributed Capital		Retained Earnings
Statement of financial position 12/31/X3	$200,000	=	$60,000	+	$120,000	+	$ 20,000
19X4 gross charges	495,000	=	(15,000)				510,000
19X4 expenses	(470,000)	=	30,000				(500,000)
Statement of financial position 12/31/X4	$225,000	=	$75,000	+	$120,000	+	$ 30,000

Development of the Accrual Income Statement

Income statements attempt to match revenues realized in a given time period with costs of goods and services consumed to produce those revenues. This section examines these components of net income in detail.

Revenue Measurement and Disclosure

As seen in the illustration above, revenues increase net assets and owners' equity. Revenue realization rules establish when this increased value related to output of services should be recognized. Two logical alternatives for a medical group are to realize this increase in value when cash is collected or when the contract periods begin and the employer groups are billed. Accrual basis income statements consider the new asset created when service is performed; however, two conditions must be met: 1) The earning process must be substantially completed by providing the professional service, and 2) objective evidence must exist to show that the asset will be collected.

There are several levels or steps in the measurement of revenue. The use of gross charges represents a comprehensive method of measuring revenue. Gross charges for services is the key revenue figure because it represents the value of services provided to the medical group's patients. The medical group recognizes adjustments to gross charges whenever it provides services to patients whose payment modes fall short of reimbursing the group at full market value. The objectives of the gross charges and adjustments accounts established in this chapter are:

(1) To compile a complete and accurate record, on the accrual basis, of the market value of all services provided

(2) To maintain a record of the adjustments that reduce gross charges to adjusted gross charges (billings).

The amount of adjusted gross charges represents the dollar value of services actually billed to patients. Write-offs are the difference between amounts actually billed to patients and amounts received by the group. Net revenue is the final revenue account and, on the accrual basis, represents earned revenue for the operating period. Although the accrual income statement could begin with net revenue, the amounts of gross charges, adjustments, and allowances are important to all interested parties. The amount of resources consumed as expenses should have a direct relationship to gross charges. Services were provided and resources consumed whether cash is collected or not.

Different types of gross charges should be disclosed. Charges to patients for medical equipment and optical goods should be segregated from gross charges for professional services. Nonoperating revenues also should be disclosed separately. The group offering prepaid service on a discounted fee-for-service basis measures revenue by recording gross charges and treating the discount as an adjustment. The group offering prepaid care on a capitation basis measures revenue in the income statement as the amount of capitation payments and uses the fee-for-service equivalent of prepaid service in evaluating departmental performance.

Revenues earned from providing services to prepaid patients on a capitation basis should be disclosed and realized as the services are made available to plan participants. Professional services contracted for outside the group should be accrued as expenses in the period that patients are served. Key provisions of the prepaid plan should be included in the notes to the financial statements.

Expense Measurement and Disclosure

Expenses are resources consumed in the process of generating revenues. Groups operating on an accrual basis should match expired costs (expenses) to benefits earned (revenues) regardless of when payments or collections occur. Operating expenses are defined as expired costs incurred in the process of providing health care services to patients. These expenses are used to determine net operating income. Nonoperating expenses are those expenses generated by activities not associated with the provision of services to patients. Examples include research expenses and management of long-term investments and endowments. In the income statement, these expenses are presented after nonoperating revenues. The CRAHCA Prepaid Group Chart of Accounts organizes operating expenses in three major categories:

5000 Human resource expenses
6000 Physical resource expenses
7000 Purchased services and general and administrative expenses

Within each category are numerous detailed accounts accompanied by definitions. One possibility in preparing the income statement would be to include the three major categories above in the body of the statement, supported by schedules providing adequate detail. This degree of condensation in the body of the statement is not recommended because certain expenses within these categories have special interest for the reader. The following detail is recommended as a minimum if the items are material in amount.

5000 Human resource expenses
- 5100-5299 Physician salaries, bonuses, and benefits
- 5300-5999 Other salaries and benefits

6000 Physical resource expenses
- 6100-6399 Supplies expense
- 6410-6439 Rental and lease expenses—buildings and grounds
- 6440-6499 Other buildings and grounds expenses

	6500 and 6700	Depreciation and amortization of physical resources
	6600-6699	Rental and lease expenses—furniture, fixtures, and equipment
	6800-6899	Other furniture, fixtures, and equipment expenses
	6900-6999	Other physical resource expenses
7000	Purchased services and general and administrative expenses	
	7100-7199	Purchased services — nonprepaid professional and medical
	7200-7299	Purchased services — prepaid professional and medical
	7300-7799	General and administrative expenses
	7800-7899	Interest expenses

In an incorporated medical group, all salaries are expenses of the corporate entity. In a partnership, however, owners' salaries may either be recognized in a similar manner or be treated as a portion of the resultant net income that provides the basis for distributions to the partners. For comparisons between groups and between years in the same group, separate disclosure of physicians' compensation appears to be necessary for owners to assess the progress and potential of the group.

Other salaries and benefits and purchased professional and medical services also are of direct interest to owners. Adding staff or purchasing services should be analyzed for their impact on the cost of services received by patients and on gross charges.

All expenses that are "book charges," such as depreciation and amortization, should be disclosed separately because they do not decrease cash or working capital in the current period. The accounting profession requires the reporting entity to disclose in the financial statements or notes thereto a general description of depreciation by major classes of assets, the balances of these major classes, and accumulated depreciation by class or in total.

Other physical resource expenses include items such as supplies, utilities, insurance, property taxes, maintenance, repairs, and cost of goods sold to patients. Creditors may be interested in details about cost of goods sold, maintenance, and repairs. If the medical group sells equipment, medicine, or other items, it is useful to know both the revenue from and the cost of these items to determine their contribution. To a certain extent, maintenance and repairs may be deferred or accelerated on either the accrual or cash basis because there is some discretion on the part of management with regard to their timing. It is important, therefore, to compare one period's expenditure with that of others. Insurance, particularly professional liability insurance, is a sensitive expense for which accurate information should be readily available.

Disclosure of Leases
Operating or capital noncancellable leases call for a great deal of disclosure in the financial statements and their accompanying notes. Capital leases are accounted for in a manner similar to that of the purchase of a depreciable fixed asset on the installment plan. Operating leases, on the other hand, are accounted for much like month-to-month rentals, but with a great deal more disclosure because of their noncancellable nature.

For operating leases having an initial or remaining term in excess of one year, the following must be disclosed.

- Minimum rental payments in aggregate as of the latest balance sheet date, and the minimum rentals for each of the five succeeding fiscal years.

- Total minimum rentals to be shown under noncancellable subleases as of the latest balance sheet date.

- Rental expense for each period an income statement is presented, with separate amounts for minimum rentals, contingent rentals, and sublease rental income. Rental payments under leases with terms of a month or less that were not renewed need not be recorded.

The general description of leasing arrangement terms also must be disclosed. Requirements are largely the same for both operating and capital leases.

Interest expenses are disclosed separately for several reasons. Among these is the fact that capital lease payments, particularly in their early years, include relatively large amounts of interest. By separating out interest expenses, comparison of a group using large amounts of debt financing with a group using mainly financing by owners' equity is facilitated. Interest expenses also are deductible in arriving at both taxable income and net income. Dividends paid to stockholders are not deductible in determining either of these amounts.

Disclosure of Income Taxes
Income taxes are included in the income statement if the entity is subject to these taxes and if there is taxable income. If there are no timing differences of the nature discussed in the statement of financial position chapter, the income tax expense in the statement and in the tax return will be the same. Where timing differences do exist, the income tax expense and the actual amount of taxes to be paid will be different. This difference will increase or decrease the deferred income tax account(s) in the balance sheet.

Income taxes may be reduced by investment tax credits obtained by purchasing qualified depreciable assets. These credits are used to satisfy tax liabilities and thus save the taxpayer cash; however, the question of how to account for these credits remains. The major alternatives are: to flow the credits through the income statement in the year the qualified asset is purchased and thus reduce reported taxes in that single year; or to spread the tax reduction effect of the credits over the life of the related asset. In a medical group corporation, investment tax credits are used to offset corporate taxes. If the flow-through method is used (assuming there are income tax expenses to be offset), book value of the capital stock is increased immediately by the amount of the credit. This increase takes place gradually if the impact of the investment credit is spread over the life of the asset that created the credit.

In a partnership, a policy should be established with respect to passing the benefit of the investment tax credits through to partners to use on their individual income tax returns.

Reporting the Results of Operations— Accrual versus Cash Basis

Because of the wide use of the cash basis of accounting in medical groups, a similar comparison to the one provided in Chapter 5 is also provided in Exhibit 6-1. The accrual income statement is compared with the statement of revenues collected and expenses on the cash basis.

In a given year, differences between expense amounts reported using the cash basis approach and those reported in the accrual basis income statement are a matter of timing. If accounting periods were longer, for example three years, there would be fewer differences between these two income statement approaches. In accrual accounting, there is a deliberate effort to match expenses with revenue produced on a yearly or interim basis. This is not too difficult for items having a direct cause-and-effect relationship between revenues and expenses, such as supplies used, cost of goods sold, and purchased professional and medical services. For these items, the cash basis allows the period of the payment to govern expense recognition. Payment could either precede, follow, or match the period in which the resource is consumed.

In theory, the cost of long-lived assets is expensed over the life of the assets through depreciation under accrual basis accounting and expensed in the year cash is paid under cash basis accounting. In practice, depreciation and amortization, representing a systematic, rational allocation of the cost of long-lived assets, are treated in the same manner under the accrual basis as under the cash basis. The reason for this similarity is due largely to the influence of the Internal Revenue Code, which has required modification of the cash basis in order to use accrual treatment for long-lived assets. Accrual modifications to the cash basis may also be called for if inventories become material.

When it is difficult to match expenses with revenues on a cause-and-effect basis or by employing systematic allocations, accrual accounting expenses are recorded in the year of their incurrence if there is no specific identifiable

EXHIBIT 6-1
RESULTS OF OPERATIONS—ACCRUAL AND CASH BASES

SEAVIEW MEDICAL GROUP
OPERATING STATEMENT
For the Year 19X4

	Income Statement (Accrual Basis)	Statement of Revenues Collected and Expenses (Cash Basis)
Revenues:		
Gross charges	$2,000,000	
Contract revenues	337,600	
Total revenues	$2,337,600	
Adjustments and allowances	(240,000)	
Net revenues	$2,097,600	
Cash collected from patients		$2,260,000
Operating expenses:		
Nonphysician salaries and benefits	$ 450,000	$ 455,000
Supplies	120,000	139,000
Rent	84,000	84,000
Depreciation and amortization	47,500	41,500
Interest	9,300	9,300
Purchased services—prepaid professional and medical	98,000	172,000
Other operating expenses	196,000	202,000
Total operating expenses	$1,004,800	$1,102,800
Available for distribution to physicians	$1,092,800	$1,157,200
Distributions to physicians	1,157,200	1,157,200
Net loss before taxes	$ (64,400)	$ 0

future benefit. A good example is research and development. On the cash basis, this type of cost is always expensed when the cash outlay is made, regardless of when the cost is incurred.

In summary, in a given year, expenses other than depreciation, amortization, and possibly cost of goods sold tend to be different when using the accrual basis rather than the cash basis. Individual expense transactions will, of course, yield the same result if cash outlay for the expense is in the same period that the resource is consumed.

The revenue section used in the comparative illustration of the income statement and the statement of revenues collected and expenses—cash basis—introduces differences that are unique to medical groups in addition to those that commonly exist between the accrual and cash bases. The income statement illustration in the exhibit begins with gross charges. Gross charges are not a measure of revenue to be collected when adjustments are routinely granted or required and write-offs occur. Although this information is important, as stated previously, the accrual income statement could start with net revenue (gross charges minus adjustments and allowances), which is equivalent to the net billings to patients or third-party payors less write-offs. Because the group has a prepaid component, contract revenue is recorded as it is earned on the accrual basis and as cash is received on the cash basis.

The difference between the cash basis and the accrual basis is again one of timing. Because of unevenness of collection efforts, problems may arise in evaluating operations for a given period. During periods in which cash collected from patients exceeds net billings for services performed, revenues and net income under the cash basis will be greater than revenues and net income reported on the accrual basis and vice versa. Delaying recognition of revenues until cash is collected, as the cash basis usually does, generally tends to magnify differences between the cash and accrual bases. This tendency can result in a later reporting of net income on the cash basis income statement and lower amounts of assets and retained earnings on the statement of assets and liabilities. For a rapidly expanding medical group, these differences are more severe on the income statement than for a mature organization that has attained a stable level of operations. For the group adding or significantly expanding a prepaid component, the lag in the payment of claims payable on referrals can also create problems for a given period. A major increase in the level of claims from one period to the next can dramatically affect the group's financial position. A good example of the impact of this timing difference on the income statement can be seen in Exhibit 6-1, which shows Purchased Services—Prepaid Professional and Medical to be $98,000 on the accrual basis and $172,000 on the cash basis. One should recognize these differences when deciding which basis of accounting to use in a medical group.

Income Statement Formats

Two broad types of income statement formats are used in external financial reporting. The single-step format groups net revenues together, regardless of source, followed by a listing of each of the expense captions to arrive at net income. A second format, the multistep income statement, emphasizes the segregation of income derived from operations and nonoperating revenues and expenses. Other subtotals are included, such as gross profits on sales, when they are considered material.

Another variation in either the single- or multistep income statement, as well as in the statement of revenues collected and expenses, is to combine the income statement with the retained earnings statement. The retained earnings statement details changes in the balance of retained earnings from the beginning of the period to the end, including net income (loss), dividends declared, and, in rare instances, correction of prior year's income. Combining the two statements allows less chance of overlooking these corrections and also stresses the relationship between revenues, expenses, net income, and retained earnings. Internal operating statements prepared for departments and for each prepaid plan may employ any format that proves to be useful to managers and owner physicians. These internal reports will be discussed in Part III, *Financial Planning and Control*.

Summary

This chapter illustrated the relationship between the statement of financial position (balance sheet) and the income statement of a medical group. Next, the principles of revenue measurement and revenue disclosure were discussed followed by expense disclosures. An illustration of an income statement for a medical group with a prepaid component was then presented and compared with a statement of revenues collected and expenses prepared on a cash basis. The chapter concluded with a brief discussion of various income statement formats.

Chapter 7

Statement of Changes in Financial Position

The status of a group's assets, liabilities, and owners' equity in the statement of financial position and the summary of operations in the income statement present only a limited picture of the financial activities of the group. Comparative statements of financial position help to show what assets were purchased or sold and what liabilities were increased or paid off. The income statement shows the amount of resources provided by operations. Neither statement, however, provides a full picture of the resources provided and the uses to which they were put during the period.

The statement of changes in financial position presents information on the financing and investing activities of a group. Two common approaches to the statement of changes in financial position are: first, to define resources as cash flows, and second, to define resources as working capital flows. Although the second method is the most widely used in industry, the cash approach is more useful for a medical group. Therefore, only the cash approach will be described and illustrated.

There is a significant difference between the statement of changes in financial position and a conventional cash flow statement. In the conventional cash flow statement, a transaction that has no effect on cash, such as the purchase of equipment on credit, is not reported. The statement of changes in financial position includes any change that affects the financing and investing aspects of a group. In the instance of acquiring equipment by giving a note, the issuance of the note is treated as a source of cash and the acquisition of equipment is treated as a use of cash even though no cash was actually involved in the transaction.

A diagram illustrating the types of events and transactions that are reflected in the statement of changes in financial position is presented in Exhibit 7-1.

EXHIBIT 7-1
DIAGRAM OF STATEMENT OF CHANGES IN FINANCIAL POSITION

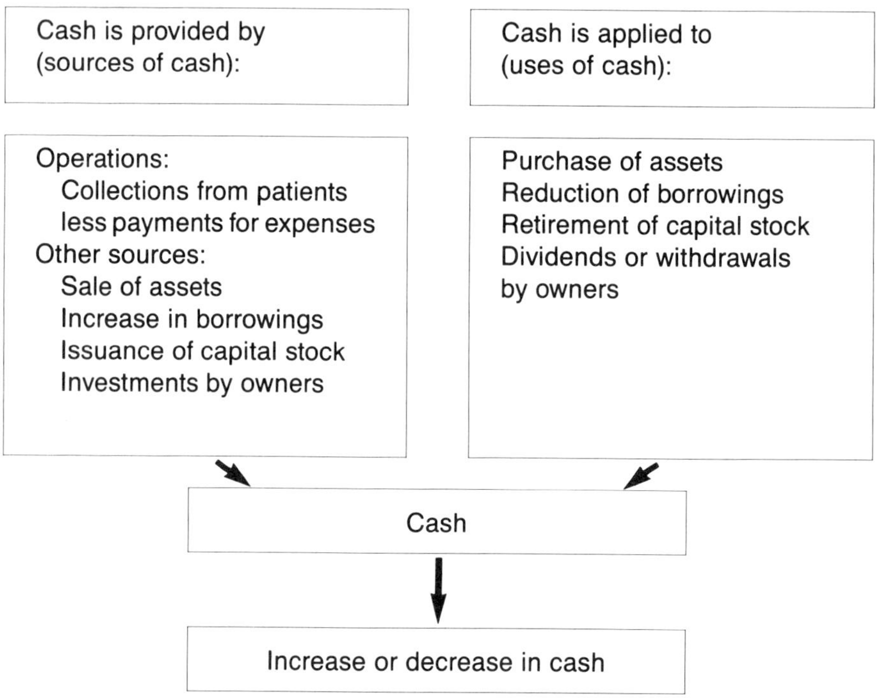

Development of Statement of Changes in Financial Position

Exhibit 7-2 shows the financial position of Seaview Medical Group as of the beginning and ending of the year in the first two columns. The amount of change in each component of financial position is shown in the third column, and the fourth column identifies by code what items are related to the change in the cash balance during the year. In this last column, code (1) indicates an item is related to both cash and an income statement account (operations). To arrive at cash collected from operations, the amount reported on the income statement as net revenues is adjusted for the decrease in accounts receivable and the increase in deferred prepaid revenues as follows:

Net revenues per income statement	$2,097,600
Decrease in accounts receivable (caused by collecting more from patients than the year's billings)	140,000
Increase in deferred prepaid revenues (caused by an increased prepayment by prepaid patients)	22,400
Cash collected from operations	$2,260,000

Operating expenses are also converted from the accrual amount to the cash basis by taking related balance sheet changes into account.

Operating expenses (other than depreciation, amortization, and physician salaries)	$ 957,300
Increase in supplies on hand	10,000
Increase in prepaid expenses	6,000
Decrease in accounts payable	9,000
Decrease in contract claims payable	74,000
Decrease in accrued liabilities	5,000
Cash paid for operating expense items	$1,061,300

According to the income statement, cash distributed to physicians amounted to $1,157,200. When this amount and the other cash operating expenses of $1,061,300 are subtracted from cash collected from operations, the resulting figure is the cash flow from operations. Depreciation and amortization expenses require no cash to be paid out in the current period, because they are "book charges" that are based on cash expenditures made in an earlier period.

Cash provided or applied by operations should be set out separately because the cash flow can be improved for a time by borrowing money or selling assets, but it is operations in the long term that generates money to pay back these debts and replace assets.

EXHIBIT 7-2

COMPARATIVE BALANCE SHEET AND INCOME STATEMENT
SEAVIEW MEDICAL GROUP
19X4

COMPARATIVE BALANCE SHEET

	Year's Beginning	Year's Ending	Amount of Change	Cause of Change
Current assets:				
Cash	$ 60,000	$ 74,300	$ 14,300	
Marketable securities	1,500	1,500	0	(2)
Accounts receivable (net)	480,000	340,000	(140,000)	(1)
Supplies	22,000	32,000	10,000	(1)
Prepaid expenses	24,000	30,000	6,000	(1)
Total current assets	$587,500	$477,800	$(109,700)	

EXHIBIT 7-2 (continued)

Investments:				
Property held for future use	$ 76,000	$ 76,000	0	(2)
Fixed assets:				
Land	0	100,000	100,000	(2)
Furniture, fixtures, and equipment	240,000	240,000	0	(2)
Accumulated depreciation	(150,000)	(186,000)	(36,000)	(3)
Total fixed assets	$ 90,000	$154,000	$ 64,000	
Intangible assets	46,500	35,000	(11,500)	(3)
Total assets	$800,000	$742,800	$ (57,200)	
Current liabilities:				
Accounts payable	$ 49,000	$ 40,000	$ (9,000)	(1)
Contract claims payable	104,000	30,000	(74,000)	(1)
Notes and loans payable	7,000	0	(7,000)	(2)
Current portion of long-term debt	10,200	11,300	1,100	(2)
Accrued liabilities	17,000	12,000	(5,000)	(1)
Payroll withholdings	9,000	9,000	0	(1)
Deferred prepaid revenues	7,600	30,000	22,400	(1)
Deferred income taxes	2,000	(6,000)	(8,000)	(3)
Total current liabilities	$205,800	$126,300	$ (79,500)	
Long-term liabilities:				
Long-term debt	$ 67,800	$146,500	$ 78,700	(2)
Deferred income taxes	5,000	0	(5,000)	(3)
Total long-term liabilities	$ 72,800	$146,500	$ 73,700	
Total liabilities	$278,600	$272,800	$ (5,800)	

EXHIBIT 7-2 (continued)

Owners' equity:				
Common stock	$ 60,000	$ 60,000	0	(2)
Capital in excess of par	6,000	6,000	0	(2)
Retained earnings	455,400	404,000	(51,400)	
Total owners' equity	$521,400	$470,000	$ (51,400)	
Total liabilities and owners' equity	$800,000	$712,800	$ (57,200)	

(1) Changes related to operations
(2) Changes related to financing and investing
(3) No effect on resources

INCOME STATEMENT

Gross charges	$2,000,000
Contract revenues	337,600
Adjustments and allowances	(240,000)
Net revenues	$2,097,600
Operating expenses	$ 957,300
Depreciation and amortization	47,500
Distributions to physicians	1,157,200
Total expenses	$2,162,000
Net loss before taxes	$ (64,400)

Exhibit 7-3 shows the statement of changes in financial position prepared by Seaview Medical Group for 19X4. It lists among the other sources of cash a mortgage of $90,000 that was used to finance 90 percent of the purchase of the real estate listed among other uses of cash at $100,000. This "all resources" approach to the statement of changes in financial position provides much more relevant information than merely including only the down payment of $10,000 as a use of cash.

EXHIBIT 7-3
STATEMENT OF CHANGES IN FINANCIAL POSITION
SEAVIEW MEDICAL GROUP
19X4

Cash collected from operations		$2,260,000
Cash paid for expenses	$1,061,300	
Cash paid to physicians	1,157,200	2,218,500
Cash provided by operations		$ 41,500
Other sources of cash:		
Issuance of mortgage		90,000
Total sources of cash		$ 131,500
Other uses of cash:		
Reduce debt	$ 10,200	
Retire note	7,000	
Purchase of real estate	100,000	117,200
Increase in cash during year		$ 14,300

Summary

The accrual income statement is not intended to be a source of information as to the amount of cash provided by operations in a single accounting period. Therefore, several income statement amounts are adjusted to reflect cash flows by using information from a comparative balance sheet on changes in assets and liabilities that are related to operations. Even a cash basis income statement (statement of revenues collected and expenses) must be adjusted to obtain cash provided by operations because it contains expenses that are "book charges" such as depreciation and amortization.

In addition to operating sources of cash, the statement of changes in financial position includes all other sources and uses of cash. When the various components of sources and uses are examined for several accounting periods to determine their changing importance over time, valuable information is revealed. Finally, the "all resources" approach to the statement of changes in financial position requires major noncash transactions to be reported.

Chapter 8

Summary of Part I

Prepaid medical care has experienced rapid growth during the last few years. From a survey conducted by the authors, it appears that two of the major reasons for this growth are to enable medical groups to meet competition for patients and to expand the number of patients served. When a medical group's entry into the prepaid field involves a capitation contract, the need for increased accounting information and utilization data arises immediately. It is the purpose of this text to provide practical financial management tools to assist medical groups in meeting this emerging need.

Part I has provided a data accumulation system and illustrative financial statements for a medical group with a prepaid component. It also presented a brief overview of the entire text.

Part II will outline a cost accounting system that develops the costs of serving prepaid patients to be used in controlling operations and renegotiating contracts.

Part III will demonstrate tools for budgetary planning and control that should be useful to the management of a group with capitation contracts.

For groups that restrict their entries into prepaid plans to those contracts that are essentially discounted fee-for-service, no changes are necessary in their accounting systems. *Practical Financial Management for Medical Groups* published by CRAHCA in 1979 should serve their needs very well.

In Chapter 2 an overview of the CRAHCA Prepaid Group Chart of Accounts, which is the heart of the data accumulation system, was presented with an explanation of the four fields of the coding structure. Also described in this chapter was the relationship between the flexible coding structure and the information needs of the group.

Chapter 3 described in detail the CRAHCA Prepaid Group Chart of Accounts. Summary and detailed accounts were delineated and explained fully. The chart facilitates meeting the unique information needs of a prepaid medical group and at the same time facilitates its participation in MGMA's cost survey and Performance Efficiency Evaluation Report (PEER).

Chapter 4 discussed generally accepted accounting principles underlying the preparation and presentation of general purpose financial statements by a medical group with a prepaid component. The cash and accrual bases of accounting were also examined and compared. It was concluded that although the cash basis is often adopted by the medical group for tax reporting, it has two major weaknesses for financial reporting. First, performance evaluation is often distorted by cash inflows that either precede or follow the period when patient services are actually provided and also by cash outflows for expenses that do not take place in the period when resources are actually consumed. Second, many important assets and liabilities are left off the balance sheet. For example, patient accounts receivable, claims payable for purchased medical services, and deferred prepaid revenue are omitted.

Chapters 5, 6, and 7 discussed and illustrated the three general purpose financial statements that have evolved as a result of years of experience: Chapter 5, the statement of financial position (balance sheet); Chapter 6, the income statement; and Chapter 7, the statement of changes in financial position (funds flow or cash flow statement). In Chapters 5 and 6 the financial statements were presented on the accrual basis and compared with their respective cash basis counterparts, followed by the conclusion that the accrual basis provides better information. However, because the statement of changes in financial position is focused on explaining the factors affecting the group's financial liquidity, the cash approach for that statement was supported in Chapter 7.

PART II

COST ACCOUNTING FOR PREPAID MEDICAL GROUPS

Chapter 9

Introduction to Part II

As a medical group moves from fee-for-service practice to prepaid practice, the primary emphasis moves from revenue production to cost control. While cost data are important to the management of a fee-for-service medical group, they are critical for a medical group offering prepaid care. There is a great deal of confusion, however, about how costs should be accumulated and how they should be used. Different purposes require different cost data. Cost information generated for one purpose may actually be misleading if used for another purpose that requires a different array of costs.

Uses of Cost Data

In many different situations, cost data should be tailor-made to fit; five situations are introduced in this chapter.

- Income measurement
- Distribution of income to physicians
- Cost control
- Overall planning
- Decision making in specific situations

The cost concepts introduced in these five situations will be fully developed later in this section.

Income Measurement

When general purpose financial statements are prepared, expenses must be matched with revenues to measure income. Fortunately, medical practices do not face the income determination problems found in manufacturing or other types of businesses with complex inventory cost measurements. The basic issue in measuring expenses is the choice between cash and accrual bases of accounting. Throughout the text it is emphasized that the accrual basis of accounting provides the best measure of income for groups with a sizeable prepaid component.

The reasons for choosing one form of accounting over another are as much philosophical as practical. Cash basis measurements are widely used in fee-for-service medical practices for three practical reasons. The first is that they are simple and easy to use. Except for depreciation and payroll withholdings, revenues equal cash collected and expenses equal cash paid. Until the activities of the practice become sufficiently complex to require more valid information, the benefits of the accrual measurement of expenses may not be apparent.

Second, payments to partners or physician-owners essentially have been a distribution of the income remaining after expenses are paid. When a practice uses cash basis accounting, net income (except for depreciation expense) equals the income available for distribution. If a practice uses accrual accounting, this is not true. The variation in activity between time periods (the current period in which revenues and expenses are matched versus previous and subsequent time periods) will cause different revenue and expense amounts to be recorded than are actually received or paid "out-of-pocket." The accrual records will indicate that income available for distribution to physicians may be more than, less than, or equal to the amount of cash available. It may be difficult to explain to physicians that the practice must borrow to pay their salaries and bonuses or that available cash exceeds the amount of physician salaries and bonuses to be paid.

Finally, medical practices, and most small businesses, are concerned that financial statements and tax returns be consistent. There is the common belief that it is wrong to prepare financial statements on the accrual basis and to prepare the tax return on the cash basis. The tax code requires that if the tax return is prepared on a cash basis the books of account must support the tax return with cash basis measurements. Accrual accounting records, however, can be maintained for managerial purposes. The practice's financial statements should reflect the most meaningful measurements of revenues and expenses for management needs, while the tax return must comply with the tax code. As the prepaid component grows, the tax advantage provided by cash basis accounting will decrease and it may become more advantageous to use accrual basis measurements for tax purposes.

For planning, control, and most short-range decisions, accrual measurements of revenues and expenses are essential. The measurement of incurred but unreported claims for hospital and referral services is critical for evaluation of performance and determination of distributions to physicians. Measurement of performance and management of cash require different, although interdependent, sets of information. When the financial information system focuses on only one dimension, the other must suffer.

Distribution of Income to Physicians

The organization of the practice and the specific income distribution method chosen by the medical group determine the information needs. In fee-for-service medical groups the move to production-based income distribution methods has accelerated over the past decade. The information needed for income distribution is provided by the billing system and the conventional cash basis income statement. With the added emphasis of rewarding for production, fee-for-service medical groups also tend to relate direct costs to revenue produced either by individual physician or, more commonly, by specialty. In addition to the billing system and income statement for the group as a whole, fee-for-service medical groups have adopted cost accounting systems that relate direct costs to specialties and departments.

Production-oriented income distribution systems are not consistent with prepaid medical care. Rather than treat more sick patients (or treat them more often), the motivation is to keep patients well. Assuming the quality of care remains high, there are financial incentives for preventive care rather than curative care. In prepaid medical groups income distribution methods have tended to move away from being heavily production-oriented to compensating the physicians by salary with incentives. The incentives may be related to care utilization and referral control or other measures to control costs. The information needs shift to better cost information such as cost per member per month and cost per unit of activity.

Cost Control

The third major purpose of gathering cost data is to control costs. There are two dimensions of cost control. First, costs must be related to the activity that is being performed. Control of activities, and therefore control of costs, is carried out by the practice's responsibility centers. Costs must be traced to the center responsible for their incurrence. Second, the manager must know what costs should be. A base point, generally a budget, must be established to serve as a frame of reference by which to evaluate actual costs.

In Part I, a responsibility center was defined as a part of the organization that has responsibility for certain activities. A large medical practice may have responsibility centers for each doctor or for each doctor and group of doctors by specialty; for each ancillary department such as laboratory or radiology; and for several support activities such as reception and appointments, data processing, occupancy, business office, and administrator and staff. A small medical practice may identify responsibility centers such as the practice, laboratory, radiology, administration, and occupancy.

The ability to control costs depends upon how clearly responsibility center activities have been defined. Usually, activities to be performed in a particular responsibility center are specifically defined. Although not necessarily stated in writing, job descriptions also are reasonably well-defined. A view that is often held in medical practices maintains that the manager of a responsibility center, particularly a physician who heads a specialty, should devote his or her time to carrying out activities of the responsibility center and leave cost control to the administrator. As a result, the administrator has responsibility for costs incurred by someone else in the organization. This sharing of responsibility for costs leads to lack of control. In such a case, the responsibility center manager does not want responsibility for cost control and the administrator cannot exercise control.

In a fee-for-service/prepaid medical group there may be no distinction between the delivery of care to fee-for-service patients and to prepaid patients of the group. A particular lab test or immunization or other procedure is the same regardless of the patient. To control costs for the prepaid patient, the group must develop a cost control system for the entire practice. Cost per procedure data would then be used to develop the cost per member per month for the prepaid practice. The cost system, however, is developed for the entire practice. As a result, the fee-for-service practice should benefit as well.

The first step in establishing a cost control system is to identify responsibility centers to which costs are to be related and to establish a system for tracing costs to the center responsible for their incurrence. To carry the point further and for purposes of control, costs over which a manager does not have responsibility should not be allocated to his or her responsibility center. For example, from a control standpoint, it is doubtful whether building rent or depreciation, group administration costs, or other common costs should even appear in the operating statements provided to responsibility center managers.

The second dimension of cost control is related to establishing a base point or frame of reference as to what costs should be. Every medical group has some type of budget. Some groups formally prepare a budget reflecting their best judgment of what revenues and costs should be for the coming year. Other groups use the past years' data as a basis for planning the upcoming year's activities and for evaluating performance later. When past years' data are used, it is assumed that conditions will not change; otherwise, adjustments must be made to the data, at least informally. In both cases the group is, in reality, using a budget.

Data about the past are relevant to budgeting only to the extent that conditions have not changed. They are relevant when they provide a base for evaluation of current costs and prediction of future costs. When conditions have changed, care must be exercised to reflect the impact of the changes in the analysis. The concept of a flexible budget is very useful (and in some cases necessary) when the actual level of activity is significantly different from the planned level of activity. The revised budget for evaluating performance will reflect what costs and revenues should be at the actual level of activity. The real contribution of a flexible budget is that the impact of changes in volume (activity) is removed from revenues and costs, and the manager is able to focus upon the effects of efficiency, pricing, and mix of services.

Overall Planning

Although all medical practices have a planning process, most of the fee-for-service practices surveyed or interviewed do not use a formal budgeting system. In the past, doctors in a fee-for-service practice have been able to meet increases in expenses and generate higher personal income through higher fees and increased productivity. There will soon be a point, however, if it has not already been reached, when fee increases must be justified by cost of services provided. When a prepaid component is added, budgeting soon follows. The survey also indicated that 72 percent of the groups with small prepaid components and all of the groups with large prepaid components prepare and utilize a budget. Planning and control of operations require two dimensions of information: first, a knowledge of what happens to revenues and costs as activity changes; and second, a knowledge of when cash will be collected and when cash must be paid. Meaningful cost projections must be based on the amount of resources consumed for the amount of services performed. For this purpose, accrual measurement of expenses and a knowledge of cost behavior patterns are necessary.

Decision Making in Specific Situations

Because decisions involve the future and changes in the practice, cost data must be tailored to each specific situation. Some decisions, such as what fees to charge, are routine, and the financial information system provides most of the data necessary to make the decisions. Other decisions do not recur often, such as whether to perform a laboratory test inhouse or to purchase the service outside, and may need much more data from outside the practice. As examples of decisions and information needs, consider the following three decisions:

- What fees to charge fee-for-service patients or what capitation to negotiate for prepaid patients
- Whether to perform a laboratory test inhouse or purchase the service outside
- When to add a physician for prepaid patients

What Fees to Charge or Capitation to Negotiate? For the profession as a whole, fees are set to recover the cost of rendering the service and to provide the doctor with a desired level of income. The relevant cost is the full cost of providing a particular service. Full cost of a service is the sum of the costs directly incurred to provide the service plus a fair share of support costs such as occupancy and administration. The resulting cost for a particular service is an aid in setting the fee for that service; however, the prevailing rates in the community for the service must also be considered.

Capitation may be based upon either the fee-for-service equivalent fees for the services to be provided or the costs of the services to be provided. The fee-for-service equivalent basis requires discounting the fee-for-service fees to adjust for collection expenses and bad debts. If fee-for-service equivalents are used, determining the capitation rate is not substantially different from setting the fee-for-service fees. Ultimately, the fees or capitation payments must cover all costs. Development of cost by procedure and then cost per member per month allows the group to determine areas where costs are in excess of revenues and may suggest further analysis or action.

Perform a Laboratory Test or Purchase Outside? For this type of decision, usually termed "make or buy" in business literature, the entire cost of purchasing a test from an outside laboratory is relevant, while the relevant inhouse costs are only the incremental expenses of performing the test. The full cost (i.e., allocated indirect costs plus direct costs) of performing the test inhouse is not relevant to the make or buy decision, since some of the costs included in the full cost, such as allocated occupancy and administration costs, will not change as a result of performing the test inhouse. The incremental costs (which may contain both variable and fixed costs) can be compared with the cost of purchasing the service outside in order to reach a decision.

When to Add a Physician? In a growing prepaid practice that is responsible for referral costs as well as for costs of services performed within the group, the point will be reached when it should cost the group less to add a doctor and perform a particular service inside the group than to continue to refer outside. Only the costs incurred by adding the doctor on one hand, and the referral costs on the other hand, are relevant to the decision. Allocated administration and other fixed costs that will not change as a result of adding a doctor are not relevant to the decision. While this text addresses the issue of costs, there may be other factors that are more important to the decision of whether to add a new doctor. These include the long-range goals of the practice and its relationships with other providers in the community.

Structuring the Cost System

There are recurring needs for cost data that must be met on a regular basis by the financial information system. Data needed include those costs incurred by and directly traceable to each responsibility center and the cost behavior pattern of each cost. Periodically, it also is necessary to know the full cost of providing a service to determine if revenue is adequate. Cost per member per month must be determined for the prepaid patients. When the need arises, it is necessary to determine the costs relevant to certain decisions.

In computing unit costs, dollars of cost are related to units of activity, with cost of providing a medical service divided by the number of procedures or patients. One difficulty arises when the accounting system is maintained on a cash basis. The units of activity—number of procedures per doctor, number of laboratory procedures, and number of x-ray procedures, for example—usually are accumulated for the period in which the services are performed. On the cash basis, however, costs are recorded when cash is paid, which may not occur in the same period in which the services requiring the costs were performed. Only accrual basis measurements will provide reliable and comparable cost data. The fee-for-service/prepaid medical group must do its cost analyses with accrual basis measurements.

Outline of Part II

In the remainder of this section various aspects of cost accounting are discussed and subsequently related to the data accumulation system in Part I. Chapter 10 is concerned with the behavior of costs as the level of activity changes. Techniques for separating costs into their variable and fixed components are examined. The chapter concludes with a discussion of cost-volume-profit analysis and the use of cost behavior patterns in planning and control of costs.

Chapter 11 discusses responsibility centers and examines the problems of tracing costs to these centers. The chart of accounts presented in Part I provides for a responsibility center field that allows all costs to be identified with a specific responsibility center. Chapters 12 and 13 discuss the problems of allocating the costs of support departments to revenue-producing departments so that the full cost of services may be determined. Chapter 12 examines the techniques of allocation and Chapter 13 some philosophical issues in allocation. A discussion of various bases used for allocation also is included. Chapter 14 describes and provides illustrations of a cost accounting system for a fee-for-service/prepaid medical group. Chapter 15 provides a summary of Part II.

Chapter 10

Cost-Volume-Profit Relationships

How costs behave as activity changes must be known before accurate forecasts of costs can be prepared. One of the keys to cost prediction is found in understanding and using cost behavior patterns. In addition to projecting costs, a knowledge of cost behavior patterns is important for a proper evaluation of performance in controlling costs. If a cost is to be controlled, management must know whether the cost is expected to change under various operating conditions and how much it is expected to change. Other types of businesses have developed methods of determining cost behavior patterns and performing cost-volume-profit analyses. Only recently has the ambulatory health care industry determined and used cost behavior patterns in financial management and accounting.

This chapter is devoted to a study of how costs behave as activity changes. It presents techniques of separating costs into their fixed and variable components and demonstrates the use of cost-volume-profit analysis in a medical group setting.

Cost Behavior Patterns

The behavior of costs falls into four basic patterns of change. These patterns are illustrated in Exhibit 10-1 and are defined in this section.

Fixed Costs

Fixed costs are those that do not change as activity changes. For example, a group pays $1,000 per month to lease a piece of equipment. Regardless of the number of patient visits, the lease expense does not change from month to month. From the standpoint of management control, fixed costs fall into two categories: committed and managed. Committed fixed costs are those that relate to the investment in buildings, equipment, and key personnel. These costs cannot be changed in the short run. Control of committed costs is exercised when the asset is purchased or the equipment is leased. Managed fixed costs are subject to the discretion of management and may be reduced or increased in the short run. Examples include maintenance, promotion, convention and meeting expenses, and some support personnel.

Variable Costs

Variable costs are those that change in proportion to changes in activity. The amount of medical supplies used is directly related to the number of patient visits and the types of procedures performed. Each x-ray procedure requires additional film and other supplies.

Semivariable Costs

Semivariable costs are those containing both variable and fixed components. A common example is processing patient receivables through a service bureau. The contract with the service bureau provides for a fixed charge per month plus a charge per entry or per line.

Step-fixed Costs

Step-fixed costs are those that are fixed over a range of activity and increase in stairstep fashion. Most personnel costs fall into this category. For example, the addition of another physician, another nurse, or another receptionist will take place in steps. Personnel tend to be added as levels of activity are reached. Assuming that an additional nurse is necessary for a physician to increase production to more than $200,000 in gross charges, an increase in activity beyond $200,000 would require the addition of another nurse (perhaps shared with another doctor).

EXHIBIT 10-1
ILLUSTRATION OF FOUR COST BEHAVIOR PATTERNS

COST-BEHAVIOR PATTERNS

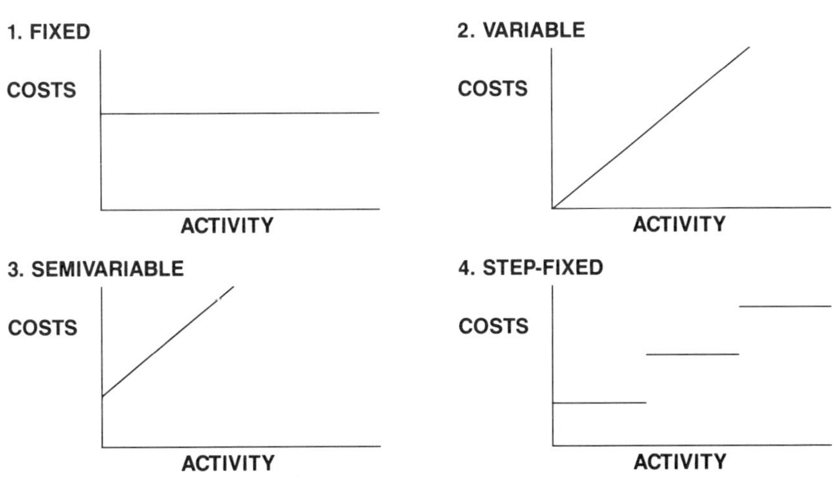

Relevant Range of Activity

Costs fall into one of the four cost behavior patterns when both a period of time and a range of activity are considered. As the time period becomes shorter, more costs become fixed. For example, most of the costs incurred by a medical practice for an hour or a day do not change regardless of the number of procedures performed. As the increment of time increases, more and more costs change as activity changes. Within a specific time period, very few costs are completely variable. In the event of a drastic change in volume, management would take action to reduce costs considered fixed, which would not be appropriate if activity continued at a normal level. On the other hand, as capacity within existing facilities is reached, some costs increase disproportionately, such as overtime premiums and the additional insurance coverage that may be required.

The range over which there is knowledge of cost behavior patterns is called the relevant range. It would be a mistake to believe that the relevant range extends from zero activity to the full capacity of existing resources. Care must be exercised in projecting costs outside the relevant range of activity.

The Flexible Budget

Accountants call a plan for control of cost behavior patterns a flexible budget. For simplicity, accountants use straight-line relationships to explain and work with cost behavior patterns. If it is assumed that all costs can be identified as fixed or variable, and that a semivariable cost can be separated into its fixed and variable components, the following equation will express the cost behavior pattern of any cost.

Total costs = Fixed costs per period + (Variable cost per unit of activity × Activity level)

Accountants have chosen a set of symbols to express these relationships. The equation becomes:

$$TC = FC + VC(x)$$

where: TC = projected total costs
FC = fixed costs for a given period of time
VC = variable cost per unit of activity
(x) = activity level during a given period of time

To illustrate the flexible budget, assume that Best Medical Center has formed an HMO, Bestcare. Because of growing enrollments in an area some distance from Best Medical Center, a satellite office providing only primary care is to be opened in the eastern suburbs. The office will be staffed with two salaried physicians. Assume only five costs (to simplify the example) for the satellite office:

Office and equipment rent—$2,500 per month

Support staff salaries—$4,000 per month

Supplies—$2 per patient visit

Other costs—$500 per month plus $1 per patient visit

Associate physician salaries—$8,000 per month

The flexible budget for each of the costs and the total satellite office costs follows.

	Flexible budget		
	TC = FC	+	VC(x)
Fixed cost—office and equipment rent	$2,500	+	$0(x)
Fixed cost—support staff salaries	4,000	+	0(x)
Variable cost—supplies	0	+	2(x)
Semivariable cost—other	500	+	1(x)
Fixed cost—physician salaries	8,000	+	0(x)
Total costs	$15,000	+	$3(x)

Costs may now be projected for any level of activity within the relevant range by substituting the estimate of patient visits in place of (x) in the equation. In the example below, if there are 1,000 patient visits in a particular month, the total costs would be $18,000 and the individual costs would be as follows:

	TC	=	FC	+	VC(x)
Office and equipment rent	$ 2,500	=	$ 2,500	+	$0(1,000)
Support staff salaries	4,000	=	4,000	+	0(1,000)
Supplies	2,000	=	0	+	2(1,000)
Other costs	1,500	=	500	+	1(1,000)
Physician salaries	8,000	=	8,000	+	0(1,000)
Total costs	$18,000	=	$15,000	+	$3(1,000)

The average cost of a patient visit is $18 ($18,000/1,000). This average cost is correct only at the level of 1,000 patient visits. If the cost behavior patterns remain unchanged, what are total costs and unit cost if activity drops to 800 patient visits? Total costs are now $17,400 [$15,000 + $3(800)] and unit cost is $21.75 ($17,400/800) per patient visit.

With these flexible budgets, costs can be projected when a planning budget (profit plan) is developed for a future period. What costs should have been in a particular period can be determined when a performance budget is prepared to evaluate cost control at the end of the period. The flexible budgets are also useful for any decision that requires information at different levels of activity.

A few assumptions are made in preparing the flexible budget. If they are not true, the resulting cost projections may be inaccurate. These assumptions are:

The cost behavior patterns can be determined and are linear

Prices remain unchanged

Mix of services remains unchanged

Production is within the relevant range of activity

Techniques for Determining Cost Behavior Patterns

Two practical means for determining cost behavior patterns have been developed by accountants: inspection of accounts and study of past cost behavior patterns. The methods differ in the sources of data used.

Inspection of Accounts

The most intuitive method of determining whether a cost is fixed or variable is to examine the nature of each cost in the chart of accounts. Many costs are fixed or variable by their nature; their cost behavior patterns are determined readily by examination. Because this method is both intuitive and arbitrary, it is subject to a higher degree of error than other methods. In situations where analysis is not very sensitive to error in classification of fixed and variable costs, this method may provide a quick and inexpensive measure of cost behavior.

To illustrate account analysis, a number of accounts from the chart of accounts in Part I are presented in Exhibit 10-2 with an indication of their probable cost behavior patterns. A special warning is necessary. Each medical group is different. The cost behavior patterns must be determined from the contracts, staffing patterns, and style of practice in the particular group.

EXHIBIT 10-2
ILLUSTRATION OF INSPECTION OF ACCOUNTS

Determination of Cost Behavior Patterns

Account	Account Title	Cost Behavior Pattern
5100	Physician Salaries, Distributions, and Bonuses	Fixed—Amount of distributions to doctors depends upon many factors other than activity level. A salary based upon production should be segregated and classified as a variable.
5200	Physician Benefits	Fixed—See explanation for Account 5100.
5400	Ancillary Department Salaries	Step-fixed—Most medical practice personnel are hired in steps, resulting in a stairstep pattern.
5500	Medical Support Salaries	Step-fixed—See explanation for Account 5400.
5600	Administrative Salaries	Fixed—Most medical practice administrative personnel costs will not depend upon activity levels.
5700	Housekeeping, Maintenance, and Security Salaries	Fixed—See explanation for Account 5600.
5800	Other Salaries	Fixed—These salaries depend more on style of practice than activity level.
5900	Nonphysician Employee Benefits	Fixed—Benefits are largely fixed by contract. To the extent that some of the salaries are variable, a portion of the benefits may also be variable.
6100	Supplies Expense	Variable—With minor exceptions supplies relate to patient visits.
6200	Ancillary Department Supplies Expense	Variable—See explanation for Account 6100.

EXHIBIT 10-2 (continued)

6400	Occupancy and Use—Buildings and Grounds	Fixed—These costs relate to the provision of capacity rather than to various levels of activity in the use of capacity.
6500	Occupancy and Use—Building Depreciation	Fixed—See explanation for Account 6400.
6600	Occupancy and Use—Furniture, Fixtures, and Equipment	Fixed—See explanation for Account 6400.
6700	Occupancy and Use—Furniture, Fixtures, and Equipment Depreciation	Fixed—See explanation for Account 6400.
6800	Occupancy and Use—Other Furniture, Fixtures, and Equipment Expenses	Fixed—See explanation for Account 6400.
7100	Purchased Services—Nonprepaid Professional and Medical	Variable—Amount will depend upon the style of practice.
7200	Purchased Services—Prepaid Professional and Medical	Variable—Amount will depend upon the amount of care the group must refer outside.
7300	General and Administrative—Purchased Services	Fixed—Amount will depend upon factors other than level of activity.
7400	General and Administrative—Employee-related	Fixed—Most expenses in this category are discretionary and do not relate to volume of service.
7500	General and Administrative—Liability Insurance	Fixed—This expense relates to the number of doctors and the types of specialties.
7600-7700	Other General and Administrative Expenses	Fixed—These expenses relate to the style of practice and discretion of management.
7800	Interest Expenses	Fixed—These expenses have no direct relationship to level of activity.

8200	Nonoperating Expenses	Fixed—These expenses have no relationship to operations.

Study of Past Cost Behavior Patterns

Analysis of past experience assumes that data are accurate and that future cost behavior will duplicate past cost behavior. When accurate past cost data are available, they provide empirical evidence of cost behavior patterns. The issue of accuracy becomes important when accounts are maintained on the cash basis. Unless the use of resources is recorded in the period of use, rather than in the period of cash payment, a distorted cost behavior pattern may result.

To measure cost behavior patterns from past data, the accountant "fits" a straight line to the data. The assumption is made that these data vary linearly. Mathematically, one may fit a straight line to any set of two or more points. Evaluating the quality of the fit and the reliability of the resulting flexible budget requires judgment.

Recall that the mathematical statement of a straight line is the equation TC = FC + VC(x), which is also the flexible budget formula. This equation is illustrated graphically in Exhibit 10-3.

EXHIBIT 10-3
ILLUSTRATION OF FITTING A STRAIGHT LINE TO COST AND ACTIVITY DATA

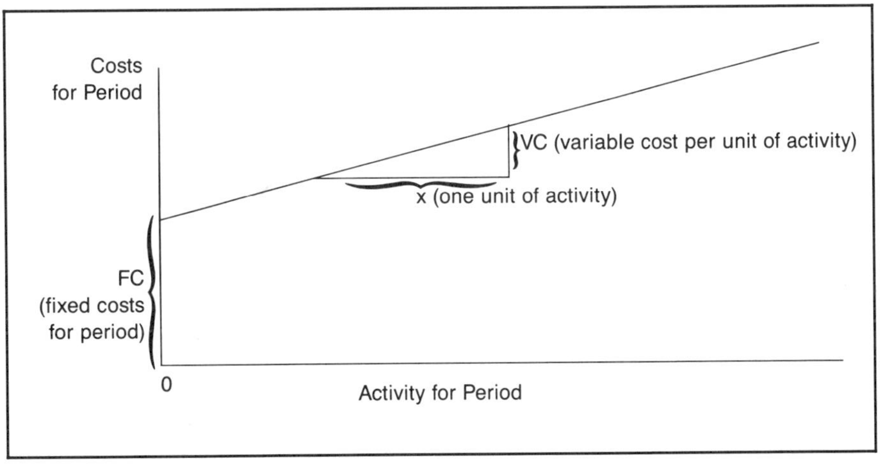

There are three general methods of determining cost behavior patterns from past data to arrive at a flexible budget formula.

(1) Scattergraph approach, which relies upon a visual fit using a graph

(2) High-low point method, which fits a line to two representative points of data

(3) Linear regression analysis, which fits a line to several observations using statistical methods

To illustrate separation of past cost data into fixed and variable costs, assume that the laboratory cost and activity data presented in Exhibit 10-4 were developed from the accounting records of the past year.

EXHIBIT 10-4

COST AND ACTIVITY DATA OF LABORATORY FOR DETERMINING COST BEHAVIOR PATTERNS

	Number of Laboratory Tests	Total Laboratory Costs
January	4,500	$21,500
February	5,000	$24,000
March	5,200	$23,000
April	4,800	$22,500
May	4,500	$22,000
June	4,000	$20,000
July	3,000	$18,000
August	4,500	$21,000
September	4,800	$22,000
October	4,500	$20,000
November	4,000	$19,500
December	3,000	$17,000

Scattergraph Estimate. A scattergraph is a graphic presentation of actual data, with total costs (TC) represented on the vertical axis and activity (x) represented on the horizontal axis. Each observation is plotted on the graph shown in Exhibit 10-5. There are 12 months of data and, therefore, 12 plottings for the laboratory.

The scattergraph allows an image to be drawn of the relationship between costs and activity. Do the costs fall into one of the four cost behavior patterns presented in Exhibit 10-1? Is the pattern a straight-line pattern, a curved line pattern, a stairstep pattern? The simplest way to fit a line to the scattergraph plottings is to draw a line by visual inspection so that about half the plots lie above the line and about half below the line.

As an image of the pattern of the costs is drawn, an image of the reliability of the fit should also be drawn. The closer the plotted points cluster around the line drawn, the more reliable conclusions about the cost behavior pattern become. Any highly unusual plotted points should be investigated—and ignored if conditions were unusual or data erroneous.

EXHIBIT 10-5

ILLUSTRATION OF SCATTERGRAPH ESTIMATE

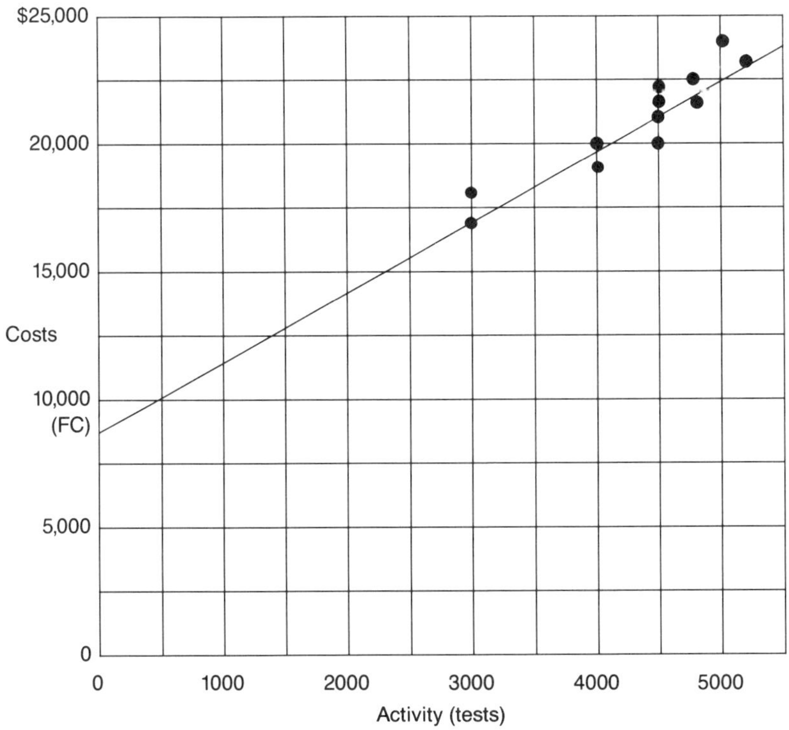

$$\begin{aligned} \text{FC} &= \$8{,}500 \\ \text{Total variable costs} &= \text{TC} - \text{FC} \\ &= \$22{,}500 - \$8{,}500 \\ &= \$14{,}000 \end{aligned}$$

$$\begin{aligned} \text{VC} &= \text{Total variable costs/Number of tests} \\ &= \$14{,}000/5{,}000 \\ &= \$2.80 \end{aligned}$$

$$\text{TC} = \$8{,}500 + \$2.80(x)$$

What can be said about the pattern of the data in Exhibit 10-5? The data can be visually summarized by a straight line. The point where the fitted line crosses the vertical axis is the estimate of fixed costs designated by (FC). In the example, fixed costs are approximately $8,500. The variable costs can be determined at any level by subtracting $8,500, the estimate of fixed costs, from the total costs at any activity level on the fitted line. For example, at 5,000 tests total costs are estimated to be $22,500 from the data on the scattergraph. Therefore, total variable costs for 5,000 tests are $14,000 ($22,500 – $8,500) and the variable cost per unit is $2.80 ($14,000/5,000). The flexible budget for the laboratory is $8,500 per month plus $2.80 per test.

A mistake in fitting the line could result in a large error. Within the range of activity represented here by past data, however, the error should not be large. Failure to control costs during a period should not be allowed to distort the flexible budget.

High-Low Point Estimate. A quick and yet effective way of determining cost behavior patterns involves the use of data for one period of high activity and one period of low activity. A straight-line relationship is then determined from these two sets of data. The periods selected should be representative periods of costs for each level of activity. Care should be exercised in the selection of the periods and in investigating the cost data to avoid abnormal data.

The high-low method involves five steps.

Step 1. Select a representative high month and a representative low month of activity (number of laboratory tests).

	Costs	Tests
High activity—March	$23,000	5,200
Low activity—December	$17,000	3,000

Step 2. Determine the change in costs and activity.

Change	$ 6,000	2,200

Step 3. Determine variable cost per test by dividing the change in costs by the change in activity.

$$\text{Variable cost per test} = \frac{\text{Change in costs}}{\text{Change in activity}}$$

$$= \frac{\$6,000}{2,200} = \$2.73$$

Step 4. Determine the total variable costs at either the high or low level of activity. Multiply the variable cost per test by either the high or low level of activity.

$$\begin{aligned} \text{Total variable costs} &= \text{Number of tests} \times \text{Variable cost per test} \\ &= 3{,}000 \times \$2.73 \\ &= \$8{,}190 \end{aligned}$$

Step 5. Determine the total fixed costs by deducting the total variable costs at either level of activity from the total costs at the same level of activity.

$$\begin{aligned} \text{Fixed costs} &= \text{Total costs} - \text{Total variable costs} \\ &= \$17{,}000 - \$8{,}190 \\ &= \$\ 8{,}810 \end{aligned}$$

The months of March and December appear reasonable and were selected as the representative high and low months. The resulting flexible budget formula is TC = \$8,810 + \$2.73(x).

Linear Regression Analysis. Linear regression analysis is a statistical technique that determines the relationship between two variables, in this case, cost and activity. The regression line is an average line, free from subjective error; it is the line of "best fit." This method contains two mathematical properties that make regression a more accurate method. Both properties are missing in other methods described earlier. First, the algebraic sums of the positive and negative deviations from the lines equal zero. Second, the sum of the squares of these deviations is less than the sum of the squared vertical deviations from any other line. Because of this last mathematical property, the method is often called least-squares regression.

Because linear regression utilizes squared deviations from the fitted line, any abnormal observation has a disproportionate effect on the line and can result in an unrealistic cost behavior pattern. For example, consider a normal observation with deviation of \$1 from the regression line and an abnormal observation \$10 from the regression line; when squared the deviations become 1 and 100. The abnormal deviation has 100 times the effect of the normal observation in fitting the line. It is critical that abnormal data be identified and removed from the analysis.

Some important assumptions must be kept in mind when using linear regression analysis. First, the method assumes a linear relationship between two variables, cost and activity. Second, it assumes that the cost data are independent; that is, the cost for March is not dependent upon the cost for February, April, or any other month. Third, there is uniform dispersion of actual costs around the regression line. This means that costs are scattered around the regression line at low levels of activity in roughly the same way as at high levels.

Last, differences between actual costs and the regression line plotted for any level of activity will yield a normal (bell-shaped) curve.

Exhibit 10-6 presents the determination of cost behavior patterns for the laboratory using linear regression analysis. Note that two equations have been adopted from statistics. It is beyond the scope of this volume to show the mathematical proof of the equations. The equations are solved in Exhibit 10-6 using the 12 months of data from Exhibit 10-4. The resulting flexible budget is: TC = \$9,040 + \$2.74(x).

EXHIBIT 10-6
ILLUSTRATION OF LINEAR REGRESSION ANALYSIS

Month	Number of Laboratory Tests x (000)	Total Laboratory Costs y (000)	xy (000,000)	x^2 (000,000)
January	4.5	\$ 21.5	\$ 96.75	20.25
February	5.0	24.0	120.00	25.00
March	5.2	23.0	119.60	27.04
April	4.8	22.5	108.00	23.04
May	4.5	22.0	99.00	20.25
June	4.0	20.0	80.00	16.00
July	3.0	18.0	54.00	9.00
August	4.5	21.0	94.50	20.25
September	4.8	22.0	105.60	23.04
October	4.5	20.0	90.00	20.25
November	4.0	19.5	78.00	16.00
December	3.0	17.0	51.00	9.00
	51.8	\$250.5	\$1,096.45	229.12

$$FC = \frac{\Sigma y \Sigma x^2 - \Sigma x \Sigma xy}{n(\Sigma x^2) - (\Sigma x)^2} \qquad VC = \frac{n(\Sigma xy) - \Sigma x \Sigma y}{n(\Sigma x^2) - (\Sigma x)^2}$$

Where:

Σ = Sum
Σx = Total activity
Σy = Total costs
n = Number of time periods
FC = Total fixed costs
VC = Variable cost per unit of activity
Σxy = Costs times activity summed
Σx^2 = Activity squared summed
$(\Sigma x)^2$ = Total activity squared

$$FC = \frac{(250.5 \times 229.12) - (51.8 \times 1{,}096.45)}{(12 \times 229.12) - (51.8 \times 51.8)}$$

$$= \frac{57{,}394.56 - 56{,}796.11}{2{,}749.44 - 2{,}683.24}$$

$$= \frac{598.45}{66.2} = 9.040 \text{ or } \$9{,}040 \text{ fixed costs per month}$$

$$VC = \frac{(12 \times 1{,}096.45) - (51.8 \times 250.5)}{(12 \times 229.12) - (51.8 \times 51.8)}$$

$$= \frac{13{,}157.40 - 12{,}975.90}{66.2} = \$2.74 \text{ variable cost per test}$$

Total costs or flexible budget = \$9,040 fixed costs + \$2.74 per laboratory test

---

When regression analysis is used, it is also possible to tell how well the flexible budget fits the past data, how statistically significant the equation is, and how much variation should be expected between estimated and actual data. Most computer programs that compute the regression equation also provide these measures of goodness of fit. Three tests of the goodness of fit are:

The r value

The r^2 value

The standard error of the estimate

The r value is the correlation coefficient. When the plottings fall perfectly along a straight line, the r value will be +1.0. No relationship between activity and cost would result in an r value of 0. The square of r value is the coefficient of determination. It is a measure of the percentage of variation in one variable explained by the variation in the other. The r^2 value can vary from 0 to 1.0. The standard error of the estimate shows how far the actual observations deviate from the regression line.

Summary of Techniques for Determining Cost Behavior Patterns

The flexible budgets determined by the three techniques are very similar. Any time the data fall in a tight, straight-line pattern similar to the pattern in Exhibit 10-5, all methods of fitting a straight line should yield similar results. The three flexible budgets are as follows:

Scattergraph TC = \$8,500 + \$2.80(x)

High-Low	TC = \$8,810 + \$2.73(x)
Linear regression	TC = \$9,040 + \$2.74(x)

Any of the three flexible budgets is sufficiently accurate for most purposes.

The cost of obtaining relevant information should not exceed the benefits from its use. The purpose of determining cost behavior patterns and identifying costs as fixed and variable is to provide management with relevant data for planning, control, and decision making. In those cases where decisions are very sensitive to errors in cost estimation, care must be used in determining cost behavior patterns. Linear regression should provide the most accurate measure of fixed and variable costs when mixed costs are analyzed. In addition, regression analysis generates data to measure the reliability of the relationship between the two variables (the correlation coefficient). A discussion of these tests is beyond the scope of this chapter.

In those cases where decisions are not sensitive to errors in cost estimation, a technique such as the high-low method may be used. It is quick, simple, and inexpensive. Because the high-low point method involves only two periods of data, the data could be obtained by sampling if historic records are inadequate.

The important point is that several techniques are available. The prepaid practice wishing to determine cost behavior patterns should select the technique that provides the desired level of accuracy. The scattergraph technique, however, should be used to supplement other methods and to determine whether a straight line is appropriate and whether the dispersion of the plotted points is too great to provide a reliable cost behavior pattern.

One caution is in order. During periods of inflation, as experienced in the past decade, past data may give an impression of a higher level of variable costs than actually exists. For example, if the rate of growth is approximately the same as the rate of inflation, a fixed cost over time will look like a variable cost on a scattergraph. When the rate of inflation is high, past data should be deflated to allow a clear picture of cost behavior.

Cost-Volume-Profit Analysis

Ways in which knowledge of cost behavior patterns are useful to management of a practice were identified earlier. This section provides illustrations of cost-volume-profit analysis or the impact of a change in activity on costs and profit.

Cost-Volume-Profit Analysis through Graphs

The easiest way to visualize and understand cost-volume-profit analysis is graphically—through a break-even chart or a profit-volume chart. A break-even chart shows much more than the point at which an organization or a practice will break even. It provides a picture of the profit or loss at all levels of activity within the relevant range of activity.

Returning to the laboratory example used to illustrate cost behavior patterns, how many tests does it require for the lab to break even? The fixed costs of $9,040 per month, variable cost of $2.74 per test, and fees of $6.00 per test are plotted on the break-even chart in Exhibit 10-7. The point at which the revenue line crosses the total costs line is the break-even point. The lab will break even at about 2,800 tests (2,773 as the equation will show in the next section). The vertical dashed lines on the break-even chart indicate the relevant range, that is, the range over which it is known that the cost-volume-profit relationships are valid. Any projection below or above the relevant range may not be reliable, because there is no experience on which to base the projection. From the graph it is possible to determine the profit at 4,000 tests (a profit of $4,000) and at 2,000 tests (a loss of $2,520), or any other level of activity within the relevant range.

Another form of break-even chart is the profit-volume chart. By plotting only the contribution margin (difference between revenue and variable costs), the profit or loss is easily determinable at any level of activity with a single line. At zero activity, the loss is equal to fixed costs. Each test performed provides a contribution margin of $3.26 (gross charges or fees of $6.00 per test less variable cost of $2.74 per test). The profit-volume chart for the laboratory is shown in Exhibit 10-7. The break-even point, the profit at 4,000 tests, and the loss at 2,000 tests are the same as shown on the break-even chart.

If the group is dissatisfied with the predicted results for the laboratory, there are at least three possible courses of action: increase the fee per test, increase the volume of tests, or decrease the costs. Exhibit 10-8 shows the impact of cost and fee changes. The long-dash line shows the impact of decreasing fixed costs by $2,000. By reducing fixed costs, the entire contribution margin line moves upward and to the left, reducing the loss or increasing the profit at each level of activity by $2,000. The break-even point decreases to about 2,160 tests. The short-dash line shows the impact of decreasing variable costs or increasing fees by $.50 per test. Both a decrease of $.50 per test in variable cost and an increase of $.50 per test in fees will increase the contribution margin by $.50 per test. The slope of the line is increased, dropping the break-even point to about 2,400 tests.

The profit-volume chart is a very useful chart for showing the impact of change graphically. The next section presents cost-volume-profit analysis through equations. Equations provide the advantage of precision and the ability to deal with several changes at one time.

EXHIBIT 10-7
ILLUSTRATION OF BREAK-EVEN CHART AND PROFIT-VOLUME CHART

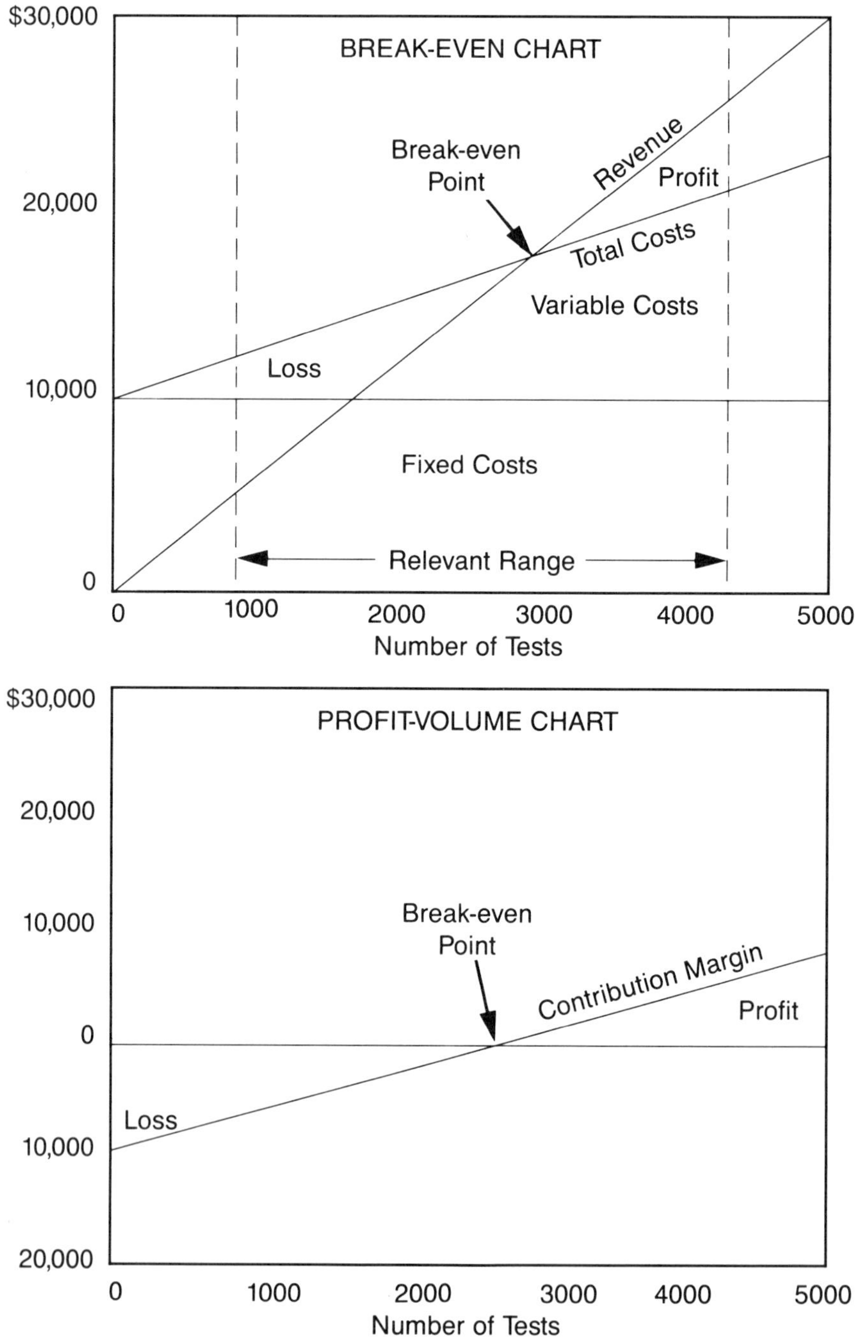

EXHIBIT 10-8
ILLUSTRATION OF THE IMPACT OF COST AND FEE CHANGES

Fixed costs decreased by $2,000:

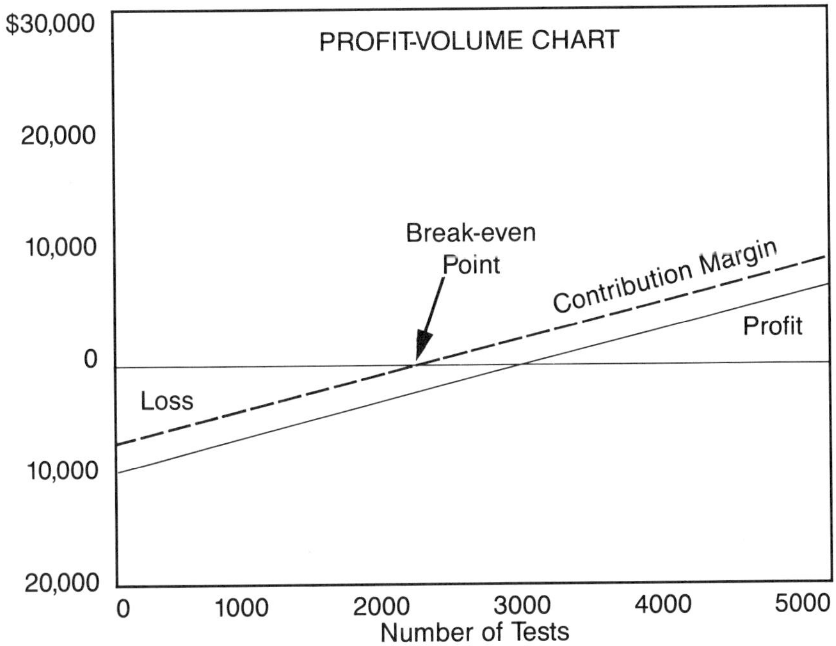

Fee per test increased by $.50:

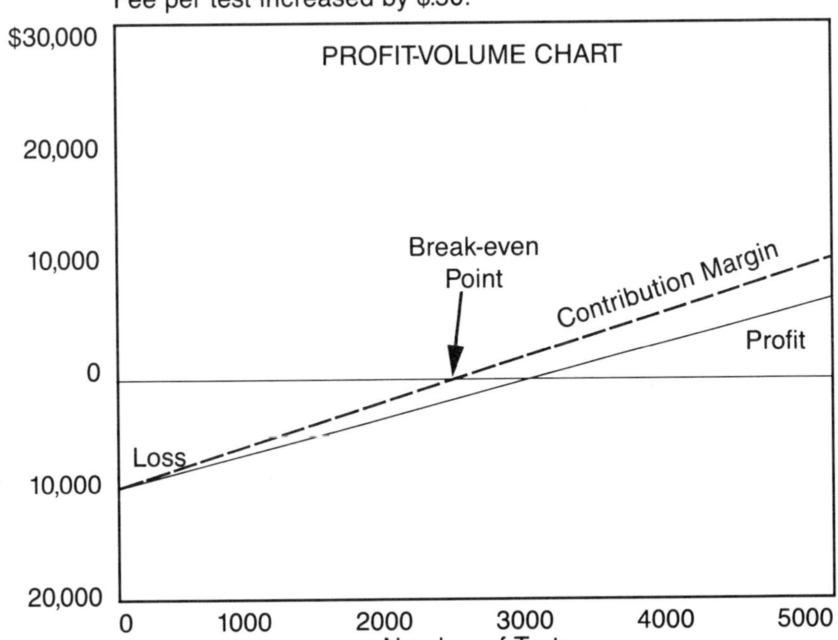

Cost-Volume-Profit Analysis through Equations

The break-even point may be determined by equation, dividing fixed costs by contribution margin per unit. The break-even point for the laboratory is 2,773 tests, approximately the amount determined by the break-even chart, computed as follows:

$$\text{Break-even point for number of tests} = \frac{\text{Fixed costs}}{\text{Contribution margin per test}} = \frac{\$9{,}040}{\$6.00 - \$2.74} = 2{,}773 \text{ tests}$$

If the practice were to decide that the laboratory should contribute $1,000 per month for administrative services performed by the main clinic, in addition to covering all costs in the laboratory, the number of tests required would be determined as follows:

$$\text{Required number of tests to generate required contribution} = \frac{\text{Fixed costs} + \text{allocated costs}}{\text{Contribution margin per test}} = \frac{\$9{,}040 + \$1{,}000}{\$3.26} = 3{,}080 \text{ tests}$$

For the laboratory to meet the desired objective of management, it must now produce 3,080 tests per month.

Cost-Volume-Profit Analysis for a Prepaid Practice

In a prepaid practice, the patients enrolled in a prepaid plan pay a monthly premium to an HMO, which in turn makes a monthly capitation payment to the practice. For the capitation payment, the practice contracts to provide all essential health care needed by the prepaid patients, including medical services provided by the practice, referrals to outside specialists, and hospitalization.

If the number of prepaid patients is used as the measure of activity, the break-even chart for the prepaid practice will look much like the typical break-even chart. The break-even chart shows the number of patients at which the plan will break even and the profit or loss at any level of activity. However, a not so subtle change occurs as the plan matures. If a constant number of prepaid patients is assumed, as may be found in a mature plan, there is a dramatic change in relationships. The break-even chart in Exhibit 10-9 shows the costs and revenue for a mature practice serving prepaid patients. The activity on the horizontal axis reflects number of patient visits. The total costs line includes the fixed costs of the practice, the variable cost per patient visit, and the variable costs for referrals and hospitalization. Revenue from capitation payments is shown as a horizontal line with break-even where revenue and cost are equal. Because revenue is fixed and cost is increasing as the prepaid patients make more visits, the practice shows a profit below the break-even point and a loss as additional activity is incurred above the break-even point.

EXHIBIT 10-9

ILLUSTRATION OF A BREAK-EVEN CHART FOR A PREPAID PRACTICE (Assumes constant enrollment level.)

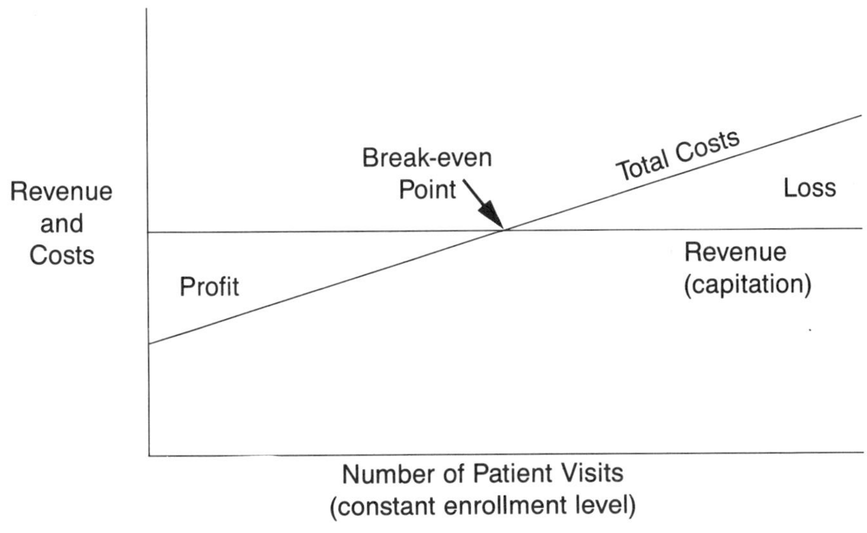

The prepaid practice is rewarded for efficient use of resources. Anything the practice can do to minimize the use of the practice's resources (yet provide quality care) will tend to increase the practice's income. In contrast, the fee-for-service group practice is rewarded for increasing patient visits and therefore revenue.

Cost-volume-profit analysis for a fee-for-service/prepaid group is further complicated because revenue and cost data are in different terms. The capitation payments are on a per member per month basis; the fee-for-service revenue and cost data are developed on a per procedure or per patient visit basis. As an example, assume the following data for Best Medical Center's satellite office.

Capitation payment for services performed at the satellite office passed on to the satellite office	$7.34 per member per month
Capitation payment for other services provided by the group and for referrals outside the medical center	$9.47 per member per month
Costs of operating satellite office	
Direct costs:	
Fixed costs per month	$15,000.00
Variable cost per visit	$3.00
Allocated costs from medical center for administration and support (14% of capitation)	$1.19
Expected utilization—3 visits per member per year	

If the variable costs are translated into per member per month data, the cost-volume-profit analysis may use enrolled members as the measure of activity. In this example, the variable cost per visit of $3.00 translates to $.75 per member per month. The contribution margin per member per month is then $5.40 ($7.34 − $.75 − $1.19). The break-even point becomes 2,778 members.

$$\text{Break-even point} = \frac{\text{Fixed costs per month}}{\text{Contribution margin per member per month}}$$

$$= \frac{\$15{,}000}{\$5.40} = 2{,}778 \text{ members}$$

The complexity of the calculation increases if different types of procedures are considered.

Summary

A knowledge of cost behavior patterns is essential in planning, in controlling costs, and in making many short-term decisions. The behavior of costs follows four basic patterns in response to changes in activity. These cost behavior patterns are termed fixed, variable, semivariable, and step-fixed. Costs that are completely fixed or completely variable are easy to identify. Semivariable costs, however, must be separated into their fixed and variable components to be able to reflect the impact of activity changes. Step-fixed costs are handled as fixed costs with a series of relevant ranges.

Four techniques for measuring cost behavior patterns were presented in the chapter. Inspection of accounts is the most intuitive and, therefore, subject to the greatest error. In the examples, the three methods using past data produced nearly identical results. For most medical practice purposes, the high-low point method produces satisfactory results. This method is simple, easy to compute, and may be used when very little past data are available. Linear regression is the most precise method and has several advantages; however, regardless of the method used, a scattergraph should be prepared to determine if a straight-line relationship exists and to observe the degree of variation in the data.

This limited discussion does not do justice to the linear regression method. The method has many uses in analysis and has many strengths. Regression is inherently more precise and therefore more accurate. As a byproduct, measures of "normal" deviation from the line and measures of the quality of fit are available; however, these measures are not discussed in this chapter.

Some of the uses of cost behavior patterns include determining how much volume is required to break even; determining impact on the break-even point and on profit or loss when fee, cost, or volume changes occur; determining whether the practice is efficient in controlling costs; and making decisions involving volume or mix of services. A further use of cost-volume-profit or break-even analysis is presented in Part III, in which planning and control are discussed.

Chapter 11

Identifying Responsibility Centers

A cost accounting system is designed to relate costs to responsibility centers. Responsibility centers are identifiable organizational units through which the activities of a medical group are performed. Each responsibility center consumes some resources of the medical group and provides some benefit, directly or indirectly, to the patient. A responsibility center may consist of the activities of a single employee or of an entire department with many employees.

It is through the tracing of costs that information is provided for cost control and distribution of income to physicians. The full cost of a responsibility center, and ultimately of a single procedure, may be determined by allocating the cost of service departments to revenue-producing responsibility centers.

Addition of a prepaid component to a fee-for-service practice places much more emphasis on costs and controlling costs. Therefore, the design and operation of the cost accounting system is most important. The techniques for determination of costs do not differ between fee-for-service and prepaid practice; however, an additional step is required in prepaid practice to translate the cost per visit or cost per procedure data into cost per member per month data.

Identification of Responsibility Centers

The ability to control costs depends upon how clearly the responsibility centers are defined. Each cost identified in the chart of accounts must be traceable to a responsibility center. Some individual in the medical group is responsible for each cost.

Identification of responsibility centers is as much a philosophical issue as a technical one. As the size of the practice expands and the organization becomes more complex, it becomes necessary to identify additional responsibility centers. Each practice is to some degree unique—whether in the mix of services, in the organizational structure chosen, or in the management style of administration. Each medical group should develop a structure of responsibility centers that best serves its needs. Responsibility centers may be developed as few as one per specialty and one for all administrative costs or may include such extensive detail as one responsibility center per physician in each specialty plus additional responsibility centers for laboratory, radiology, administration, occupancy, and data processing.

The process of identifying responsibility centers need not change as the group moves from fee-for-service practice into combined fee-for-service/prepaid practice. The group must be able to relate cost per member per month to the capitation received. When the prepaid component is small, these data may be accumulated in a responsibility center for the entire prepaid component. As the prepaid component grows in size and relative importance, the group must be able to relate its costs and fee-for-service equivalent revenues to the appropriate departments as well as to the group as a whole.

Usually, activities to be performed in a particular responsibility center are clearly defined. Though not necessarily stated in writing, job descriptions most often are implicitly understood. Responsibility for managing production and controlling costs, however, is often ambiguous. For example, a particular physician may manage the production in a given medical specialty yet leave the responsibility for cost control in the specialty to the administrator. As a result, the administrator has responsibility for costs incurred by someone else in the organization. In such cases, the physician who is responsibility center manager does not want to be accountable for control of costs, while the administrator, remote from this center, cannot effectively exercise control.

Types of Responsibility Centers

For purposes of financial management, three types of responsibility centers can be identified—expense or cost centers, profit or contribution centers, and investment centers. Each type is summarized in Exhibit 11-1. These centers differ in the amount of financial information that may be traced to each one. Basically, they differ in the criteria by which performance can be evaluated.

Expense or Cost Center

The expense or cost center is a responsibility center not serving patients directly and to which only costs may be traced. Cost centers are evaluated on their capacity to minimize costs either in total dollars or in cost per unit of service. Examples of cost centers are medical records, reception and appointments, and occupancy.

Profit or Contribution Center

The profit or contribution center is a responsibility center performing a service to patients and to which revenue for that service, as well as direct costs, can be traced. Some measure of profit or contribution may be determined. The profit or contribution centers are evaluated on their capacity to control costs

EXHIBIT 11-1
TYPES OF RESPONSIBILITY CENTERS

Type of Responsibility Center	Traceability of Financial Data	Nonfinancial Measures of Performance	Financial Measures of Performance	Evaluation Criterion
Expense or cost center	Expenses: total expenses, expenses per unit of output	Time spent and quantity of resources consumed per unit of output	Amount of expenses: actual vs. previous period, actual vs. planned, actual vs. other comparable groups	Minimize expenses: minimize dollars of expense per unit of activity
Profit or contribution center	Revenues and expenses: total revenue, total expenses, profit or contribution	Number of patients served, time spent, and quantity of resources consumed per unit of output	Amount contributed by responsibility center to cover common costs and generate income for physicians	Maximize profit or contribution
Investment center	Revenues, expenses, assets employed	Number of patients served, time spent, and quantity of resources consumed per unit of output	Return on assets employed (also measures cited above)	Maximize return on assets

and to generate a satisfactory contribution to cover common costs and provide the physicians with desired income levels. Examples of profit or contribution centers are each medical specialty, laboratory, and radiology.

Investment Center

The investment center is a responsibility center for which the amount of assets employed can be determined (in addition to revenue and costs) and a return on assets employed may be computed. While this idea is a useful tool for evaluation, it is not used widely by medical practices. Return on investment, however, is the most significant evaluation of the realty entity.

Another area in which return on assets employed should be useful is for evaluation of an ancillary department with a large investment in equipment. In this case, the ancillary department could establish fees to generate a desired rate of return on assets employed.

Cost Pools

When an appropriate allocation basis for a particular service department is determined, two assumptions must be made: first, that the service department is small enough to make expenses homogenous; and second, that at least one allocation basis per service department provides for acceptable allocation of the costs inherent to that department. When these assumptions are not valid (for example, when the organizational unit was created because of management preference rather than because of a clear definition of purpose), it may be necessary to break down the costs of the service department into cost pools. These cost pools would meet the two criteria and would be allocated to revenue-producing departments.

There are other responsibility centers in every organization to which financial data cannot be traced. Although revenues and costs cannot be related to these responsibility centers, some types of nonfinancial data are available for all responsibility centers. The nonfinancial data may include time spent, hours of operation, quantity of resources consumed, and some physical measure of output.

Accounting for Responsibility Centers

Within the structure of the chart of accounts, there are two approaches to accumulating revenue and expenses by responsibility center. The choice of approach should be made to best suit the information needs of the practice, and these needs are influenced by the number and type of responsibility centers established in the individual practice.

Use of the Basic Field for Ancillary Departments

The smaller medical groups surveyed indicated a desire to limit the number of responsibility centers and confine the account structure to four digits. These groups wanted to accumulate costs for responsibility centers, particularly the laboratory and radiology departments. The chart of accounts provides for several expenses to be accumulated for ancillary departments. These expenses include:

5400	Ancillary department salaries
6200	Ancillary department supplies expenses
6300	Cost of goods sold—ancillary departments
6620-6640	Rent/lease—furniture, fixtures, and equipment—ancillary departments
6720-6740	Depreciation—furniture, fixtures, and equipment—ancillary departments

6840-6880 Maintenance and repairs—furniture, fixtures, and equipment—ancillary departments

The third (or in some cases the fourth) digit identifies the ancillary department. The practical limitation on number of ancillary departments for this method is from four to six.

Use of the Responsibility Center Field

The structure of the chart of accounts presented in Part I includes a field for the identification of responsibility centers. This field is illustrated as a two-digit field following the four-digit basic field and segregated by a dash.

Basic Field	Responsibility Center Field
0 0 0 0	0 0

While the structure of the chart of accounts indicates a two-digit field, it may be one, two, or three digits depending upon the needs of the practice. Smaller practices with less than ten responsibility centers may wish to use a single digit, while larger groups may need three digits.

While an exhaustive list of possible responsibility centers with suggested coding for the responsibility center fields is beyond the scope of this volume, Exhibit 11-2 provides a list of possible responsibility centers and suggested coding based upon the results of the survey and inoffice interviews.

Assume that a practice has identified the following responsibility centers:

Family Practice	01
Pediatrics	02
Radiology	40
Occupancy	70
Administration (administrator and staff)	80

Examples of accounts for this practice, using the responsibility center field approach, are:

Physician Salaries, Family Practice	5110-01
Medical Supplies, Pediatrics	6120-02

EXHIBIT 11-2
EXAMPLES OF RESPONSIBILITY CENTERS

Medicine 01-19

Family Practice
Pediatrics
Internal Medicine
Allergy and Immunology
Psychiatry
Ophthalmology
Otolaryngology
Occupational Medicine
Preventive Medicine
Dermatology
Obstetrics and Gynecology

Surgery 20-39

General Surgery
Orthopedic Surgery
Thoracic Surgery
Vascular Surgery
Colon and Rectal Surgery
Plastic Surgery
Neurological Surgery

Radiology 40-44

Other Physician 45-49

Anesthesiology
Pathology

Ancillary Medical Services 50-59

Laboratory
Radiology
Physical Therapy
Optical
EKG
Allergy
Psychology
Radiation Therapy
Nuclear Medicine

Health and Rehabilitation 60-64

Social Worker
Patient Education
Nutrition

Medical Support Services 65-69

Reception and Appointments
Medical Records
Medical Secretaries
Record Audit

Occupancy and Use 70-79

Buildings and Grounds
Maintenance
Housekeeping
Security

Administrative Services 80-89

Administration
Personnel
Employee Relations
Accounting
Electronic Data Processing
Business Office
Credit and Collections
Insurance
Purchasing
Communications

Other 90-99

Use of the Provider Field

Some practices may have more than one physician in each specialty or may wish to trace, for example, revenues and expenses to each member of the radiology responsibility center. For those practices that want even more detail than the responsibility center field provides, the provider field approach can be used.

Through the use of the provider field, revenues and costs can be accumulated not only for physicians but for each individual providing billable services to patients. The structure of the chart of accounts provides for a two-digit field to the right of the responsibility center field.

Basic Field	Responsibility Center Field	Provider Field
0 0 0 0	0 0	0 0

Like the responsibility center field, the provider field may consist of one, two, or three digits depending upon the needs of the group. By using the provider field, the practice can prepare operating statements for each provider of medical care.

To illustrate, assume a medical practice has identified the following responsibility centers and provider codes:

	Responsibility Center Code	Provider Code
Family Practice	01	
Physician A		01
Physician B		02
Pediatrics	02	
Physician C		03
Physician D		04

Revenues and costs can be accumulated using the responsibility center code and provider code, as the following examples show.

Salary, Physician A	5110-01-01
Nurse's Salary, Physician C	5510-02-03
Drugs and Medications, Physician B	6110-01-02
Gross Charges, Physician D	3100-02-04

Summary

Identification of responsibility centers is a key step in any cost accounting system. For purposes of control, revenues and costs are traced to the centers responsible for their incurrence. Control reports should not include costs over which the responsibility center manager does not have control.

The nature of the responsibility center will determine the criterion that should be used to evaluate the responsibility center's performance. A cost or expense center is responsible only for costs and therefore is evaluated on a cost minimization criterion. A profit or contribution center is responsible for revenues as well as costs and should be evaluated on the maximization of profit or contribution. Finally, an investment center is responsible for assets employed, as well as revenues and costs, and should be evaluated on the maximization of return on assets employed.

Chapter 12

Determining Full Cost

Discussion so far has focused on identification of cost behavior patterns, break-even analysis, and tracing costs to responsibility centers. This body of accounting may be termed "responsibility accounting." Its primary purpose is cost control. The purpose of this chapter is to explain the concept of full cost and to develop the process of measuring the full cost of a costing objective. The usual costing objectives for medical practices are revenue-producing responsibility centers and procedures. The full cost of each procedure is a valuable aid in setting fees or negotiating capitation payments.

Direct and Indirect Costs

Throughout the accounting process, revenues and costs are classified, segregated, and traced to specific focal points or costing objectives. Three broad classifications are time periods, products and services, and responsibility centers. Some costs, called direct costs, are capable of being traced to and logically associated with a specific focal point. Other costs, called indirect costs, are common to several costing objectives and are therefore not logically assignable to a specific costing objective without some type of allocation process. This chapter and the next two chapters will discuss and illustrate the process of allocating indirect costs to specific costing objectives. The specific costing objectives will be services or procedures performed by a fee-for-service/prepaid medical group.

Cost per Member per Month

Traditional costing techniques of fee-for-service medical groups develop the cost of operating a particular responsibility center and the cost of performing a specific procedure or service. In prepaid practice, the unit of cost is the cost per member per month. Cost per procedure and cost per member per month use different activity bases. The translation of cost per procedure into cost per member per month involves an additional step in the cost accounting process. The cost of each procedure (or group of procedures) is applied to the procedures performed for the prepaid patients to arrive at the total cost of serving prepaid patients for the month. This total cost is divided by the average number of members enrolled for the month to arrive at cost per member per month.

Cash versus Accrual

A question of accuracy and comparability arises when the accounts of the medical group are maintained on a cash basis. Ideally, costs would be analyzed and compared with a "budget" monthly. Monthly comparisons are meaningful on the accrual basis because expenses are measured as the resources are consumed in providing services to patients. In a fee-for-service/prepaid group, the early receipt of revenues and the long delay before paying some costs makes the accrual basis mandatory for control of costs. On the cash basis, the practice may pay cash and therefore recognize the expense before, in the same period as, or after the resources are consumed. On the cash basis, a longer period of time, such as a quarter, must be used to provide a more comparable measure of expenses. The analyses in this text assume accrual accounting or else a sufficiently long period of time to offset timing differences.

Measurement of Full Cost

To arrive at the cost of a unit of service, some measure of cost (direct cost, variable cost, full cost, etc.) is divided by the units of activity performed by the responsibility center. When procedures differ widely within a responsibility center, some relative unit of measure may be necessary to define a unit of service. One procedure may involve one unit of service, while another involves three units of service.

Measurement of the full cost of a service or procedure involves four steps. A fifth step translates cost per procedure to cost per member per month for the prepaid practice.

Step 1 Identify responsibility centers.

Step 2 Trace all revenues and costs to the center responsible for their incurrence.

Step 3 Allocate costs of service departments to revenue-producing responsibility centers to determine full cost (direct plus allocated costs) of each center.

Step 4 Determine the cost of each procedure or service by dividing the full cost of the responsibility center by the number of procedures or services performed.

Step 5 Translate cost per procedure or service data into cost per member per month for the prepaid practice.

The first two steps were discussed in Chapter 11. The last three steps are explained and illustrated in the remainder of this chapter. The focus in this chapter is on the techniques of cost allocation. In Chapter 13, some conceptual problems in allocating the costs of service departments to revenue-producing departments are discussed.

Step 1 Identify Responsibility Centers
Chapter 11 contains a full discussion of responsibility centers. The responsibility center identified in any practice should reflect the organizational structure and style of practice adopted by the physicians. The primary consideration in identifying responsibility centers is the control of revenues and costs. Distribution of income to physicians is important, but as a secondary consideration.

Step 2 Trace Revenues and Costs to Responsibility Centers
Like Step 1, this step was examined earlier. The use of the responsibility center field requires each revenue and cost to be identified with a particular responsibility center. Again, it should be pointed out that the primary consideration in tracing costs should be revenue and cost control.

Step 3 Allocate Costs of Service Departments to Revenue-producing Responsibility Centers
There are three procedural issues to be considered in allocating costs.

Technique of allocation

Order of allocation

Basis of allocation

Technique of allocation—Should service department costs be allocated directly to revenue-producing responsibility centers or should they be allocated to other service departments as well?

Order of allocation—Which service department's costs are allocated first, second, and so on?

Basis of allocation—Should costs be allocated on the basis of square footage, revenue production, patient visits, or some other basis?

For each of the three issues there is no one right way. Allocation of costs is an arbitrary action. The process should be fair, equitable, and understandable. A different technique, a different order of allocation, or a different basis of allocation may produce different total costs for a particular responsibility center; however, total costs for the entire practice will remain unchanged.

The last two issues, order of allocation and basis of allocation, are discussed as issues in cost allocation in the next chapter. The first issue, technique of allocation, is examined below.

Technique of Allocation
Three techniques of allocation are presently in use.

Direct allocation

Step-down allocation

Simultaneous equations or matrix algebra allocation

Direct Allocation. Direct allocation is the simplest method, requiring a minimum of clerical effort. Costs of each service department are allocated directly, and only to revenue-producing responsibility centers. No costs of services are allocated to other service departments.

In a complex organization with many shared services, the direct allocation method has a major disadvantage. Direct allocation fails to recognize that services performed by one service department may benefit another service department and, consequently, does not develop the full cost of operations in service departments.

Step-down Allocation. The step-down technique is relatively simple. Its precision is dependent upon the manner of identifying responsibility centers and the order of allocation. The step-down technique involves allocating the costs of each service department in a predetermined order. Allocation of the costs of each service department is a separate step. As the costs of a service department are allocated to revenue-producing responsibility centers and the remaining service departments, there is a step-down or continuation to the next service department. Once the costs of a service department are allocated, that service department is considered closed and no subsequent allocations to it from other service departments are made. Because no subsequent allocations are made to a closed service department, the step-down technique does not produce the full cost of each service department.

The step-down technique is the most widely used method of cost allocation and the one recommended in this text. It is reasonably accurate for most purposes. In addition, it is a systematic approach involving only moderate clerical effort.

Simultaneous Equations or Matrix Algebra Allocation. This technique provides precise information and develops full costs for each center through use of simultaneous algebraic equations. Such a technique can be effectively employed by a large organization with highly sensitive cost data, if benefits from using the method exceed the costs of using it. Because special computer software is required for the complex calculations, matrix algebra is more difficult for most medical practices to implement. The illustration of this technique will include a very simple setting.

Illustration of Cost Allocation Techniques

For the purpose of demonstration, assume that a medical group has only two revenue-producing departments, medical and ancillary, and two service departments, occupancy and administration. Exhibit 12-1 contains the data to be used in illustrating the techniques of cost allocation. To simplify the example, activity data are presented in percentage form. The revised data for square feet of space and number of employees reflect eliminating the allocation of the costs of a particular responsibility center to itself.

EXHIBIT 12-1

DATA FOR COST ALLOCATION ILLUSTRATIONS

		Revenue-producing Departments		Service Departments	
	Total	Medical	Ancillary	Occupancy	Administration
Direct costs (traced to the departments)	$200,000	$100,000	$20,000	$30,000	$50,000
Data for bases of allocation:					
Patient visits	100%	60%	40%	—	—
Revenue production	100%	90%	10%	—	—
Square footage	100%	20%	40%	10%	30%
Personnel count	100%	40%	10%	10%	40%
Square footage (revised)	100%	22%	45%	—	33%
Personnel count (revised)	100%	66%	17%	17%	—

Illustration of Direct Allocation Techniques. To illustrate direct allocation, two examples are presented, one in Exhibit 12-2 and one in 12-3. In the first illustration (Exhibit 12-2), occupancy and administration costs are allocated directly to the medical and ancillary departments on the basis of number of patient visits. Because there are no allocations to other service departments, the order of allocation is unimportant. When service department costs are allocated on the basis of patient visits, full cost of operating the medical department is $148,000 and the ancillary department $52,000.

In the second example (Exhibit 12-3), service department costs are allocated directly to the medical and ancillary departments on the basis of revenue production. In this case, the full cost of operating the medical department is $172,000 and the ancillary department $28,000. Note that the full cost of operating the ancillary department is approximately 1.9 times larger when patient visits are used as an allocation base than when revenue production is used.

EXHIBIT 12-2
ILLUSTRATION OF DIRECT ALLOCATION TECHNIQUE 1

	Total	Medical	Ancillary	Occupancy	Administration
Direct costs	$200,000	$100,000	$20,000	$30,000	$50,000
Allocate service departments' costs on basis of patient visits		48,000	32,000	(30,000)	(50,000)
Full cost	$200,000	$148,000	$52,000	$ 0	$ 0

EXHIBIT 12-3
ILLUSTRATION OF DIRECT ALLOCATION TECHNIQUE 2

	Total	Medical	Ancillary	Occupancy	Administration
Direct costs	$200,000	$100,000	$20,000	$30,000	$50,000
Allocate service departments' costs on basis of revenue production		72,000	8,000	(30,000)	(50,000)
Full cost	$200,000	$172,000	$28,000	$ 0	$ 0

Illustration of Step-down Allocation Techniques. The third example uses the step-down technique, first allocating occupancy costs on the basis of square footage and next allocating administration costs on the basis of revenue production (Exhibit 12-4).

The fourth (Exhibit 12-5) and fifth (Exhibit 12-6) illustrations use number of patient visits and personnel count to allocate administration costs. Note that in each case the occupancy department is considered closed and no administration costs are allocated to occupancy.

EXHIBIT 12-4
ILLUSTRATION OF STEP-DOWN TECHNIQUE 1

	Total	Medical	Ancillary	Occupancy	Adminis-tration
Direct costs	$200,000	$100,000	$20,000	$30,000	$50,000
1. Allocate occupancy costs on basis of square footage		6,600 (22%)	13,500 (45%)	(30,000)	9,900 (33%)
2. Allocate administration costs on basis of revenue production		53,910 (90%)	5,990 (10%)		(59,900)
Full cost	$200,000	$160,510	$39,490	$ 0	$ 0

Medical	20%	(20/90)	=	22%	× 30,000	=	$ 6,600
Ancillary	40%	(40/90)	=	45%	× 30,000	=	13,500
Administration	30%	(30/90)	=	33%	× 30,000	=	9,900
	90%			100%			$30,000

EXHIBIT 12-5
ILLUSTRATION OF STEP-DOWN TECHNIQUE 2

	Total	Medical	Ancillary	Occupancy	Adminis-tration
Direct costs	$200,000	$100,000	$20,000	$30,000	$50,000
1. Allocate occupancy costs (square footage)		6,600 (22%)	13,500 (45%)	(30,000)	9,900 (33%)
2. Allocate administration costs (patient visits)		35,940 (60%)	23,960 (40%)		(59,900)
Full cost	$200,000	$142,540	$57,460	$ 0	$ 0

EXHIBIT 12-6
ILLUSTRATION OF STEP-DOWN TECHNIQUE 3

	Total	Medical	Ancillary	Occupancy	Adminis-tration
Direct costs	$200,000	$100,000	$20,000	$30,000	$50,000
1. Allocate occupancy costs (square footage)		6,600 (22%)	13,500 (45%)	(30,000)	9,900 (33%)
2. Allocate ad ministration costs (personnel count)		47,920 (80%)	11,980 (20%)		(59,900)
Full cost	$200,000	$154,520	$45,480	$ 0	$ 0

Illustration of Simultaneous Equations or Matrix Algebra Allocation Technique. The final example sets up simultaneous equations for allocating costs of occupancy to administration and costs of administration to revenue-producing departments (Exhibit 12-7). In this way, there is no need to be concerned about order of allocation. In addition, it provides a total cost for each service responsibility center. The total cost of administration is $63,460 not $50,000. To use this method in a more complex and realistic setting, the group must use a computer and matrix algebra. Further illustration is beyond the scope of this text.

EXHIBIT 12-7
ILLUSTRATION OF SIMULTANEOUS EQUATIONS OR MATRIX ALGEBRA TECHNIQUE

	Total	Medical	Ancillary	Occupancy	Adminis-tration
Direct costs	$200,000	$100,000	$20,000	$30,000	$50,000
Allocate occupancy		8,973 (22%)	18,355 (45%)	(40,788)	13,460 (33%)
Allocate adminis-tration		41,884 (66%)	10,788 (17%)	10,788 (17%)	(63,460)
Full cost	$200,000	$150,857	$49,143	$ 0	$ 0

EXHIBIT 12-7 (continued)

Let S1	= Total costs of occupancy
Let S2	= Total costs of administration
S1	= $30,000 + .17(S2)
S2	= $50,000 + .33(S1)

Substitute S2 into S1

S1	= $30,000 + .17[$50,000 + .33(S1)]
.944(S1)	= $30,000 + 8,500
S1	= $40,788

Substitute S1 into S2

S2	= $50,000 + .33($40,788)
S2	= $63,460

Comparison of Techniques of Allocation

A summary comparison of the methods is presented in Exhibit 12-8. Medical responsibility center costs range from a low of $142,540 to a high of $172,000. Ancillary costs range from $28,000 to $57,460. As precision is added to the calculation, the range narrows. The simultaneous equations method is the most accurate with costs of $150,857 for medical and $49,143 for ancillary.

Selection of the method should depend upon its cost, sensitivity to error, and the ability of the people performing the cost analysis. For most purposes the step-down method will provide results that are satisfactory.

EXHIBIT 12-8

FULL COST OF REVENUE-PRODUCING RESPONSIBILITY CENTERS

	Medical	Ancillary	Total
Direct allocation techniques:			
1. (Exhibit 12-2)	$148,000	$52,000	$200,000
2. (Exhibit 12-3)	$172,000	$28,000	$200,000
Step-down allocation techniques:			
1. (Exhibit 12-4)	$160,510	$39,490	$200,000
2. (Exhibit 12-5)	$142,540	$57,460	$200,000
3. (Exhibit 12-6)	$154,520	$45,480	$200,000
Simultaneous equations technique:			
1. (Exhibit 12-7)	$150,857	$49,143	$200,000

Step 4 Determine the Cost of Each Procedure or Service

The last step in measuring full cost involves determination of the unit costs of services or procedures performed by the revenue-producing departments. This amount should be used in establishing billing and capitation rates, in seeking reimbursements, and in making other decisions involving fees. In a fee-for-service/prepaid practice this amount becomes the basis for determining the per member per month cost. The full cost for each revenue-producing department is divided by the measure of service or number of procedures performed. If there is a wide range of services or procedures performed, it may be necessary to use some relative weighting scale to equate the services or procedures. One procedure might have a value of eight units while another is worth two. The procedure worth eight units would have a unit cost four times that of the procedure worth two units.

To calculate cost per unit, assume that during the year patient visits amounted to 6,000 for the medical department and 4,000 for the ancillary department. The unit costs are presented in Exhibit 12-9. With such wide divergence in unit costs—from $23.76 to $28.67 for the medical department and from $7.00 to $14.37 for the ancillary department—what is the best measure of cost? There is no one right answer. Each unit cost is an arbitrarily determined amount. Care must be used in identifying the responsibility centers, in tracing the costs to responsibility centers, in choosing the order of allocation, and in selecting the bases of allocation. The next chapter examines some of the more philosophical issues in cost allocation.

EXHIBIT 12-9
DETERMINATION OF COST PER UNIT OF PROCEDURE OR SERVICE

	Medical (6000 patient visits)		Ancillary (4000 patient visits)	
	Full Cost	Unit Cost	Full Cost	Unit Cost
Direct allocation techniques:				
1. (Exhibit 12-2)	$148,000	$24.67	$52,000	$13.00
2. (Exhibit 12-3)	$172,000	$28.67	$28,000	$ 7.00
Step-down allocation techniques:				
1. (Exhibit 12-4)	$160,510	$26.75	$39,490	$ 9.87
2. (Exhibit 12-5)	$142,540	$23.76	$57,460	$14.37
3. (Exhibit 12-6)	$154,520	$25.75	$45,480	$11.37
Simultaneous equations technique:				
1. (Exhibit 12-7)	$150,857	$25.14	$49,143	$12.29

Step 5 Determine Cost per Member per Month
To determine cost per member per month, the costs of providing health care to prepaid patients must be related to the number of members. Utilization records will indicate the number of prepaid patient visits to medical and ancillary responsibility centers. Assume the following data for prepaid patients:

Number of members enrolled for which capitation payment was received	9,600
Prepaid patient visits within the group:	
Medical visits during month by prepaid patients	2,400
Ancillary visits during month by prepaid patients	1,440
Cost of referrals outside the group	$32,640

Cost per member per month may be determined by multiplying number of patient visits by the unit cost per visit and dividing the product by number of enrolled members.

$$\frac{2{,}400 \times \$25.14}{9{,}600} = \$6.28 \text{ medical cost per member per month}$$

$$\frac{1{,}440 \times \$12.29}{9{,}600} = \$1.84 \text{ ancillary cost per member per month}$$

$6.28 + $1.84 = $8.12 total cost per member per month for services provided to prepaid patients within the group

$$\frac{\$32{,}640}{9{,}600} = \$3.40 \text{ referral cost per member per month for services referred outside the group}$$

The cost per member per month of $8.12 may be compared with the monthly capitation for services within the group and the $3.40 with the capitation for referred service. Both must be compared with the planned cost per member per month.

Other methods of determining cost per member per month have been suggested. One method determines the fee-for-service equivalent charges for the services performed. Instead of using cost per procedure, one multiplies the fee-for-service charge (discounted for appropriate adjustments and allowances) by the utilization data for the services actually used by prepaid patients. The resulting figure should be comparable to the capitation payment but does not reflect actual cost. A second method would allocate total costs between fee-for-service and prepaid practice on some aggregate measure of service usage such as relative value units.

Summary

One of the most troublesome areas in accounting is the measurement of full cost. The purpose of this chapter has been to explain the concept of full cost and to determine the full cost of some costing objective. Measuring full cost involves: first, tracing direct costs to the costing objective, then, allocating a fair share of indirect costs to the costing objective.

Three techniques of allocation were illustrated: direct allocation, step-down allocation, and the simultaneous equations allocation method. Also demonstrated was the determination of unit cost per procedure as the last step in measuring full cost. An additional step for a fee-for-service/prepaid practice translated the cost per procedure to the cost per member per month.

Chapter 13

Issues in Cost Allocation

Techniques of allocation were discussed at length in Chapter 12. This chapter focuses on some of the issues concerning cost allocation for medical practices. To a large extent these issues are philosophical, with no right or wrong approach. When a decision is to be made regarding which technique, order of allocation, or basis of allocation to adopt, the needs and characteristics of the particular organization should be considered. The size, organizational structure, and scope of operations are all deciding factors. The methods chosen should best meet the needs of the organization and should be financially justifiable. If the cost structure is relatively insensitive to less precise calculations, the financial burden of a precise allocation method would hardly be justified.

Four qualitative tests should be applied to each choice made.

Is the method fair?

Is it equitable?

Is it understandable?

Do the benefits from the method justify the costs to the organization?

Any method that meets the four criteria can be considered a correct choice.

Behavioral Impact

When the cost allocation methods most appropriate to the organization are decided upon, the behavioral impact of implementing different methods must be considered. It is recommended that, for purposes of control and for most decisions relating to mix and volume of services, revenues and costs be traced to responsibility centers and that arbitrary allocations of cost not be allowed to distort the responsibility for revenues and costs. The full cost of a responsibility center is useful for setting fees but not for cost control or for decisions concerning volume or mix of services.

When establishing allocation methods, the responsibility center managers should agree upon the technique of allocation, the order of allocation, and the basis of allocation before any numerical data are used. These philosophical issues should be decided on the basis of fairness, equity, understandability, and cost to implement. Once these issues are decided, then numerical data may be used and the results evaluated. A presentation of alternative methods together with their impact on actual data will often cause managers to shop for the methods that will improve their positions.

Allocation of Individual Costs versus Allocation of Pools of Costs

In addition to any issue of precision in allocation of costs, there is the basic question of cost control. To achieve control of costs, every cost in the chart of accounts must be traced to some responsible manager. For this reason, it is critical to identify responsibility centers, so that responsibility for costs is clearly evident. The first two steps in a good cost control system should be identical to the first two steps in a good cost allocation system.

Step 1 Identify responsibility centers.

Step 2 Trace all revenues and costs to the center responsible for their incurrence.

If these steps are followed, cost control and cost allocation to measure full cost should be compatible. The process of cost allocation is arbitrary, and wide differences in measuring full costs for a particular responsibility center may occur if different techniques and/or bases of allocation are employed. There is no one right way to allocate costs. If cost centers are emphasized, the allocation of entire pools of cost (total costs of a responsibility center) provides better overall results than allocation of individual costs. For example, accumulating the costs of occupancy and allocating a single figure for occupancy or internal rent is superior to allocating rent, depreciation, utilities, and so forth individually. Because these costs are not controlled by the responsibility center to which they are allocated, the added precision of individual allocation is not warranted, and there is less chance of distorting results for cost control.

Order of Allocation

When the step-down technique of cost allocation is used, an order of allocation must be established. Different orders of allocation may produce a significantly different full cost for a particular responsibility center. The broad guideline that should direct the order of allocation is:

> Begin with the responsibility center that provides the most services to other responsibility centers but uses the least services from other responsibility centers.

Fairness and equity will be greatest when this guideline is followed. Application of this guideline will usually result in the following order of allocation:

Occupancy

Administration

Data processing

Purchasing

Reception and appointments

Judgment is required to apply the guideline. The order should progress from the responsibility center that provides the most services to others (particularly other service departments) to the responsibility center that serves only the revenue-producing centers.

Allocation Criteria

Allocation bases fall into three broad criteria categories. It is useful to recognize these criteria, for they may have serious behavorial implications. They are:

Cause and effect

Facilities provided

Ability to bear

Cause and Effect

Under this criterion the relationship between the cost to be allocated and the responsibility center receiving the allocation must be clear; in other words, the user relationship must be clear and traceable. Unfortunately, in most cases the relationship is at best casual or indeterminant. It may be possible to maintain records of usage and to establish an internal billing rate or transfer price for some services. For example, the use of an automobile owned by the practice may be charged to users. The cause and effect criterion is a logical framework for ascertaining allocation bases, as it normally results in fair and equitable, and therefore mutually acceptable, cost allocations.

For some responsibility centers, such as administration, there is no adequate measure of cause and effect. Attempts to develop some measure of cause and effect, such as an allocation based on the time the administrator devotes to each responsibility center, will usually cause more problems than they solve.

Facilities Provided
The underlying logic is that facilities are provided for all users, and the decision of whether or not to use them is made by each responsibility center manager. Each manager, therefore, should bear a share in relationship to facilities' possible use, not their actual use. Occupancy costs fit this criterion.

Ability to Bear
Ability to bear is a common, arbitrary basis of allocation, under which costs are allocated to those centers most able to cover additional costs. The fairness of this measure is questionable, especially in view of the fact that costs of services are often independent of their results. Any allocation that uses revenues, gross charges, contributions, or a similar allocation base without consideration of services provided in roughly the same proportion may be considered to be based on ability to bear.

Allocation Bases

To apply allocation bases to costs, two assumptions should be made: 1) the cost center is small enough that expenses are homogeneous, and 2) at least one allocation basis per cost center provides for acceptable allocation of the costs inherent to that center. Some of the more common bases are:

- Square footage—derived from the number of square feet occupied by each responsibility center and converted to a percentage of total square feet. This basis fits the criterion of facilities provided.

- Utilization—based on the number of units (hours, etc.) of usage derived for the individual responsibility centers. Such utilization patterns can be established through studies over a period of months during which records of utilization are kept and an average utilization amount for each center arrived at, subject to annual review and revision. Another and simpler method is to report actual utilization by each responsibility center on a monthly basis.

- Patient visits—derived from the number of patient visits to the medical practice.

- Personnel count—derived from the number of employees in each responsibility center and converted to a percentage of total employees. Subdivisions can be determined in which services are provided exclusively for one stratum of the staff, for example, a personnel count of all physicians in order to allocate costs of a service provided only for them.

- Specific identification—established through use of monthly tally cards, time reports, or number of requisitions.
- Revenue production—determined by the billing system to indicate the amount of gross charges or adjusted gross charges and the capitation revenue or fee-for-service equivalent charges. This would fit the criterion of ability to bear.
- Direct costs of responsibility centers—derived from the cost accounting records. To some extent this fits the criterion of ability to bear.
- Gross payroll—determined from the payroll records or from the cost accounting system. Labor-related services may use this basis.

To facilitate a practical understanding of the different allocation bases and their relationship to cost centers, a list of possible allocation bases is presented below.

Cost Center or Pool	Allocation Bases
Occupancy (rent, depreciation, property taxes, maintenance)	Square footage Utilization
Administration	Personnel count
Business and insurance offices	Personnel count Utilization
Data processing (rental, depreciation, maintenance, computer lines)	Utilization Combination—square footage plus utilization
Accounting	Personnel count Revenue production
Cafeteria	Personnel count Combination—square footage plus utilization
Reception and appointments	Physician count (provider count) Patient visits
Medical records	Patient visits

Central supplies and purchasing	Specific identification

Use of Multiple Bases

When it is possible to determine cost behavior patterns for service responsibility centers, some medical practices use more than one basis of allocation. The fixed costs of a service responsibility center may be allocated according to the criterion of facilities provided, and the variable costs may be allocated according to the cause and effect (use) criterion. Some practices use multiple bases related to cost behavior patterns for the purpose of distribution of income to doctors. In these practices fixed costs are allocated equally and variable costs are allocated on the basis of production.

Summary

The most serious issues in cost accounting are the behavioral issues. Determining the technique of allocation, the order of allocation, and the basis of allocation involves policy decisions. To a large extent the issues are philosophical, with no right or wrong approach. These issues should be resolved before any allocations are made.

Four qualitative tests should be applied to any choice. Is it fair? Is it equitable? Is it understandable? Do the benefits of the method justify its costs to the organization? When the practice can answer yes to these questions for any of the issues discussed in the chapter, policy has been correctly established.

Chapter 14

Illustration of a Cost Accounting System

This chapter presents a detailed illustration of cost accounting for a fee-for-service/prepaid medical group. Although the data were developed from a number of representative groups, the illustration should not be used as a norm. Focus is on the costing process rather than on the numbers or results.

Measuring Full Cost

Determination of the full cost of services or procedures is useful for a number of purposes. The primary purpose is as an aid in setting fees or negotiating capitation rates. For this purpose, budgeted or estimated data should be used. Past data may be useful for developing a fee schedule; however, if conditions are expected to change, the costs of services and procedures developed from historical data must be adjusted to reflect the anticipated changes. Other uses of full cost data include identification of problem areas to be studied further.

Measurement of the full cost of a service or procedure involves four steps. A fifth step translates cost per procedure to cost per member per month for the prepaid practice.

Step 1	Identify responsbility centers.
Step 2	Trace all revenues and costs to the center responsible for their incurrence.
Step 3	Allocate costs of service departments to revenue-producing responsibility centers to determine full cost (direct plus allocated costs) of each center.
Step 4	Determine the cost of each procedure or service by dividing the full cost of the responsibility center by the number of procedures or services performed.
Step 5	Translate cost per procedure or service into cost per member per month for the prepaid practice.

As each of the five steps is demonstrated, measurement and other problems are examined.

Step 1 Identify Responsibility Centers

Best Medical Center has identified six revenue-producing departments (contribution centers) and four service departments (cost centers). They are shown in Exhibit 14-1. In larger groups the cost centers for administration and occupancy would be further detailed. The number of responsibility centers selected should be determined by the need for information to control operations.

EXHIBIT 14-1
IDENTIFICATION OF RESPONSIBILITY CENTERS

Contribution Centers:	
Family practice	01
Pediatrics	03
Internal medicine	05
Obstetrics/gynecology	13
Laboratory	51
Radiology	53
Cost Centers:	
Reception and appointments	65
Medical records	66
Occupancy	70
Administration	80

Step 2 Trace Revenues and Costs to Responsibility Centers

The primary purpose of a cost accounting system should be control of operations. This step relates the revenues and costs to the center responsible for their incurrence. Exhibit 14-2 shows a summary of fee-for-service gross charges, direct costs, and some nonfinancial data for each of the 10 responsibility centers.

Departmental operating statements are prepared from these same data. For example, the data relevant for control in the pediatrics department are presented in Exhibit 14-3. Individual responsibility centers are credited with the fee-for-service equivalent charges for prepaid patients. Fee-for-service charges are discounted by 12 percent for fee-for-service equivalents. Greater expense detail would be presented in practice. It is important that data for control are not distorted by arbitrary allocations of costs incurred in other departments.

EXHIBIT 14-2
DATA FOR MEASURING FULL COST OF RESPONSIBILITY CENTERS

	Fee-for-Service Gross Charges	Direct Costs[1]	Square Footage % of Total	Personnel Count	Patient Visits
Contribution Centers:					
01 Family practice	$ 752,400	$ 726,810	25%	14	42,801
03 Pediatrics	265,814	256,126	12	5	12,806
05 Internal medicine	276,640	272,006	10	5	15,896
13 Obstetrics/ gynecology	277,056	342,759	10	5	10,253
51 Laboratory	770,182	256,667	8	3	105,465
53 Radiology	510,469	175,743	10	2	12,427
Cost Centers:					
65 Reception and appointments		38,400	4	3	
66 Medical records		68,150	6	4	
70 Occupancy		266,400	0	1	
80 Administration		248,348	15	6	
	$2,852,561	$2,651,409	100%	48	199,648

[1]Direct costs include distributions and benefits to physicians.

Step 3 Allocate Costs of Service Departments to Revenue-producing Responsibility Centers

It is at this point that the data needs for control and data needs for fee-setting decisions separate. The amount of costs finally allocated to each revenue-producing department depends upon three policies: the technique of allocation, the order of allocation, and the basis of allocation. These issues should be determined before any numbers are involved. Consider again the qualification criteria identified earlier in this volume to evaluate allocation policies. Is it fair? Is it equitable? Is it understandable? Do the benefits exceed the cost of the methods selected?

EXHIBIT 14-3
ILLUSTRATION OF DEPARTMENTAL OPERATING STATEMENT

BEST MEDICAL CENTER
PEDIATRICS OPERATING STATEMENT
For the Year Ended December 31, 19X4

Gross charges—fee-for-service		$265,814
Adjustments and allowances		(15,949)
Net revenues—fee-for-service		$249,865
Fee-for-service equivalent charges for services to prepaid patients		23,058
Net revenue		$272,923
Direct costs:		
Staff salaries	$32,400	
Staff benefits	6,480	
Supplies	15,896	
Professional liability insurance	7,200	
Equipment rental	1,200	63,176
Contribution of pediatrics toward distributions to physicians and common costs		$209,747
Distributions and benefits to physicians		192,950
Contribution of pediatrics toward common costs		$ 16,797

The order of allocation and bases of allocation are presented in Exhibit 14-4. The allocation worksheet is presented in Exhibit 14-5. The step-down method of allocation is used.

EXHIBIT 14-4
ORDER AND BASIS OF ALLOCATION

	Order of Allocation	Basis of Allocation
Cost Centers:		
65 Reception and appointments	3	Patient visits
66 Medical records	4	Patient visits
70 Occupancy	1	Square footage
80 Administration	2	Personnel count

Costs of the occupancy department are allocated first. This department benefits the largest number of other departments and draws the least from them. The percentage of square footage occupied by each department was presented in Exhibit 14-2. Occupancy costs allocated to family practice and administration are determined as follows:

Family practice	$266,400 × 25% = $66,600
Administration	$266,400 × 15% = $39,960

In the step-down method, when the costs of a service department are allocated, that department is considered closed. No further costs will be allocated to a service department once it is closed. For example, costs of the administration department are the second to be allocated. No administration costs will be allocated to occupancy or to itself. The administration costs to be allocated now include direct costs of $248,348 and costs allocated from occupancy of $39,960, making a total of $288,308. Administration costs are allocated on the basis of the number of employees in other departments. The amount of administration costs allocated to family practice and medical records are determined as follows:

Family practice	$288,308 × 35% = $100,909
Medical records	$288,308 × 10% = $ 28,831

$$\frac{\text{14 employees in family practice}}{\text{41 employees in departments other than administration and occupancy}} = 35\%$$

(Rounding error was added to family practice.)

The process of allocating service department costs to revenue-producing departments does not change the total costs. Additional steps must be taken before a full cost may be determined that will serve as a basis for setting fees. First, if physician salaries and benefits are not included in direct costs, distributions to physicians in each department must be added to arrive at total costs. Second, adjustments and allowances must be allocated to the revenue-producing departments.

Adjustments and allowances represent deductions from gross charges for amounts that will never be collected. Some adjustments that are determined by the physicians in each department may be traced directly to the department in Step 2 of the cost accounting. The balance of the adjustments and allowances that cannot be identified directly with a department must be allocated. In Exhibit 14-5, all adjustments and allowances are allocated on the basis of gross charges. It has been assumed that adjustments and allowances represent 6 percent of gross charges; therefore, the allocation to each department is equal to 6 percent of its gross charges. The amount of adjustments and allowances allocated to family practice and radiology are determined as follows:

Family practice	\$752,400 × 6% = \$45,144
Radiology	\$510,469 × 6% = \$30,628

The full cost for each revenue-producing department is computed in Exhibit 14-5.

Step 4 Determine the Cost of Each Procedure or Service

The full cost determined for each department in Step 3 may now be divided by the number of services or procedures performed by each department to arrive at the cost of each unit of service or procedure. For example, in the family practice department, the full cost amounts to \$979,548 and the number of patient visits amounts to 42,801, resulting in a cost per patient visit of \$22.89. This is the average cost incurred for each patient seen by the family practice department. Does this method provide a good basis for setting fees or negotiating capitation rates when historical cost data are used? Only if costs and patient visits remain at this level is it a good basis for fees in the future. Because most of the costs are fixed costs, any significant change in the number of patient visits will result in a dramatic change in the full cost per visit.

Ideally, for setting fees, budgeted costs and projected patient visits should be used, since both relate to the future. In this illustration budgeted costs are used to arrive at the projected patient visit cost. Historical costs may, however, provide a good starting point.

Some departments have a wide range of services or procedures that may be very different. For example, one radiology procedure may be very simple and utilize a limited amount of resources, while another procedure may require a large amount of resources. If each is counted as one procedure, they will bear the same average cost. The use of a relative value scale allows each procedure to be weighted differently. One procedure may have a value of one unit, another two units, and another five units.

For example, assume that in the radiology department the 12,427 procedures performed consisted of three types: 5,000 Type A procedures with a value of

EXHIBIT 14-5
ILLUSTRATION OF DEVELOPMENT OF FULL COST FOR REVENUE-PRODUCING RESPONSIBILITY CENTERS

		Revenue-producing Responsibility Centers						Service Responsibility Centers			
	Total	Family Practice	Pediatrics	Internal Medicine	Ob/Gyn	Laboratory	Radiology	Recpt.& Appts.	Medical Records	Occupancy	Adminis-tration
Direct costs	$2,651,409	$726,810	$256,126	$272,006	$342,759	$256,667	$175,743	$38,400	$68,150	$266,400	$248,348
Allocation of:											
Occupancy		66,600	31,968	26,640	26,640	21,312	26,640	10,656	15,984	(266,400)	39,960
Administration		100,909	34,597	34,597	34,597	20,181	14,415	20,181	28,831		(288,308)
Medical records		24,853	6,778	9,037	5,648	59,871	6,778		(112,965)		
Reception and appointments		15,232	4,154	5,539	3,462	36,696	4,154	(69,237)			
Total	$2,651,409	$934,404	$333,623	$347,819	$413,106	$394,727	$227,730				
Adjustments and allowances	171,153	45,144	15,949	16,598	16,623	46,211	30,628				
Full cost	$2,822,562	$979,548	$349,572	$364,417	$429,729	$440,938	$258,358				
Number of patient visits		42,801	12,806	15,896	10,253	105,465	12,427				
Full cost per patient visit before adjust-ments and allowances		$21.83	$26.05	$21.88	$40.29	$3.74	$18.33				
Full cost per patient visit		$22.89	$27.30	$22.93	$41.91	$4.18	$20.79				

one unit, 6,000 Type B procedures with a value of two units, and 1,427 Type C procedures with a value of five units. What is the appropriate unit cost for the radiology department? In the example in Exhibit 14-5, the unit costs are determined both including and excluding adjustments and allowances. However, because in this case there are no bad debts or other adjustments and allowances, the cost per unit should exclude adjustments and allowances.

Procedure Type	Number of Procedures	Units per Procedure	Total Units	Cost per Unit[1]	Cost per Procedure
A	5,000	1	5,000	$9.44	$ 9.44
B	6,000	2	12,000	$9.44	$18.88
C	1,427	5	7,135	$9.44	$47.20
	12,427		24,135		

[1] $\frac{\$227,730}{24,135} = \$9.44$

Step 5 Determine Cost per Member per Month

Cost per member per month is an accepted measure of unit cost in prepaid practice. It is in the same terms as the capitation payment and may be used to compare the group's performance with other prepaid groups. There are at least three ways to determine cost per member per month in a fee-for-service/prepaid medical group. Two may be considered as macro methods, the third a micro method.

Fee-for-Service Equivalent Method. The first method uses gross charges and fee-for-service equivalent gross charges to allocate total costs of the group between fee-for-service practice and prepaid practice. This is at best a crude measure. In the Best Medical Center illustration, fee-for-service gross charges are $2,852,561, the discounted fee-for-service equivalent for services to prepaid patients amounts to $241,905, and the member months (total number of months that members have been enrolled) amount to $23,345. The cost per member per month would be determined as follows:

$$\text{Cost of services to prepaid patients} = \frac{\text{Total costs} \times \text{fee-for-service equivalent gross charges}}{\text{Total gross charges (fee-for-service and prepaid)}}$$

$$= \frac{\$2{,}822{,}562 \times 241{,}905}{\$3{,}094{,}466}$$

$$= \$220{,}649$$

$$\text{Cost per member per month} = \frac{\text{Cost of services to prepaid patients}}{\text{Member months}}$$

$$= \frac{\$220{,}649}{23{,}345}$$

$$= \$9.45$$

Relative Value Method. The second method allocates total costs between the fee-for-service practice and the prepaid practice on the basis of relative value units for each. This is a more refined method and should provide a more precise result than the first method. Relative value units have not been determined in this example; therefore, this method will not be illustrated.

The major criticism of the relative value method is that it determines only the total cost per member per month. This method does not determine the cost per member per month by specialty or by type of procedure. A second criticism is that the relative value method assumes that costs relate to the relative value units. This is not necessarily true, particularly in the ancillary departments.

Cost Accounting Method. The third method translates the unit costs determined in Step 4 into cost per member per month data. The cost per member per month data may be as detailed as the costing process. Further, this method shows the actual cost per member per month for each responsibility center.

Exhibit 14-6 demonstrates the computation. The number of prepaid patient visits is multiplied by the cost per visit to arrive at total prepaid cost; this total cost is divided by the number of member months. The resulting cost per member per month of $9.95 is considerably higher than the fee-for-service equivalent method cost per member per month of $9.45.

Summary

This chapter has presented an extended illustration of cost accounting for a fee-for-service/prepaid medical group. Two major purposes are served by a cost accounting system. The information needs for each differ, and they should not be confused. The primary purpose of a cost accounting system is to provide information for cost control. This is accomplished by tracing revenues and costs to the departments responsible for their incurrence. The second purpose of a cost accounting system is to provide the full cost of services and procedures

EXHIBIT 14-6
ILLUSTRATION OF COMPUTATION OF COST PER MEMBER PER MONTH

	Prepaid Patient Visits	Cost per Visit[1]	Total Prepaid Cost	Cost per Member per Month[2]
Family practice	3,201	$21.83	$69,878	$2.99
Pediatrics	1,426	$26.05	$37,147	1.59
Internal medicine	1,606	$21.88	$35,139	1.51
Ob/gyn	893	$40.29	$35,979	1.54
Total cost of physician specialties				$7.63
Laboratory	9,193	$ 3.74	$34,382	1.47
Radiology	1,083	$18.33	$19,851	.85
Total cost per member per month				$9.95

[1]Unit cost before adjustments and allowances
[2]Member months = 23,345

as an aid to setting fees and negotiating capitation rates. Ideally, the group will know its costs by responsibility center and procedure when negotiating a capitation rate. The full costs for negotiating capitation rates should be computed from budgeted costs and projected services or procedures; however, historical costs may provide a starting point.

The illustration of the cost accounting system presented in this chapter involves five steps. The first two steps, "Identify responsibility centers" and "Trace all revenues and costs to the centers responsible for their incurrence," are essential for cost control. Steps three and four, "Allocate costs of service departments to revenue-producing departments" and "Determine the cost of each procedure or service," are added to develop full cost by unit of service. The last step translates full cost data into cost per member per month data.

Full cost data were developed in this chapter with either budgeted or historical costs. In Part III, *Financial Planning and Control*, which involves planning and control systems for fee-for-service/prepaid medical groups, a budget for a medical group with a prepaid practice will be developed. Data generated in Step 2 of the cost accounting system must be compared with a budget for proper cost control. The cost per member per month developed in Step 5 should be compared with the capitation rate and with cost per member per month data from peer groups.

Chapter 15

Summary of Part II

It is important to recognize that different purposes require different cost data. Cost data generated for one purpose may actually be misleading when used for another purpose. Five situations have been identified in which cost measurements must fit the situation. First, for the measurement of income, cash basis cost measurements may be significantly different from accrual basis cost measurements, whether the accrual measurements are recorded formally in the records or informally as a supplement to cash basis statements. As the fee-for-service group moves into prepaid practice, it will find cash basis cost measurements misleading. Second, for purposes of income distribution, the accounting system should emphasize the costs that reinforce the goals of the group. The move to prepaid practice leads to a shift in emphasis from production to cost control. Third, for control of costs, responsibility centers must be identified so that revenues and costs can be traced to the center responsible for their incurrence. In addition, it is necessary to know the behavior of costs so that operations may be evaluated in the light of what costs should have been at the level of operations actually achieved. Fourth, for planning, cost behavior patterns are important so that the impact of volume of activity changes on projected costs can be anticipated. Finally, in order for administrators to make decisions, it is necessary for them to know the incremental revenues and the incremental costs related to such decisions. In many cases, the fixed-variable measurement of costs will provide the relevant data for particular decisions. One decision, the setting of fees and negotiation of capitation rates, requires knowledge of the full cost of providing a service or a procedure. The common measure of cost in a prepaid practice is cost per member per month. Cost by procedure or patient visit must be translated into cost per member per month.

The chart of accounts makes it possible to trace costs to responsibility centers. Cost centers have responsibility only for costs, and the cost center manager is expected to minimize costs either in total or per unit. A profit or contribution center has responsibility for both revenues and costs, with an evaluation criterion of maximization of profit or contribution. An investment center has responsibility for revenues, costs, and assets employed. In addition to profit maximization, the investment center manager is concerned with maximization of return on assets employed. The nature of the responsibility center will necessarily have an impact on the cost accounting system.

For cost control purposes (the primary objective of the cost accounting system), arbitrary allocations of cost should not be made in the accounts or the departmental operating statements. Reports to management should be limited to revenues generated and costs incurred by the responsibility center or traced directly to the responsibility center. Responsibility center operating statements should include the fee-for-service equivalent charges for service provided to prepaid members. In this way the system measures both direct revenues and costs under the control of a responsibility center manager.

Entry into prepaid practice generates new needs for cost information. While cost data are useful and desirable in fee-for-service operations, they are critical in prepaid practice. Determining the full cost of a service or procedure requires that the costs of service responsibility centers be allocated to revenue-producing responsibility centers. Then the full cost of a service or procedure may be measured by dividing the full cost of the revenue-producing responsibility center by the number of units of service or number of procedures performed. The cost per member per month for services to prepaid patients can be derived from the full cost of services and procedures.

The full cost of a particular responsibility center may be influenced by the order of allocation, the basis of allocation chosen, and the technique of allocation used. Care must be exercised in devising the cost allocation structure. It should meet four qualitative criteria: fairness, equity, understandability, and benefit-cost relationship. Information for cost control and full cost information for setting fees and capitation rates will be compatible if arbitrary allocations are not injected into the information for control purposes.

PART III

FINANCIAL PLANNING AND CONTROL

Chapter 16

Introduction to Part III

The medical group has just completed its best year, the growth rate is favorable, and a comparison with other medical groups indicates that overhead is well managed. The physicians take home more income than their colleagues in the community, and personnel turnover has been very low. Things have never been better, so why budget?

Every medical group plans. Every medical group budgets. Every medical group attempts to control its activities. It is a question of how formal the planning and control efforts will be, not whether the group will plan and control its activities. At the one extreme, an evaluation of the activities of the past year will include an informal assessment of actions that must be taken to avoid the difficulties of the past year and to repeat or improve its favorable aspects. At the other extreme, a group will begin its planning efforts with a formal statement of goals and objectives and carry the planning through to a profit plan for each profit center, a cash budget, and a projected statement of financial position. This group will use a performance budget (profit plan adjusted for significant changes in activity) to evaluate performance and to control operations.

The planning and control efforts of most medical groups fall somewhere between these two extremes. At the present time most planning and control efforts tend toward the limited or informal end of the spectrum; however, as the activities of the practice become more complex, planning and control efforts must become more formalized.

Planning

The purpose of planning is to reduce uncertainty. For a medical group, planning involves determining goals and objectives and selecting the means of attaining them. In a profit-oriented organization, the purpose of planning is to increase the possibility of making an adequate profit. In a not-for-profit organization, the purpose of planning is to provide the desired level of services at the lowest cost. The existence of a set of plans does not ensure the success of the group. To be successful, plans must contain attainable goals and action proposals, must be properly implemented during the planning period, must serve to monitor performance and measure results, and must provide for adequate feedback.

Goals

The first stage of the planning process involves the determination of long-range goals by the owners/managers of the group. A goal is a broad statement of the direction in which the group is heading.

Objectives

Objectives represent specific short- and intermediate-term targets, usually covering a one- to three-year period. Some objectives result from specific decisions, such as the number of physicians and support personnel, the size of the facilities, and the style of practice. Other objectives result from an estimate of factors not under the owners/managers' control, such as a projection of patient demands, third-party actions, and government intervention.

Budgets

Once practice goals and objectives have been determined, a detailed plan of operations—the budget—may be developed. In its simplest terms, a budget is a dollars and cents expression of the accomplishments to be attained. It presents a means of achieving both the long-range goals and the intermediate-range objectives. The budget should also express expected results by responsibility centers in the group. These detailed budgets should motivate those responsible for achieving the desired results and also should serve as a standard against which actual results can be compared. Collectively, the detailed budgets should serve to coordinate the activities of the individual responsibility centers.

Feedback

Planning is a continuous process. As performance is monitored and actual results are compared with the plan, there should be continuous feedback for future planning. If conditions change significantly during the year, it may be necessary to revise the budget for the remainder of the year.

Control

The purpose of control is to achieve conformity to the plan. Actual performance is monitored and the results are compared with goals, objectives, and budget of the plan. Because the budget should reflect the best attainable level of performance rather than a maximum expense authorization, both favorable and unfavorable deviations from the plan are expected. Significant deviations from the plan must be identified and investigated. While past performance cannot be changed, corrective action may be taken to bring future activities back into conformity with the plan. However, if conditions have changed and the budgeted figures are no longer attainable, it may be necessary to revise or replace the budget.

The concept of responsibility accounting is crucial to the control process. This means that the financial information system should trace all revenues and costs to the responsibility centers in which they were incurred. Then, based on this information, performance reports should be prepared for each responsibility center. Each report should include only the revenues and costs controllable by the responsibility center. Indirect costs under the control of others should not be a part of the responsibility center's performance reporting system; nor should allocated costs be included in a responsibility center's performance reports that are used for control purposes. However, this procedure does not prevent the service departments' costs from being allocated to revenue-producing centers for other purposes, such as setting fees.

Outline of Part III

Chapter 17 is devoted to a discussion of strategic financial planning and the setting of goals and objectives. A questionnaire to assess priorities and formulate group goals and objectives is described. The administrator and president of the group should survey the physicians every few years to maintain a current statement of goals and objectives. Examples are given of goals and objectives that might evolve from such a process.

Chapter 18 provides an overview of budgeting. It discusses the benefits of budgeting and describes a comprehensive budget.

Chapters 19 and 20 present an integrated example of the development of a comprehensive budget (Chapter 19) and several levels of performance evaluation using the budget (Chapter 20).

An extended discussion of managing cash and other short-term resources is presented in Chapter 21. The chapter includes techniques and suggestions for the management of cash, patient receivables, and supplies.

Chapter 22 discusses the problem of estimating claims outstanding for a medical group that is obligated to provide services to members of an HMO. Nonstatistical and statistical methods are presented.

Chapter 23 presents a discussion of the information needs for decision making in a medical group. The volume closes with a brief summary in Chapter 24.

Chapter 17

Strategic Planning: Developing Goals and Objectives

The provision of health care services on a prepaid basis presents new stresses and challenges for most medical groups. In order to provide these services in a cost-effective manner and maintain the group's identity, it is crucial that the group's goals and objectives include clear directives for its involvement in prepaid care. This chapter addresses a strategic financial planning process and its desired outcomes. Even if the medical group is aware of the need to periodically assess the external and internal environment and to set direction and priorities for the group, the process may well be informal. Regardless of whether the planning process is formal or informal, the medical group will benefit from periodically applying the following planning steps.

1) Examine changes and trends in the environment
   a. External to the medical group and the prepaid plan
   b. Within the medical group and the prepaid plan.

2) Develop the goals and objectives of the group
   a. If there is a need for change in the general direction, redefine the goals.
   b. Consider the need to reestablish specific targets (objectives) and the dates for accomplishing them.

3) Establish short-term budgets consistent with the goals and objectives.

4) Compare actual results to budgets and consider the need for corrective action.

This chapter discusses the first two of the four planning steps, which are long-term or strategic in nature: examine changes and trends in the environment and develop goals and objectives. Chapters 18 and 19 address the process of establishing short-term budgets.

Examine Changes and Trends

In the last twenty years the pace of change in the health care environment has quickened in most parts of the country. Hospital-based ambulatory health care programs, government involvement in HMOs, and the establishment of Medicare and Medicaid are a few examples of changes that have occurred. The recent popularity and sudden growth of preferred provider organizations (PPOs) is another. The changes can have an impact on the medical group and can seriously influence the selection and attainment of goals and objectives. Strategic financial planning is a process of anticipating change, assessing its financial impact, formulating a response to change, and reevaluating the group's goals and objectives.

Strategic financial planning is a continuous process of evaluating long-term changes in the medical group's environment and attempting to assess their effects on the group. The process may identify a concern that can be addressed within the resources of the medical group, or one that requires cooperation with other members of the health care delivery system, or one that requires a response in the political arena. The objective of strategic financial planning, in one sense, is to avoid future unpleasant surprises. From another perspective, it is an attempt to enhance the likelihood of achieving the long-term goals and objectives of the organization. Of necessity, it is future-oriented and tends to deal with a time period of several years. There is a definite interrelationship between the strategic financial planning process, the development of goals and objectives for the organization, and the planning and evaluation of activities in the short run.

Strategic financial planning is not primarily concerned with the setting of goals and objectives, although as a by-product to the planning process it might suggest changes in the goals and objectives of the medical group. Normally, strategic financial planning is an attempt to anticipate changes in the external environment and how those changes will impact on the goals and objectives of the group. By planning far enough into the future, there should be sufficient time to take corrective action to minimize any damage to long-term goals and objectives or to make appropriate acceptable changes in them.

Strategic planning normally is oriented to the market for medical services rather than to the delivery of services or the design of clinic facilities. The primary questions become "What medical services are needed?" and "Who will purchase them?" instead of the more traditional question, "What medical services do I want to deliver?" The change in emphasis is already necessary in those portions of the country where there is an oversupply of physicians or strong competition in the health care delivery system for a static population of patients.

When strategic planning is undertaken, the focus of the plan will shift from services that the group wants to provide to services that the population will pur-

EXHIBIT 17-1
ILLUSTRATION OF THE PLANNING AND CONTROL PROCESS

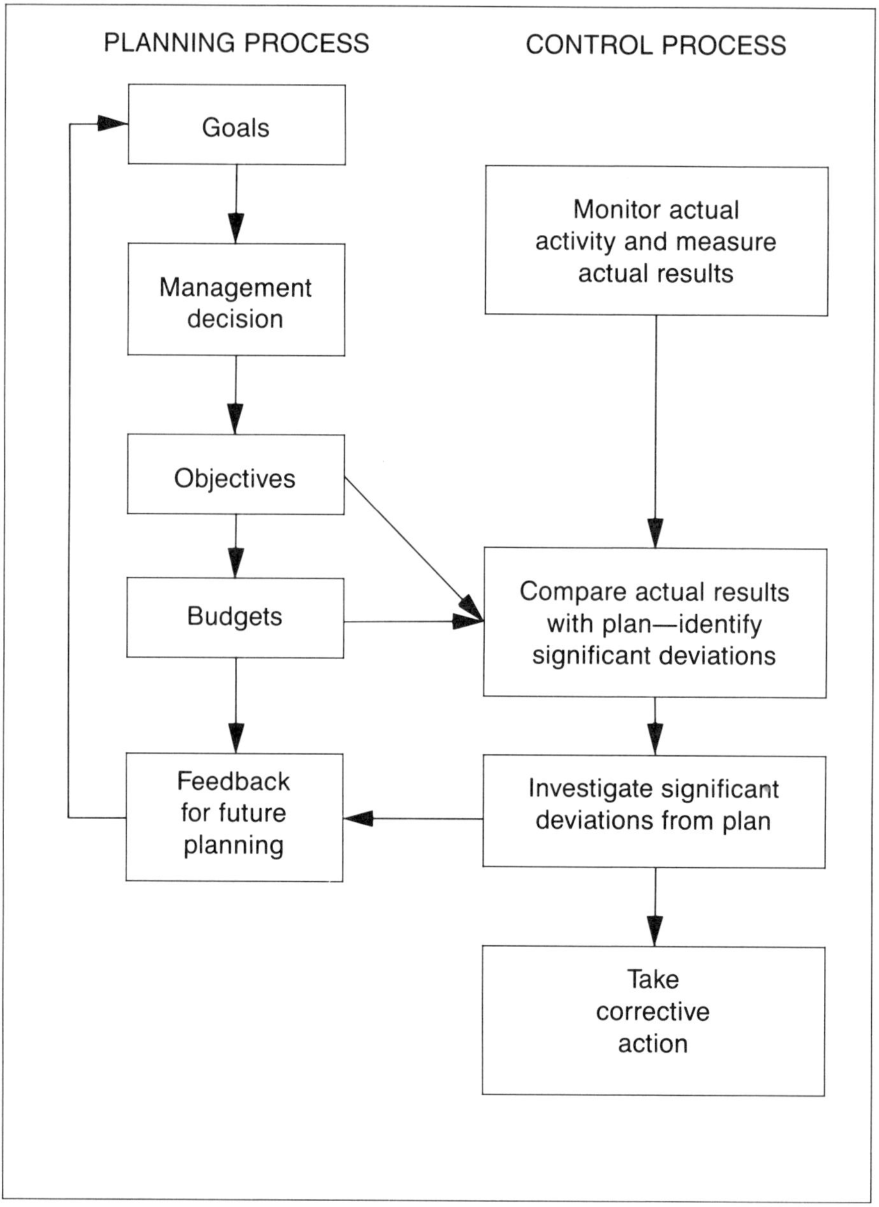

chase. Instead of focusing solely on clinic design and the present service delivery preferences of the group, the focus must broaden to include the health care needs of various segments of the general population. The shift is to more of a marketing orientation as there is a conscious attempt to anticipate the medical care needs of the population. The value of strategic planning is in increasing the ability to diagnose and respond to the needs of the market.

As a matter of long-term survival, the medical group should be aware of a broad range of possible changes in its external environment. It must also be aware of internal limitations that may affect its long-term ability to respond to changes in the outside environment. Strategic financial planning begins with an assessment of internal and external factors that may impact on the group.

Exhibit 17-1 illustrates the planning and control process in an organization. Each step in the exhibit is examined in this section.

Developing Goals and Objectives

The first stage of the planning process involves the determination of long-range goals by the owners and managers of the group. A goal is a broad statement of direction. Questions to help in developing goals include:

What patient groups are going to be served?

What kinds of services are to be provided?

Does the group wish to achieve and hold a position of leadership in the medical community?

What impact will changes in technology have on patient care?

How large a professional staff does the group want in five years? In ten years?

What impact will changes in the local health care market have on the group's share of the market, that is, its patients?

Is the general population growing or contracting and is the mix of the population changing?

Is the physician population growing or contracting and is the mix of the physician population changing?

Will the government play a greater or lesser role in the provision of health care than it has in the past?

Answering questions like these helps the group determine a broad statement of direction. Inherent in the goal-setting process should be a commitment by the physicians and administrator to a common set of targets. Further, the group should examine the relevant variables that relate to the common direction of the practice. This process will also aid in setting intermediate-range objectives for the group.

Objectives are short- and intermediate-range targets, usually covering a one- to three-year period. Specific targets are established for a number of important variables including hours of operation, units of service to be provided, gross charges, adjustments and allowances, physician compensation, desired cash and short-term resource balances, and capital acquisitions.

The planning process continues through successive steps until the projected targets are consistent with the goals. Such analysis may suggest new services, additional hours of operation, or new locations that may be necessary to meet the group's goals. When goals and objectives are consistent, the objectives should represent the best attainable estimates of activity.

Preparing Budgets

If a group is not budgeting formally at present, it is a worthwhile step to initiate a formal effort. After some experience has been gained in the budget making and review process, it is a logical extension to become more sophisticated in the analysis and to consider more than one year into the future. The starting point is a good accounting system and some experience in budgeting. With additional experience, it is appropriate and useful to start considering changes in the external environment. Budgets can be expressed in financial and non-financial terms. Financial budgets might include the following:

Operating budget—in total and per member per month
Cash budget
Capital budget
Projected balance sheet.

Nonfinancial budgets might include the following:

Personnel budget
Statistical or utilization budget (for example, patient visits or inpatient days)
Marketing or membership budget (for example, new members and patients added or total prepaid members).

Use of a Questionnaire As a Tool for Goal Setting

Goal setting is the process of deciding where the group wants to go. However, it is an iterative process, that is, a series of trials repeated until a common direction is reached. Physicians and administrators alike encounter difficulty in specifying the first steps necessary to establish group goals. Busy day-to-day schedules rarely allow the physicians and administrators to sit down and plan the destiny of the organization.

A common first step toward organizational goals and objectives is for each group member to identify his or her personal goals. Only then can he or she identify what the group's goals should be. A questionnaire can be an excellent aid in the first step of goal setting and long-range planning. Because it is tangible, it can direct the thought processes and help individuals put their views into writing. The questionnaire should focus on the basic issues the group is attempting to define, and it should be prepared in a format that is easy to answer. Clinic size, health care delivery methods, branch or satellite operations, financial considerations, style of practice, and legal structure should all be addressed. In addition, futuristic thinking should be encouraged. Obviously, for the group considering a prepaid component or sponsoring an HMO, the questionnaire should provide sufficient coverage of this consideration.

The questionnaire should conclude by identifying action priorities. A listing of key areas will allow each physician, board member, or member of management to indicate those concerns that are most important. The composite of individual responses should point to group priorities. Goals that might evolve from the use of the questionnaire are presented in Exhibit 17-2.

After each member of the professional staff has responded to the questionnaire, goals and objectives must be set and converted into action through plans and budgets. The first step is to articulate the primary goals—what members want to accomplish. A primary goal may be to satisfy the individual physicians, or to offer comprehensive medical care to a particular population, or to solve problems. The primary goals should provide overall direction to the group.

The questionnaire should assist in preparing goals that provide guidance in each of the following specific areas:

Professional services—What services will be offered?

Human resources—What kinds of personnel should be hired, and what methods should be used to train, develop, and retain them?

Physicial resources—What facilities and equipment will be needed?

Financial resources—Which funding sources should be used to finance plans? What are the financial information needs?

Innovation—What new methods of practice should be employed?

EXHIBIT 17-2
MEDICAL GROUP GOALS EXAMPLE

Provide superior quality medical care to all patients of the medical group.

Grow within the next five years to a professional staff numbering 25 physicians.

Add a prepaid component, which within five years will grow to contribute a significant portion of the group's revenue.

Expand from a single facility to one having specialities and satellite operations.

Provide a formalized capability for intra- and interdepartmental education of doctors and medical staff and educational programs for support personnel.

Maintain financial compensation to physicians and support personnel above the community average.

Positively influence the future of medical care in the community.

Productivity—What levels of productivity should be established?

Social responsibility—What should be the role of the organization in the health of the community?

Salary requirements—How much is enough?

Management information systems—What are management's information needs?

Translating Goals into Objectives

At least one specific, time-oriented objective should be set for each of the goal statements. In arriving at the timing of these objectives, it is necessary to set priorities for their accomplishment. If resources are limited, the priorities will provide the tangible guidance necessary to develop annual operating plans and budgets.

Examples of the process of setting objectives for a group are presented in Exhibits 17-3 and 17-4. The supporting goals in Exhibit 17-3 are designed to further define the primary goal to "provide superior quality medical care." For Exhibit 17-4, the primary goal is to "add a prepaid component."

EXHIBIT 17-3
SETTING OBJECTIVES

Primary Goal: Provide superior quality medical care

I. **Professional Services**
Supporting Goal: To offer comprehensive medical care.
1st Objective: To add three general practitioners within six months.
2nd Objective: To add all major specialties within five years.

II. **Human Resources**
Supporting Goal: To attract and retain only top quality professional and support staff.
1st Objective: To train two medical assistants for special procedures within one year.
2nd Objective: To train a nurse practitioner to provide a limited range of services in an urgent care clinic within two years.

III. **Physical Resources**
Supporting Goal: To provide the space and equipment needed to perform high quality work.
Objective: To provide all standard instruments in each examining room within three months.

IV. **Financial Resources**
Supporting Goal: To develop available and flexible sources of funds for all necessary capital needs.
1st Objective: To negotiate a line of credit with the local bank for working capital within three months.
2nd Objective: To set up a two-year capital budget within one month.

V. **Management Information Systems**
Supporting Goal: To develop information systems that meet all information needs of management.
1st Objective: To develop a financial information system that meets management needs within two years.
2nd Objective: To computerize patient appointment scheduling within six months.

VI. **Innovation**
Supporting Goal: To continually explore new areas of service, talent, and methods of medical care.

EXHIBIT 17-3 (continued)

1st Objective: To study and report on the feasibility of subcontracting specialty services with medical insurance carriers in the vicinity within one year.

2nd Objective: To establish a marketing plan for the group within one year.

VII. Productivity

Supporting Goal: To reward individual doctors for higher than average professional productivity.

1st Objective: To initiate a system that tracks individual production on a monthly basis within six months.

2nd Objective: To increase professional production by five percent within one year.

VIII. Social Responsibility

Supporting Goal: To take an active role in professional community affairs and to encourage all staff and employees to do so.

1st Objective: To achieve 100 percent participation in the state medical society within one year.

2nd Objective: To participate in medical awareness programs in the public schools once per year within two years.

IX. Salary Requirements

Supporting Goal: To maintain physician salaries and fringe benefits at a level above the community average.

Objective: To increase physician median income by $10,000 within two years.

EXHIBIT 17-4
SETTING OBJECTIVES—BEST MEDICAL CENTER

Primary Goal: Add a prepaid component

I. Professional Services

Supporting Goal: To offer a mixture of prepaid and fee-for-service medicine.

Objective: To contract with Bestcare HMO to provide medical care to its 3,850 members within one year.

II. Human Resources

Supporting Goal: To add necessary support personnel for the prepaid component.

1st Objective: To add an executive director within two months.

2nd Objective: To add a marketing director and a finance director within four months.

III. **Physical Resources**

Supporting Goal: To provide the space and equipment needed to perform high quality diagnostic work and minimize referrals out of the group.

1st Objective: To provide all standard diagnostic tools in each examining room within three months.

2nd Objective: To expand the equipment in the laboratory within six months.

IV. **Financial Resources**

Supporting Goal: To create an available and flexible source of funds for all necessary capital and operating needs.

1st Objective: To set up a two-year capital and cash flow budget within three weeks.

2nd Objective: To keep within the budget for two years.

V. **Innovation**

Supporting Goal: To continually explore new areas of service, talent, and methods of health care.

Objective: To study and report within six months the feasibility of purchasing a hospital within the next five years.

VI. **Productivity**

Supporting Goal: To relate physican income to professional production.

Objective: To increase professional production as defined in terms of physician office visits by five percent within one year.

VII. **Social Responsibility**

Supporting Goal: To take an active role in professional community affairs and to encourage all staff and employees to do so.

Objective: To get one staff member elected president of the Medical Society within three years.

VIII. **Salary Requirements**

Supporting Goal: To establish and maintain salaries and fringe benefits on a level with other top executives.

Objective: To increase physician median income by $10,000 within two years.

Goal setting and objective setting should be used to expand planning at different levels within the group. The first objective of the supporting goal under "Management Information Systems" provides for the development of a financial information system. This objective in turn could lead to the use of further questionnaires for developing a set of objectives to guide the establishment and maintenance of the financial information system.

Objectives are formulated as a last step in the planning process for the group—after completion of questionnaires on an individual basis, joint formulation of group goals, and the establishment of group priorities. Each major area of responsibility in the group should develop its own goals, objectives, and budget proposals that will lead to fulfillment of higher level objectives and progress toward the primary goal.

Attainable objectives cannot be set in a vacuum. Because different objectives are competing for the same resources, they must be tested through development of budgets. If the budget shows that resources are sufficient to satisfy all the objectives, the process is complete. However, if the budget shows that resources are not sufficient, a priority must be established for each objective. Thus, some objectives will have to be delayed or revised. This iterative process will continue until operating plans are developed that reconcile the priority of objectives with available resources.

In order for objectives to be accepted throughout the group, they must be communicated. The budget is an excellent device for communicating objectives and for showing what financial impact they will have when they are achieved.

One step in the budgetary control process involves corrective action when deviations from the plan are significant. Action should be taken to bring operations back into conformity with the plan. However, if the objectives are no longer attainable, they must be revised to maintain credibility of the planning process. This revision is essential to establish new priorities among objectives competing for resources. The new priorities in turn guide the preparation of revised budgets.

Planning for a Prepaid Component

Best Medical Center has set a goal to add a prepaid component and has established a series of objectives in support of that goal. Assuming the group has 12 primary physicians at present but only has a level of business to adequately support 10 physicians, a contract with Bestcare HMO would appear to bring the volume of revenues in line with the number of physicians. If Bestcare is projected to grow from 3,850 members at the end of year one to 10,245 and 19,061 at the ends of years two and three, respectively, what future impact will this have on the Best Medical Center? These projections suggest several questions for the group to consider, including the following:

> How many physicians will the group have at the end of years two and three?
>
> What physician and ancillary services will be purchased outside the group?

In Exhibit 17-2, the group set a goal to grow to 25 physicians within five years, but these projections indicate that the group will have 25 to 30 physicians by the end of year three; should the goal be reevaluated?

What impact will this growth have on the fee-for-service patients?

Can the needed physicians be readily recruited?

Can the growth be accommodated within the present facilities?

Will satellite facilities be needed to provide adequate geographic coverage in the service area?

The long-range planning process reviews these issues and others. As noted before, the process may suggest a need to reexamine goals and objectives. The value of the process is in anticipating problems and considering possible solutions so as to assure achievement of the group's goals and objectives. The group cannot plan without reliable data. If a thorough market study has been performed by the HMO, projected enrollment for the next five years should be available. Assume the following enrollment at the end of each of the next five years.

End of Year	Projected HMO Enrollment
1	3,850
2	10,245
3	19,061
4	27,734
5	34,942

Through the actuarial assumptions used to develop the premium (and therefore the medical group's capitation), expected patient visits may also be projected.

Data for the present specialties of Best Medical Center as well as for orthopedics, general surgery, and dermatology are presented in Exhibit 17-5. These data are based upon the following assumptions:

Visits per month per member	.382	
Composition of visits:		
Family practice and internal medicine		54%
Pediatrics		16
Obstetrics/gynecology		10

Orthopedics	4
General surgery	3
Dermatology	3
All others	10
	100%

It is assumed that Best Medical Center is responsible for all physician services except mental health. Therefore, the data in Exhibit 17-5 should answer many of the questions posed earlier, providing the basis for expansion of present specialties as well as the decision to add new specialties.

The data may pose other questions. Pediatrics, for example, would grow from two physicians currently to three at the end of Year 2, four in Year 3, five in Year 4, and six in Year 5. Does it want to grow this quickly? If the prepaid patients are diffused throughout the greater local area and satellite facilities are to be used, how will the different clinics be staffed? How will call schedules be arranged?

EXHIBIT 17-5
PROJECTED PREPAID PATIENT VISITS

	Number of Patient Visits Last Month of Year				
	1	2	3	4	5
Total practice	1,470	3,913	7,280	10,594	13,348
Specialty:					
Family practice and internal medicine	794	2,114	3,932	5,721	7,208
Pediatrics	235	626	1,165	1,695	2,136
Obstetrics/gynecology	147	391	728	1,059	1,335
Orthopedics	59	157	291	424	534
General surgery	44	117	218	318	400
Dermatology	44	117	218	318	400
All others	147	391	728	1,059	1,335

Summary

The influence on the medical group of changes in the environment can be quite dramatic. These changes can limit the group's ability to achieve its goals and objectives or can suggest a need for revising them. The group will benefit from periodically assessing changes in the environment and how they will affect the group.

This chapter has described goal setting as the process of deciding the future direction of a medical group. After each primary goal has been established, supporting goals must be developed in strategic areas such as services performed, human resources, physical resources, financial resources, and social responsibility. These supporting goals lead to the formation of key objectives that are quantified, time-related, and for which the responsibility of accomplishment has been established. The process of setting goals and objectives continues at the functional level by each responsibility center.

Setting objectives involves establishing priorities, since each objective requires resources within a given time frame. Certain objectives may have to be delayed to allow the timely completion of others.

Accepted objectives provide the starting point for preparing formal budgets. Once tentative budgets are prepared, an iterative process begins that may call for the reordering of objectives because of resource limitations. Given agreed upon goals and their related objectives, medical group administrators can more sensibly set and shift priorities within the resources available.

Goals and objectives also provide the framework for developing operating plans for the coming year. Objectives thus bridge the gap between the long-range goals and the short-term operating plans. Budgets are merely the results of expressing these operating plans in terms of dollars.

Chapter 18

Overview of Budgeting

The major advantage of budgeting is that it requires management personnel to plan in an organized and concentrated way. The process demands that the group set aside specific times each year to plan and that these plans be built on already established goals and objectives. The process of goal setting is valuable for any medical group, but unless goals are translated into objectives and budgets, much of the practice's planning effectiveness is lost. Most medical groups do plan, but informally, not with a formal budget that both integrates and communicates financial plans in a single comprehensive document.

To move from an informal plan to a comprehensive budget requires preparation of a profit plan, a capital expenditures budget, a cash budget, and a projected position statement for the coming year. The major purpose of this chapter is to provide an overview of a comprehensive budget, its various parts, and how the parts tie together. The next chapter will illustrate the development of a comprehensive budget.

The practice's budget, or profit plan, is an expression of its operational plan, in dollars and cents, for a specific period of time. The budget serves as a basis for determining the practice's financial ability to attain predetermined goals and for evaluating operating performance.

Functions and Benefits of Budgets

In addition to general benefits, budgeting also provides for:

- Communication and coordination of the short-range operating plans within the medical group. This becomes more important as the number of responsibility centers or departments grows.
- Anticipation of favorable conditions so that the group may take early advantage of them or, if conditions are unfavorable, minimize their impact.

- Authorization of staff personnel to use and/or acquire resources during the coming period or to expand existing activities or implement new activities. Granting this authority also demonstrates management's commitment to the plan.

- Establishment of benchmarks for the evaluation of performance. Personnel are thus motivated because they know what is expected from them.

Components of the Comprehensive Budget

A comprehensive budget consists of a series of informal projections and a number of formal statements. The components are illustrated in Exhibit 18-1. Each of the numbered steps in the exhibit will be further explained. The exhibit shows the following components.

- Cash and other short-term resources management systems. The ongoing planning and control systems for managing short-term resources provide for desired levels of short-term resources.

- The formal, comprehensive budget, which consists of a profit plan, a cash budget, a capital expenditures budget, and a projected position statement. With the exception of the capital expenditures budget, the comprehensive budget represents projections of the general purpose financial statements discussed in Part I.

Steps in the Preparation of the Comprehensive Budget

Exhibit 18-1 illustrates the steps and interrelationships in the preparation of a comprehensive budget. Each number on the exhibit indicates a step in the budgeting process. Some of the steps, particularly step (2) involving the physicians' plans, are a part of the goal- and objective-setting process discussed in Chapter 17. There is no clear point at which the setting of objectives and the preparation of a budget are separated. The steps in Exhibit 18-1 are described below. The illustration uses a cash basis example. On the accrual basis the steps are identical; however, the measurements in the profit plan and projected position statements will differ.

A group that derives a significant portion of its revenues from providing prepaid care is advised to first develop a statement of projected operations and then a balance sheet, capital budget, and a statement of cash flows. All four documents play important roles.

The steps in Exhibit 18-1 are described below.

(1) External information—The medical group must develop a picture of the environment in which it is operating, including projections of the local

economy, anticipated price increases, expected demand for medical services, competition, and any other external influences that are expected to affect the group. The HMO with which the group is contracting should provide projected enrollment and utilization data.

(2) Physicians' plans—The physician/owners must examine both their personal goals and the goals of the group. Through this process the physicians indicate their expectations and desires concerning personal income levels, changes in hours of service, changes in the style of group, changes in productivity, planned addition or reduction of providers, and planned changes in the number of nurses and medical assistants. Many of these expectations should be expressed as objectives (dated and quantified targets of planned accomplishments).

(3) Management of other short-term resources—A number of short-term resource control systems are utilized in any medical group. These systems provide planned levels for patient receivables, supplies, and short-term payables.

(4) Budgeted revenues—The group's income from prepaid contracts (HMO payments, capitation payments, patient copayments, risk-sharing payments, etc.) and the planned fee-for-service production for each provider may be projected given the changes in the environment in which the group operates, the physicians' plans for changes in the style of group, and the planned level of patient receivables.

(5) Budgeted expenses—Projected expenses fall into two broad types, variable and fixed, based upon activity changes. Because variable expenses relate to the level of production, variable expense projections are based upon the projected production determined in Step (4). Fixed costs are determined by contracts, the level of capacity, and the physicians' plans.

(6) Cash provided by operations—Budgeted revenues and expenses are on the accrual basis and include noncash items (such as depreciation). These must be removed to arrive at cash provided or used by operations.

(7) Planned acquisition or sale of assets—Planned acquisition or sale of assets will affect cash management activities. The cash budget must reflect the expected sources and uses of cash from purchase or sale of assets. The cash budget should be accompanied by a capital expenditures budget to include all capital expenditures over a specified amount. The amount and timing of these outflows can be critical and place significant demands on short-term resources.

EXHIBIT 18-1
ILLUSTRATION OF THE COMPREHENSIVE BUDGET

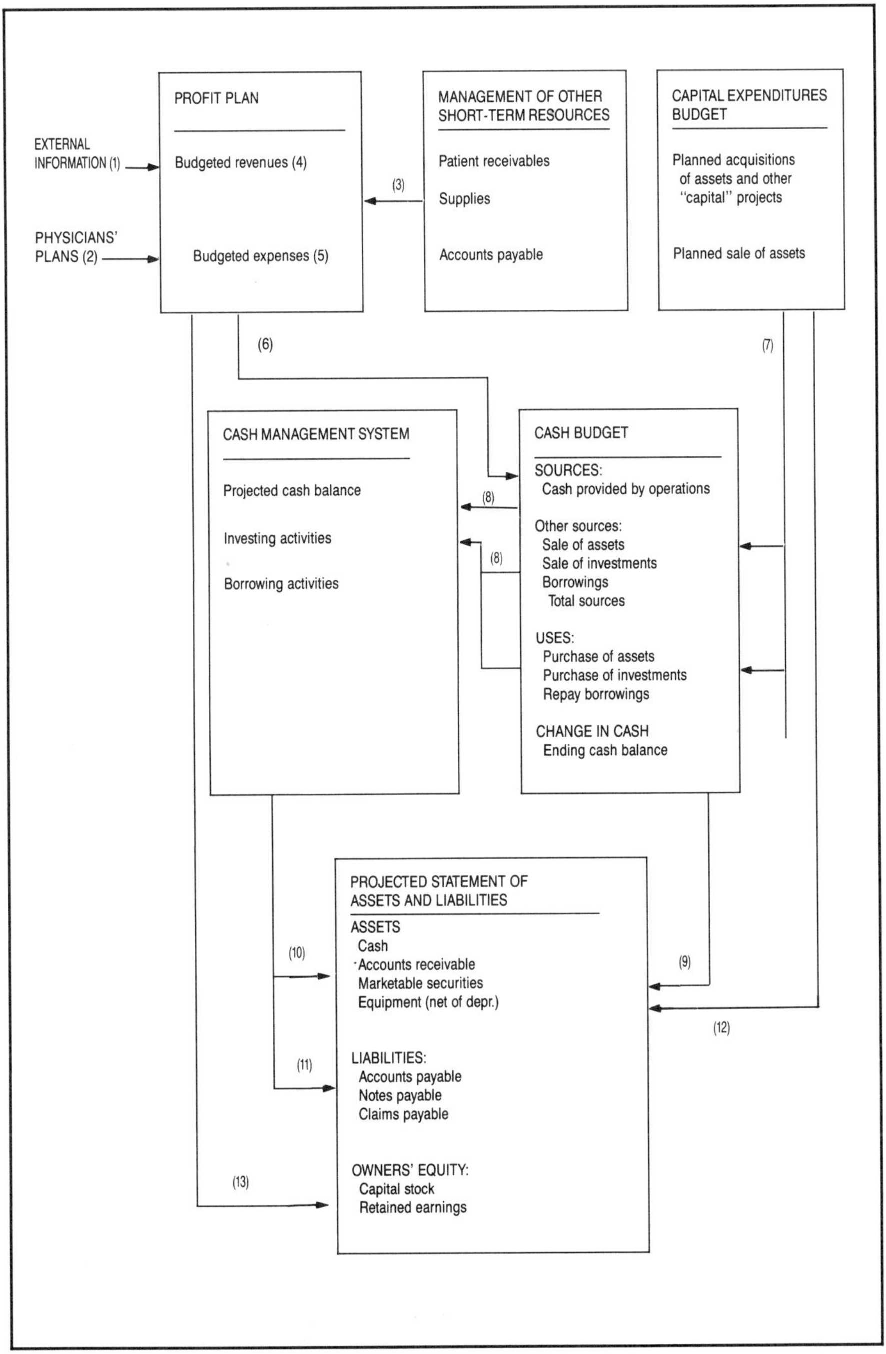

(8) Projected cash balance—Planned sources and uses of cash are determined in the process of developing the cash budget. Investing and borrowing of cash may be necessary to manage the cash position and finance the capital acquisitions of the group. These activities must be reflected in the cash budget.

Projected position statement (Steps 9 through 13)—The interrelatedness of the steps in the planning process becomes clear when the projected position statement is prepared. The beginning position statement, along with the changes generated by the previous steps, provides the information to determine the ending individual asset, liability, and owners' equity balances.

(9) Cash balance—Ending cash balance is a product of the cash budget.

(10) Accounts receivable and marketable securities—Cash management activities project the amount of estimated collection of accounts receivable and the amount of investment in marketable securities.

(11) Accounts payable, notes payable, and claims payable—Cash management activities project the amount of accounts payable for supplies, group credit cards, and outstanding bills; the amount of borrowing, repayment, and the resulting balance of notes payable; and the amount of outstanding medical claims payable.

(12) Property, plant, and equipment balances—The capital expenditures budget determines the changes in long-lived assets and, with depreciation from the profit plan, the resulting balances of property, plant, and equipment.

(13) Retained earnings—The "profit" or "loss" from the profit plan provides the change in retained earnings.

The Cash and Accrual Dilemma

The budget must provide both a planning tool (an expression of management's plans) and a control tool (a benchmark with which to compare actual results). Unfortunately, the issue of cash and accrual measurements often raises problems. On one hand, the budget should reflect what is expected to happen and provide a useful tool for control; on the other hand, the budget must relate to the actual measurements recorded in the accounting system.

Actual activities of the group involve the generation of assets through the provision of medical services to patients and the consumption of assets in providing these services. Because accrual accounting measures revenue in the period that service is performed and measures expenses in the period resources are used, a profit plan prepared on the accrual basis does a better job of reflecting the activities of the group and, therefore, provides a better basis for evaluating performance. For a medical group with a significant prepaid component, the use of the accrual basis is the only way to get a proper measurement of the results for a period of time. The natural distortions caused by a lag in collections and payments and the purposeful manipulations of cash payments and collections to reduce the tax burden distort the picture for short periods of time.

As the measurement period is lengthened, to a year for example, these cash basis distortions are significantly reduced. The value of the annual budget as a control tool, however, is also significantly reduced. Control is exercised before or as an event occurs. Once an action has taken place, nothing can be done to change it. For control purposes, the feedback of information for short periods of time is critical. Nonfinancial data, of course, are needed and used on a daily or even hourly basis.

Because of monthly distortions caused by cash basis accounting, most medical groups on the cash basis use a quarterly planning period for their operating budgets, and a balance between the level of distortion on the cash basis and the usefulness of the data is reached. As a medical group becomes more mature in financial planning and control, the accrual basis will often be used for financial planning, control, and other internal purposes, but cash basis measurements will still be used in the preparation of income tax returns.

Using the Budget

It is through the use of the budget that financial planning and control are achieved. Field research for this text identified a number of groups that did an excellent job of planning up through the development of a budget but stopped at that point. These groups did not use the budget after it was prepared. Although the planning effort was valuable, it was not complete without evaluation and feedback concerning actual activities.

A budget is a target. An attempt should be made to achieve the planned levels of activity, revenue, and expenses. Seldom, however, will actual results be identical with planned results. There are usually five major reasons for deviations from plan: 1) more or fewer patients seen than planned, 2) the pattern of cash collections changed, 3) price changes occurred in fees and/or expenses, 4) the group was either more or less efficient than budget in the use of resources, and 5) changes occurred in the level of short-term resources such as the supplies inventory.

One of the major problems in the control process is to differentiate the effects on the budget of these five reasons for variances. If a significant change in activity is accompanied by excessive use of resources, there may be a tendency to attribute the inefficiencies to the change in activity. For example, Exhibit 18-2 presents budgeted and actual results for the first quarter of 19X5 for one satellite office of the Best Medical Center, which is staffed by one physician.

During the quarter, economic conditions in the community caused a reduction in the actual number of patient visits from the budgeted level. If the mix of services did not change, how well did the Bay Boulevard office perform? There was a 16.7 percent reduction in gross charges but only a 1.6 percent reduction in expenses. Was the office efficient in controlling expenses?

EXHIBIT 18-2

OPERATING STATEMENT—BAY BOULEVARD OFFICE

Quarter 1, 19X5

	Budget	Actual	Variance
Gross charges	$120,000	$100,000	$(20,000)
Operating expenses:			
Physician salary	$ 40,000	$ 40,000	$ 0
Staff salaries	15,000	14,500	500
Laboratory services	15,000	12,000	3,000
Medical supplies	8,050	9,000	(950)
Rent and utilities	5,000	6,000	(1,000)
Other expenses	14,000	14,000	0
Total expenses	$ 97,050	$ 95,500	$ 1,550
Contribution to common costs and income	$ 22,950	$ 4,500	$(18,450)

To answer these questions, one must first know how much actual expenses should have decreased because of decreased activity. The original profit plan (budget) was prepared for a $120,000 gross charges level of activity. To evaluate performance, a new operating budget should be prepared for the $100,000 actual level of activity. By removing the change in activity from the budget, one can then concentrate upon the variances due to price changes and operating inefficiencies. A budget revised for the change in activity is called a flexible budget or performance budget. Except for the change in activity, the same assumptions are used to prepare both the profit plan and the performance budget. Exhibit 18-3 presents the actual results for the quarter (gross charges of $100,000) compared to a performance budget established at the $100,000 activity level. Only laboratory services and medical supplies are assumed to be variable expenses (those that vary with change in activity); all other expenses are assumed to be fixed (those that do not vary with change in activity). In the revised performance budget, laboratory services and medical supplies expenses are reduced in the same proportion as the level of gross charges (83.3 percent of the original budget). All other expenses are considered fixed and remain the same in the revised budget as they were originally.

EXHIBIT 18-3

ACTUAL OPERATIONS COMPARED WITH PERFORMANCE BUDGET — BAY BOULEVARD OFFICE

Quarter 1, 19X5

	Performance Budget	Actual	Variance
Gross charges	$100,000	$100,000	$ 0
Operating expenses:			
Physician salary	$ 40,000	$ 40,000	$ 0
Staff salaries	15,000	14,500	500
Laboratory services	12,500	12,000	500
Medical supplies	6,710	9,000	(2,290)
Rent and utilities	5,000	6,000	(1,000)
Other expenses	14,000	14,000	0
Total expenses	$ 93,210	$ 95,500	$(2,290)
Contribution to common costs and income	$ 6,790	$ 4,500	$(2,290)

The performance budget shows that the Bay Boulevard office should have contributed $6,790 (rather than $22,950) to the income of the group. Total deviations from plan now amount to $2,290. These may be partly explained by excessive costs in laboratory services and medical supplies. On the favorable side, the time of nurses and medical assistants and other expenses were reduced (demonstrating that some fixed expenses are not "fixed" if management wishes to change them).

Summary

The budget can be a very useful tool. It must, however, be properly prepared and properly used. Once it has been prepared, it should not be filed away; instead, actual operations should be compared to the budget at least each quarter. This periodic review insures that the budget remains an accurate projection of the practice's future performance. If changes occur that make the budget unattainable, the budget should be revised. The original budget reflects the best estimate of expected performance under specific conditions with limited information regarding the future. As information regarding the future becomes available, it is probable that the expectations of performance will also change.

Chapter 19

The Comprehensive Budget

It is through the budget that planning and control are achieved. Goals and objectives provide a vehicle for long-range planning but do not provide the benchmarks for month-to-month planning and evaluation of performance. The overview of budgeting in Chapter 18 pictured a comprehensive budget as including a series of informal projections and a number of formal statements. Exhibit 18-1 showed the interrelationships among the projections and statements. The first attempt at budgeting usually involves only a profit plan (operating budget), often using cash basis measurements. The financial risk assumed when a medical group contracts to provide medical care on a prepaid basis requires formal planning and control of operations.

This chapter discusses and illustrates the development of a comprehensive budget, using accrual accounting principles. Three portions of the comprehensive budget are presented: the profit plan, the cash budget, and the projected statement of financial position. Because the key projection in any financial plan is the amount of revenues, the chapter includes an extended discussion on budgeting revenues. The disussion on budgeting expenses relies on cost behavior patterns to project expenses. A brief discussion, including illustrations, of measuring the lag in cash payments for incurred but unreported claims is also presented.

Sequence for Developing the Comprehensive Budget

The example in this chapter involves a bottom-up approach to budgeting. After the goals and objectives are developed and communicated throughout the group, each responsibility center plans its activities and prepares a profit plan. These profit plans are then integrated into the overall profit plan. The focal point of the budgeting process in this chapter and the control process in the next chapter is the responsibility center. The illustration assumes that each responsibility center "manager" takes an active part in planning and control.

When responsibility centers are intimately involved, a typical sequence in the development of a comprehensive budget includes:

Group Owners/Stockholders of the Practice Corporation
- State goals and objectives
- Identify budgeting responsibilities
- Project overall activity levels
- Determine resources available

Administration
- Further define objectives
- Prepare working documents for responsibility center heads

Responsibility Centers
- Project activity levels
- Determine staffing
- Project direct costs of responsibility centers
- Compile preliminary profit plan for responsibility centers

Administration
- Combine preliminary profit plans into an overall profit plan
- Prepare cash budget
- Prepare projected statement of financial position

Group Owners/Stockholders of the Practice Corporation
- Review, amend, and approve the comprehensive budget

The first step in the sequence involves both the long-range planning and statement of short-term objectives or targets discussed earlier in this volume. Setting goals, objectives, and general direction is top-down planning, while the development of the budget is bottom-up planning.

Budgeting Revenues

The key projection in any operating budget is operating revenues. Expense projections, distributions to physicians, cash flow projections, and, to some extent, capital expenditure projections—all depend upon the projection of operating revenues.

Three different approaches to projecting revenues are discussed in this chapter. The first approach involves a determination of potential demand for the services of the group. It is a useful tool for planning marketing strategy, locating satellite offices, and initiating long-range planning. Because several estimates are involved, this method may have a high degree of error. It may, however, provide useful information for long-range planning and can be particularly important for the medical group providing prepaid care to patients who are members of an HMO.

The second approach involves a projection based on past activity. This approach assumes that the best measure of what will occur in the future is what has happened in the recent past. Only known changes in the group, such as additions or retirements of physicians and scheduled fee changes, are projected.

The third approach is to estimate the number of procedures or patient visits planned by each physician during the budget period. By applying the expected fee schedule to the projection of procedures or visits, budgeted production for each physician can be determined.

Unfortunately, the last two methods assume that demand for the group's services will remain constant and that the limiting resource is physician time. As competition increases, the group will be forced to consider its impact and that of other external factors on the group practice.

Projection Based on Estimate of Demand

Periodically, the group should assess future demand for medical services in its geographic area. This assessment is a key planning study when determining the medical needs of the population to be served by the prepaid practice.

The process of estimating demand for the services of the group involves three types of data: first, demographic characteristics of the area; second, patient usage rates for each department; and third, share of the market (the share of potential patient visits that the medical group expects to have). This approach is subject to a wide range of error because of the assumptions required. The group must assume both an average patient usage rate and the group's estimated share of total potential patient visits. Competition from other medical groups also must be considered in estimating the group's share of the market.

Assume that Best Medical Center accumulated the data presented in Exhibit 19-1 concerning the population and medical needs of its service area. The group is located in the Evans district of a city of about 210,000 population. This district is largely residential. Potential demand for the entire district for the specialties included in Best Medical Center is estimated to be 198,966 patient visits (Exhibit 19-2). In addition, estimated related laboratory tests are 99,483 and related radiology procedures are 39,793.

What percentage of potential patient visits should the Center plan on having? One possibility is to assume that the number of patient visits to the group will relate to the percentage of total physicians in the district that are members of the group. For example, with two-thirds of the pediatricians in the district, Best Medical Center should expect to have 26,285 pediatric patient visits. Actually, there were only 14,400 visits to the center's pediatricians. Best's share of patient visits for each specialty is presented in Exhibit 19-3. With the exception of obstetrics/gynecology, actual patient visits for other specialties of the center

EXHIBIT 19-1
DATA FOR DETERMINATION OF DEMAND

Demographic Data

Percent noncaucasian	13.5%
Average education	12.3 years
Average family income	$25,000
Average home value	$75,000

Age and Sex Distribution Summary

Age	Male	Female	Total
Under 15	6,237	6,023	12,260
15-44	9,306	10,038	19,344
45-64	5,443	5,967	11,410
65 and over	1,807	2,719	4,526
Total	22,793	24,747	47,540

Estimated Rates of Patient Visits for Fee-for-Service Patients

Overall	4.3 per year
Under 15	3.2 per year
15-44	3.6 per year
45-64	5.2 per year
65 and over	7.9 per year
Obstetrics/gynecology patients (in addition to regular visits)	.8 per year
Laboratory tests	.5 per visit
Radiology procedures	.2 per visit

are less than their estimated shares of the market. With more than 50 percent of the physicians in the district, the center is serving approximately 37 percent of estimated demand. This approach is subject to a wide range of error because of the assumptions required: first, average patient usage rate (presented in Exhibit 19-2); and second, the group's estimated share of total potential patient visits. It does, however, provide a rough estimate of market share and how well the group is competing.

It is this kind of analysis that led Best Medical Center to consider prepaid practice. In the survey of groups with some prepaid practice, the most common reason given for offering prepaid care was concern over competition and the group's ability to hold or gain patients. Assuming that Best Medical Center is considering providing physician services for Bestcare HMO, enrollment and patient visit projections would be made for five years.

EXHIBIT 19-2
COMPUTATION OF POTENTIAL PATIENT VISITS

Specialty	Population	Average Usage Rates	Potential Patient Visits
Family practice and internal medicine	35,280[1]	4.3	151,704
Pediatrics	12,260[2]	3.2	39,232
Obstetrics/gynecology	10,038	.8	8,030
Total			198,966

Ancillary Departments	Potential Patient Visits	Average Usage Rates	Ancillary Department Visits
Laboratory	198,966	.5	99,483
Radiology	198,966	.2	39,793

[1]Excluding population under 15
[2]Population under 15

EXHIBIT 19-3
ESTIMATED DEMAND—BEST MEDICAL CENTER

		Physicians					
Specialty	Potential Patient Visits	Total in Area	No. in Group	% of Total	Group's Share of Patient Visits	Group's Actual Patient Visits	Percent Actual of Potential
Family practice	101,136[1]	13	6	46%	46,523	39,600	39%
Pediatrics	39,232	3	2	67%	26,285	14,400	37%
Obstetrics/ gynecology	8,030	2	2	100%	8,030	9,360	117%
Internal medicine	50,568	7	2	29%	14,665	10,080	20%
Total	198,966	25	12		95,503	73,440	37%

[1]Family practice visits assumed to be 2/3 and internal medicine 1/3.

Bestcare HMO's enrollment and patient visit projections by month for the first year and for the last month of years two through five are presented in Exhibit 19-4. The projected prepaid patient visits to Best Medical Center for the first year are 7,135, an addition of approximately 10 percent to the present year's patient visits. If Best Medical Center maintains its present fee-for-service patients (73,440 annual visits or an average of 6,120 per month), the prepaid component will represent nearly one-sixth of the total patient activity by the end of the first year (1,177 prepaid and 6,120 fee-for-service visits in December).

Best Medical Center's projected patient visits for the pediatrics department are presented in Exhibit 19-5. Prepaid patients will generate 235 patient visits per month at the end of the first year, growing to 2,136 patient visits per month at the end of five years. If it materializes, this demand will necessitate the addition of at least three pediatricians by the end of the fifth year.

EXHIBIT 19-4

PROJECTED ENROLLMENT AND PATIENT VISITS—PREPAID PRACTICE

Month	Projected Enrollment (member months)	Projected Patient Visits		
		Care Provided Inhouse	Referred Outside	Total
1	130	40	10	50
2	216	66	17	83
3	328	100	25	125
4	1,165	356	89	445
5	1,721	526	131	657
6	1,875	573	143	716
7	1,976	604	151	755
8	2,426	742	185	927
9	2,590	791	198	989
10	3,290	1,006	251	1,257
11	3,778	1,154	289	1,443
12	3,850	1,177	294	1,471
24	10,245	3,131	783	3,914
36	19,061	5,825	1,456	7,281
48	27,734	8,475	2,119	10,594
60	34,942	10,678	2,670	13,348

Projection Based on Past Activity

Many groups believe that the best indicator of a physician's activity level for the next year is what he or she is doing today. This assumes that the conditions for the next year will not change significantly and is the method generally used by fee-for-service practices. It assumes that demand for the group's

EXHIBIT 19-5
PROJECTED PATIENT VISITS—PEDIATRICS

	Fee-for-Service		Prepaid		Total	
Month	Patient Visits	Gross Charges[1]	Patient Visits	Fee-for-Service Equivalent[2]	Patient Visits	Gross Charges
1	1,150	$ 21,126	8	$ 129	1,158	$ 21,255
2	1,060	19,472	13	210	1,073	19,682
3	1,200	22,044	20	323	1,220	22,367
4	1,210	22,228	71	1,148	1,281	23,376
5	1,200	22,044	105	1,698	1,305	23,742
6	1,200	22,044	115	1,860	1,315	23,904
7	1,250	22,962	121	1,957	1,371	24,919
8	1,100	20,207	148	2,393	1,248	22,600
9	1,300	23,881	158	2,555	1,458	26,436
10	1,300	23,881	201	3,250	1,501	27,131
11	1,300	23,881	231	3,735	1,531	27,616
12	1,200	22,044	235	3,800	1,435	25,844
	14,470	$265,814	1,426	$23,058	15,896	$288,872

[1]Fee-for-service average fee = $18.37
[2]Discounted fee-for-service equivalent fee = $16.17 (88%)

services remains constant and that physician time will be the limiting resource.

The projection starts with each physician's production for the past year or year-to-date (annualized) if the budget is prepared before the end of year. For example, if the budget for 19X5 is being prepared in November 19X4 and production of one physician for the first 10 months of 19X4 amounted to $164,178, production for 19X4 is annualized as follows:

$$\$164{,}178 \times \frac{12 \text{ months}}{10 \text{ months}} = \$197{,}014 \text{ annualized}$$

Annualizing in this manner assumes even production throughout the year. Any seasonal pattern must be considered in annualizing the data. For example, in the illustration above, production for the first 10 months is assumed to account for approximately 83 percent (10/12) of annual production. If November and December are the lowest months of production, usually accounting for only 14 percent of annual revenues, production would be annualized at $190,905 ($164,178/86 percent).

After the current year's data are annualized, expected changes are applied to the current year's data. Changes for a particular physician would include: expected changes in hours of work (for example, a physician nearing retirement may wish to reduce his workload or a physician may want to expand or contract hours worked for personal reasons), changes in the mix of procedures (thereby changing the average fee charged), or changes in the fee schedule. By applying these changes to the current year's production, the production for the next year can be projected. An example of projecting production by adjusting past activity is presented in Exhibit 19-6.

EXHIBIT 19-6
PROJECTION OF PRODUCTION BASED ON PAST ACTIVITY

	Actual Quarter 1 19X5	Changes	Projected Quarter 1 19X6
Physician A	$27,889	Increased production due to additional hours—$837. Increase in fee schedule during 19X5 (approx. 10%) —$2,822.	$31,548
Physician B	24,122	No changes proposed in activity. Increase in fee schedule during 19X5 (approx. 10%)—$2,412.	26,534
Total production	$52,011		$58,082

Exhibit 19-6 involves only one quarter. The process for a year, however, should not be significantly different. Beginning in the new year, Physician A will increase his hours by approximately three percent (any significant projected increase in fee-for-service business should be supported by requests for appointments by patients). The major change is to adjust for an increase in fees during the last quarter of 19X4. The predictions do not consider the impact of prepaid patients. Past experience indicates what the physicians have done, not what they can do or must do.

Projection Based on Number of Procedures or Patient Visits

A final method of projecting revenues involves estimating either the number of procedures or the number of patient visits the physician expects to handle each month during the budget year. Because of the large number of possible procedures a medical group must deal with, groups generally use the number of patient visits. Another approach is to estimate the number of days each physician will work each month. The disadvantage of projecting only days worked, and therefore production per day, is that seasonality in patient load is not considered. If good data are available by week or month for the last two years or more, it is possible to consider seasonality in a meaningful fashion. Because the use of either the number-of-procedures or the projection-of-patient-visits method involves estimates by physicians, there will be a stronger attempt by the physicians to meet the target. Therefore, the projections should be more accurate if proper feedback takes place during the year.

To use this approach, the administrator of the group must provide each physician with a worksheet showing: 1) number of days the group will be open during each month of the budget year; 2) number of patients the physician saw each month of the past year; 3) blank spaces for the number of days the physician expects to work each month; 4) blank spaces for estimated patient visits each month. The worksheet for a pediatrics department physician is presented in Exhibit 19-7. Use of this worksheet allows the physician to indicate when he or she plans to be away from the practice (for vacations, meetings, etc.) and to show planned changes in practice patterns. It also allows the administrator and medical director to identify potential staffing problems. Because this schedule reflects only working days and patient visits, it will not necessarily meet the demand for the group's services. How will the prepaid patients be served? It should be easy to add the 8, 13, and 20 expected prepaid patient visits during the first three months; however, 235 additional visits are expected during the last month of the year (see Exhibit 19-5). Relying upon past experience does not ensure that this need will be met.

EXHIBIT 19-7
WORKSHEET FOR PROJECTION OF PATIENT VISITS—PEDIATRICS

	Jan	Feb	Mar	Quarter[1] Total	Total Year
Total available working days	21	20	23	64	258
Physician A					
Revenues last year					$118,570
Patients seen	600	520	580	1,700	7,100
Average revenue per patient visit					$16.70
Estimated working days	___	___	___	___	___
Estimated patient visits	___	___	___	___	___
Average revenue per patient visit					$18.37
Estimated revenues (completed by controller)	___	___	___	___	___

EXHIBIT 19-7 (continued)

Completed Worksheet

Physician A					
Revenues last year					$118,570
Patients seen	600	520	580	1,700	7,100
Average revenue per patient visit					$16.70
Estimated working days	21	20	20	61	233
Estimated patient visits	620	520	610	1,750	7,300
Average revenue per patient visit					$18.37
Estimated revenues	$11,390	$9,552	$11,206	$32,148	$134,100

Summary for Department

Revenues last year					$240,480
Patients seen					14,400
Average revenue per patient visit					$16.70
Estimated working days	39	40	43	120	465
Estimated patient visits	1,150	1,060	1,200	3,410	14,470
Average revenue per patient visit					$18.37
Estimated revenues	$21,126	$19,472	$22,044	$62,642	$265,814

Budgeting Expenses

One of the key topics in Part II, *Cost Accounting for Prepaid Medical Groups*, is cost behavior patterns and the resulting flexible budget. The importance of a knowledge of cost behavior patterns for projecting costs is stressed. The four patterns of cost behavior are variable, fixed, semivariable, and step-fixed. Variable costs change in proportion to changes in activity, while fixed costs do not change as activity changes. Some costs exhibit both characteristics (semivariable), while other costs increase in stairstep fashion (step-fixed). The flexible budget is a mathematical statement of the relationship between activity and costs.

$$\text{Total costs} = \text{Fixed costs} + (\text{Variable cost per unit of activity} \times \text{Activity level})$$

By expressing costs as fixed or variable, the flexible budget allows costs to be projected for any activity level. To project variable costs, the relationship between costs and activity must be known. For purposes of projection, fixed costs can be identified as committed or programmed. Committed fixed costs arise from long-range decisions and usually remain unchanged for long periods of time. Examples of committed fixed costs include depreciation of buildings and equipment, lease expense, insurance, and property taxes. Programmed fixed costs are set by short-range decisions and changed by management action. Programmed fixed costs are usually stairstep in pattern and include most of the staff salaries, employee benefits (particularly professional development), repairs, and marketing costs. Exhibit 19-8 lists the costs of the pediatrics department of Best Medical Center, classifies them by behavior pattern, and indicates the flexible budget based on last year's (19X4) costs.

EXHIBIT 19-8
CLASSIFICATION OF COSTS—PEDIATRICS

Costs	Cost Behavior Pattern	Flexible Budget 19X4 (average month)	Expected Changes in 19X5
Physician salaries	Programmed fixed	$11,500	Increase on Jan. 1 to $12,600
Physician benefits	Programmed fixed	a) 20% of salaries b) 2% of salaries—meetings and professional development	a) No change b) Increase to 5% of salaries
Staff salaries	Programmed fixed	$2,700	Increase at anniversary dates—approx. 10%
Staff benefits	Programmed fixed	20% of salaries	No change
Supplies	Variable	$1.00 per patient visit	No change
Equipment rental	Committed fixed	$100 per month	No change
Professional liability insurance	Committed fixed	$300 per month per physician	No change

Seasonal expenses (such as utilities) and fixed expenses that vary widely from month to month (such as telephone expense) should be projected by applying the expected increases to monthly amounts for the previous year. In addition to the expenses, adjustments and allowances must be considered. In the example, they are approximately six percent of production. The previous year's flexible budget for total costs was: TC = $17,970 per month + $1.00 per patient visit. Considering the expected price and rate increases, the current flexible budget for total costs becomes: TC = $20,014 per month + $1.00 per patient visit.

Preparing the Profit Plan

Planning, control, and decision making are most effective when the profit plan and subsequent performance reporting are related to responsibility centers. Most medical groups are organized along responsibility center lines, with each medical specialty a separate responsibility center. (Part II discussed the process of identifying responsibility centers and tracing direct costs for responsibility centers.)

Responsibility Center Profit Plan

Using the revenue projections and cost behavior patterns developed in Exhibit 19-8, a profit plan for Pediatrics is presented in Exhibit 19-9. The profit plan illustrated in this chapter will include figures for each of the three months in Quarter 1, and for the total year. (Quarters 2, 3, and 4 are omitted to simplify the exhibits.) Only expenses directly traceable to the responsibility center are included in the responsibility center's profit plan.

Prepaid Practice Profit Plan

It is critical for the group entering prepaid practice to establish accountability for its prepaid component. Each medical and ancillary responsibility center providing service to prepaid patients should be given fee-for-service equivalent credit for the patient visits or the procedures performed in the responsibility center. This rewards each responsibility center with a satisfactory revenue measure. It does not, however, provide an evaluation of the prepaid practice. A separate responsibility center should be created for this purpose.

Revenues in the prepaid practice responsibility center are the capitation payments from the HMO. Expenses include the cost of service provided to prepaid patients, expressed in fee-for-service equivalents, and the cost of outside referrals. If there are incremental costs traceable to the prepaid practice (for example, a nurse or clerk assigned to utilization review and control), these costs should be included in the profit plan of the prepaid practice and in subsequent reporting.

The real cost for inside service is the cost per member per month (explained in Part II, *Cost Accounting for Prepaid Medical Groups*). The difference

EXHIBIT 19-9
PROFIT PLAN—PEDIATRICS

	Jan	Feb	Mar	Quarter 1 Total	Total Year
Fee-for-service gross charges	$21,126	$19,472	$22,044	$62,642	$265,814
Adjustments and allowances	(1,268)	(1,168)	(1,323)	(3,759)	(15,949)
Fee-for-service net revenues	$19,858	$18,304	$20,721	$58,883	$249,865
Prepaid gross charges (fee-for-service equivalent)	129	210	323	662	23,058
Total revenues	$19,987	$18,514	$21,044	$59,545	$272,923
Operating Expenses:					
Physician salaries	$12,600	$12,600	$12,600	$37,800	$151,200
Physician benefits	3,150	3,150	3,150	9,450	37,800
Staff salaries	2,970	2,970	2,970	8,910	35,640
Staff benefits	594	594	594	1,782	7,200
Supplies	1,158	1,073	1,220	3,451	13,804
Equipment rental	100	100	100	300	1,200
Professional liability insurance	600	600	600	1,800	7,200
Total expenses	$21,172	$21,087	$21,234	$63,493	$254,044
Contribution to common costs and income	$(1,185)	$(2,573)	$ (190)	$(3,948)	$ 18,879

between the fee-for-service equivalent for service provided to prepaid patients and the real cost of serving the patients is included in the reports of the medical and ancillary responsibility centers. The cost per member per month should be included as a note to the profit plan of the prepaid practice.

In Exhibit 19-10, the prepaid practice projects a contribution to income of $17,691 for the year. A further gain will be shown in the reports of the medical and ancillary responsibility centers for the difference between the cost per member per month of $9.95 and the fee-for-service equivalent for service provided. This example does not consider the potential risk of hospital costs. If the group is at risk for a portion of excess costs resulting from excessive hospital utilization, they will experience a financial loss. Conversely, if hospital utilization is less than expected, then a gain will be reflected in the reports of the prepaid practice responsibility center.

EXHIBIT 19-10
PROFIT PLAN—PREPAID PRACTICE

	Jan	Feb	Mar	Quarter 1 Total	Total Year
Enrollment (member months)	130	216	328	674	23,345
Revenues:					
Capitation—inside services	$1,446	$2,402	$3,647	$ 7,495	$259,596
Capitation—outside referrals	1,008	1,674	2,542	5,224	180,924
Total revenues	$2,454	$4,076	$6,189	$12,719	$440,520
Expenses:					
Inside services to prepaid patients (fee-for-service equivalent)	$1,358	$2,238	$3,433	$7,029	$241,905
Outside referrals	1,008	1,674	2,542	5,224	180,924
Total expenses	$2,366	$3,912	$5,975	$12,253	$422,829
Contribution to common costs and income	$ 88	$ 164	$ 214	$ 466	$ 17,691

Capitation for inside services	$11.12
Capitation for outside referrals	7.75
Total capitation for services	$18.87
Projected cost per member per month for inside services	$9.95
Projected cost per member per month for outside referrals	7.75
Total projected cost per member per month	$17.70

Compilation of Responsibility Center Profit Plans into a Profit Plan for the Group

The purpose of the profit plan for the group is to forecast whether total revenues will be sufficient to cover total expenses and provide an adequate level of income. Responsibility center profit plans are compiled into the overall profit plan in Exhibit 19-11. Production, adjustments and allowances, and net

EXHIBIT 19-11
PROFIT PLAN — BEST MEDICAL CENTER

	Jan	Feb	Mar	Quarter 1 Total	Total Year
Fee-for-service gross charges	$227,089	$209,115	$227,412	$663,616	$2,852,561
Adjustments and allowances	(13,625)	(12,547)	(13,645)	(39,817)	(171,153)
Fee-for-service net revenues	$213,464	$196,568	$213,767	$623,799	$2,681,408
Capitation—inside services	1,446	2,402	3,647	7,495	259,596
Capitation—outside referrals	1,008	1,674	2,542	5,224	180,924
Total revenues	$215,918	$200,644	$219,956	$636,518	$3,121,928
Expenses by responsibility center:					
Family practice	$ 60,168	$ 59,930	$ 60,335	$180,433	$726,810
Internal medicine	22,499	22,435	22,553	67,487	272,006
Pediatrics	21,208	21,123	21,000	63,331	256,126
Obstetrics/gynecology	28,265	28,094	28,379	84,738	342,759
Laboratory	20,028	19,284	20,114	59,426	256,667
Radiology	14,090	13,787	14,125	42,002	175,743
Prepaid practice—outside referrals	1,008	1,674	2,542	5,224	180,924
Reception and appointments	3,200	3,200	3,200	9,600	38,400
Medical records	5,598	5,554	5,603	16,755	68,150
Occupancy	22,200	22,200	22,200	66,600	166,400
Administration	20,290	20,068	20,316	60,674	248,348
Total expenses	$218,554	$217,349	$220,367	$656,270	$2,832,333
Net income (loss)	$ (2,636)	$ (16,705)	$ (411)	$(19,752)	$ 289,595

revenue are presented as single amounts for the entire group. Expenses, however, are presented by responsibility centers. An alternative presentation would be to list the contribution of each responsibility center, then deduct common costs from the total contribution for the group. Presentation of total production has been chosen because most medical groups want to see total revenues for the group in the budget and in the income statement.

The profit plan may be prepared several times, using different projections of production and expenses, if the physician-owners are not satisfied with the overall income level. If they are not dissatisfied with the final net income (after profit sharing), they may go back to individual responsibility centers to consider cost reductions, fee increases, or increases in the level of production.

Preparing the Cash Budget

The second part of the comprehensive budget is the cash budget. After the profit plan is prepared and plans for capital expenditures are finalized, the cash budget is prepared. Ideally, both the profit plan and the cash budget should be structured as "rollover budgets," adding a new month at the end of each month (and a new quarter at the end of each quarter), always showing the next three months and three quarters. In this way the profit plan and cash budget are always current.

The lag in cash outflows resulting from incurred but not reported claims for outside referrals is, however, sufficiently significant that the impact of the lag on the cash budget should be understood. Measurement of cash flows for outside referrals is the "other side" of measuring incurred but unreported claims. The typical fee-for-service medical group does not have a liability for services provided outside the group. The medical group that has agreed to provide services to members of an HMO on a capitation basis typically has a liability for physician services outside the group to the prepaid patients. Chapter 22 discusses the need for estimating outstanding claims and gives several examples of how the liability may be measured.

Exhibit 19-12 shows the budgeted referral expenses for the first year of prepaid service in the continuing example. The amounts are on the accrual basis and thus show the expense in the month in which the service was rendered. For simplicity's sake, the effect of seasonality in the use of services is omitted.

Exhibit 19-13 shows the months in which the claims were actually paid in Year 1 and the amount of outstanding claims at the end of the year. Month 1, for example, shows that $362 was paid and that the $362 was for services incurred in Month 1. Month 2 shows a total of $964 paid, with $363 and $601 for services incurred in Months 1 and 2, respectively. By the end of Year 1, $145,268 had been paid for services rendered during the year. Claims of $180,927 were presented (assuming events turn out as projected) in Year 1, and thus a liability exists for $35,659 for claims not yet received.

Exhibit 19-13 shows that the amounts and timing of the payment of claims are dramatically different from the projected timing of services as shown in Exhibit 19-12. The differences need to be taken into consideration in developing the cash budget for the group.

EXHIBIT 19-12
BUDGETED REFERRAL EXPENSES BY MONTH

Month	Enrollment (member months)	Referral Cost per Member per Month	Referral Expenses
1	130	$7.75	$ 1,008
2	216	$7.75	1,674
3	328	$7.75	2,542
Qtr 1	674		5,224
4	1,165	$7.75	9,029
5	1,721	$7.75	13,338
6	1,875	$7.75	14,531
Qtr 2	4,761		36,898
7	1,976	$7.75	15,314
8	2,426	$7.75	18,802
9	2,590	$7.75	20,073
Qtr 3	6,992		54,189
10	3,290	$7.75	25,498
11	3,778	$7.75	29,280
12	3,850	$7.75	29,838
Qtr 4	10,918		84,616
Year	23,345		$180,927

Preparing the Projected Statement of Financial Position

The third and final step in developing the comprehensive budget is the preparation of a projected statement of financial position. Exhibit 18-1 in Chapter 18 illustrated the flow of data through the profit plan and cash budget to the projected statement of financial position. Development of the cash budget produces many of the ending balances of assets and liabilities for the projected statement of financial position. For example, projection of the cash payments lag for incurred but unreported claims also produces the balance of the liability for incurred but unreported claims. The projected statement of financial position has limited uses. Its major purpose is to tie the planning documents together and show the estimated financial position at the end of the planning period. Are the physician-owners and the creditors satisfied with the balances and the relationships presented in the projected position statement? If the group has active cash management, a strong credit and collection function,

EXHIBIT 19-13

PAYMENT OF CLAIMS IN YEAR 1 AND INCURRED BUT NOT REPORTED CLAIMS (IBNR) AT YEAR END

Incurral Month	Month in Which Claims Were Paid												Total Claims	Budgeted Referral	
	1	2	3	4	5	6	7	8	9	10	11	12	Paid	Expenses	IBNR
1	$362	$363	$ 106	$ 81	$ 41	$ 20	$ 15	$ 19	$ -	$ -	$ -	$ -	$ 1,006	$ 1,008	$ 2
2		601	603	176	134	69	33	25	32	-	-	-	1,672	1,674	2
3			913	915	267	203	104	51	38	48	-	-	2,539	2,542	3
4				3,241	3,250	948	722	370	181	135	172	-	9,020	9,029	9
5					4,788	4,802	1,400	1,067	547	267	200	253	13,324	13,338	14
6						5,217	5,231	1,526	1,162	596	291	218	14,241	14,531	290
7							5,498	5,513	1,608	1,225	628	306	14,778	15,314	536
8								6,750	6,769	1,974	1,504	771	17,767	18,802	1,035
9									7,206	7,226	2,108	1,606	18,146	20,073	1,927
10										9,154	9,179	2,677	21,010	25,498	4,488
11											10,511	10,541	21,052	29,280	8,228
12												10,712	10,712	29,838	19,126
Total Year 1	$362	$964	$1,621	$4,413	$8,481	$11,258	$13,005	$15,321	$17,542	$20,625	$24,592	$27,084	$145,268	$180,927	$35,659

and a good supply control system, the balances on the projected position statement should produce very few surprises.

Summary

The planning process illustrated in this chapter is an extension of the goal and objective setting discussed in Chapter 17. Objectives provide the quantified targets upon which the profit plan and cash budget are built. A comprehensive budget includes a profit plan, a cash budget, and a projected statement of financial position. The comprehensive budget involves both top-down and bottom-up processes. The goals and objectives come from the top down. In response to the goals and objectives, the profit plan is prepared through a bottom-up approach by each responsiblity center and then consolidated into an integrated profit plan for the group as a whole. By using responsibility centers as the basis for the profit plan, motivation to succeed should increase. Projection of revenues is based on past production, or the projection by patient visit method, or an estimate of demand for the group's services. Projection of expenses is built upon a knowledge of cost behavior patterns. The cash budget should be a part of both the comprehensive budget and an ongoing program of cash management.

Chapter 20

Performance Evaluation: The Control Process

Financial planning is intended to ensure that resources will be used in an efficient manner, thereby achieving desired goals and objectives. However, financial planning is not complete without monitoring actual performance and comparing it to the plan. The control process cannot stand alone; there must be benchmarks by which to evaluate performance. The budget links these two processes—planning and control. A medical group's commitment to provide care on a prepaid basis not only involves a potentially large financial risk but also requires more effective planning and control over the use of the group's resources. The day-to-day procedures must be appropriate for the task, and the quality and breadth of the planning process must be enhanced when a prepaid component is added to a fee-for-service practice.

In addition to the financial measures of performance discussed in this chapter, there are a number of nonfinancial measures of performance that are used in the day-to-day management of the group. For example, the physicians' appointment schedules are routinely reviewed for open hours, and steps can be taken to fill these time slots by calling patients for regular checkups or to reschedule missed appointments. The emphasis on financial analysis in this chapter should in no way diminish the use of any proven nonfinancial measure.

Dimensions of Analysis

In reviewing the adequacy of its planning and control processes, the group should consider several dimensions of analysis. The results of operations may be analyzed in terms of:

Responsibility centers

Goals and budget

External comparisons

General questions with regard to each of the different dimensions of analysis are:

- Responsibility Centers—Control is exercised at the responsibility center level. How did each center perform for the period? Each revenue and expense is traced to the center responsible for its incurrence. It is particularly important that care is exercised in identifying responsibility for and controlling the costs that are related to the group's commitment to provide prepaid care.

- Goals and Budget—How did the group do in relation to its goals, objectives, and budget? This dimension of analysis examines significant deviations from the planned use of resources and attempts to determine the cause of the deviations.

- External Comparisions—How is the group doing compared to other groups? How is the prepaid component doing compared to other prepaid components and HMOs? Comparison with other groups provides useful information for identifying areas to be investigated and for establishing goals and objectives.

These dimensions of analysis are not mutually exclusive. They are in fact complementary, and all should be performed.

Responsibility Centers/Performance Evaluation

The concept of responsibility centers was introduced in Part II, *Cost Accounting for Prepaid Medical Groups.* This concept, often called responsibility accounting, is an integral part of the control process and dictates that the results of operations be reflected on a responsibility center basis. The responsibility center is a unit within the organization that can and should exert control over performance and the consumption of resources. The laboratory and the pediatrics department are examples of two responsibility centers. The entire prepaid practice should also be accounted for as a responsibility center for performance evaluation. For the medical group offering prepaid care, when the prepaid component does not exceed about 25 percent of the total practice, it is probably sufficient that the revenues and costs of the prepaid component be reported as a separate responsibility center. The other responsibility centers within the group would report fee-for-service equivalents as revenue surrogates for providing care to the prepaid patients. The effect of this is twofold:

1. Responsibility for treatment of prepaid patients in a cost effective fashion is diffused throughout the group, and no one individual or group of individuals is clearly accountable. The primary care physician comes closest to having full responsibility for a particular patient's care when serving in a gatekeeper role. However, no one person has a similar responsibility for the entire prepaid practice.

2. Performance is expressed in terms that are meaningful to the fee-for-service environment, and outcomes are monitored in these terms. The prepaid environment, on the other hand, requires different performance and outcome criteria and, therefore, expresses itself in terms that are not necessarily consistent with fee-for-service practice.

For the group with less than 25 percent of its revenues from prepaid care, these effects are probably not significant. However, when prepaid revenues exceed 25 percent of a group's revenues, it probably will be necessary for the group to change not only its financial information system but the rewards system as well. One option is for the group to switch from crediting individual responsibility centers with fee-for-service equivalents to crediting the centers with a pro rata share of the capitation for physician services. Similarly, instead of being charged to a single responsibility center for prepaid care, the cost of outside referrals would be charged to the responsibility center of the referring physician. On the surface this may not appear to be a significant shift; however, it represents a shift from the fee-for-service orientation of increasing production to an orientation toward managing costs within a fixed income. This may lead to the individual physician becoming a responsbility center for cost control. The unit of performance measurement would in turn become the cost per member per month.

The purpose of responsibility center operating statements is to focus upon financial control. Therefore, the statement should include only those revenues and costs over which the particular responsibility center has control. Arbitrary allocation of common costs should not be included in control reports. Exhibit 20-1 shows the results for the pediatrics department for the first quarter of 19X5. The report includes the actual results for the quarter, results for the same quarter last year, the budget for the quarter, and deviation from the budget.

Goals and Budget/Performance Evaluation

The group must evaluate its performance in relation to its own goals, objectives, and budget. Data from the past and from outside the group may be useful in establishing objectives and identifying areas for investigation, but unless relevant information is really comparable it should not be used as a standard and may not be applicable for determining efficiency.

Comparison of actual results with a budget prepared for a single level of activity involves three reasons for deviation from the plan. They are:

A change in activity from the planned level of activity

More or less efficiency in the use of practice resources

Changes in the prices of resources purchased.

Since deviation from the budget cannot be attributed solely to any one of the above reasons, performance is often difficult, if not impossible, to evaluate.

EXHIBIT 20-1
OPERATING STATEMENT—PEDIATRICS

	Actual Quarter 1 19X4	Budget Quarter 1 19X5	Actual Quarter 1 19X5	Variance (unfavorable)
Fee-for-service gross charges	$52,011	$57,682	$56,960	$(722)
Adjustments and allowances	(3,120)	(3,461)	(3,418)	43
Fee-for-service net revenues	$48,891	$54,221	$53,542	$(679)
Prepaid revenues (fee-for-service equivalent)	0	663	1,617	954
Total revenues	$48,891	$54,884	$55,159	$ 275
Operating expenses:				
Physician salaries	$34,500	$37,800	$37,800	$ 0
Physician benefits	7,590	9,450	9,000	450
Staff salaries	8,100	9,000	9,000	0
Staff benefits	1,620	1,800	1,850	(50)
Supplies	3,110	3,181	3,400	(219)
Equipment rental	300	300	300	0
Professional liability insurance	1,800	1,800	1,800	0
Total expenses	$57,020	$63,331	$63,150	$ 181
Contribution to common costs and income	$ (8,129)	$ (8,447)	$ (7,991)	$ 456
Patient visits—fee-for-service	3,110	3,140	3,200	60
Patient visits—prepaid	0	41	100	59

EXHIBIT 20-2

OPERATING STATEMENT—BEST MEDICAL CENTER
ACTUAL VS. BUDGET
Quarter 1, 19X5

	Budget	Actual	Variance (unfavorable)
Fee-for-service gross charges	$663,616	$640,000	$(23,616)
Adjustments and allowances	(39,817)	(39,680)	137
Fee-for-service net revenues	$623,799	$600,320	$(23,479)
Capitation—inside services	7,495	8,896	1,401
Capitation—outside referrals	5,224	6,200	976
Total revenues	$636,518	$615,416	$(21,102)
Expenses by responsibility center:			
Family practice	$180,433	$180,000	$ 433
Internal medicine	67,487	68,000	(513)
Pediatrics	63,331	63,150	181
Obstetrics/gynecology	84,738	82,000	2,738
Laboratory	59,426	60,000	(574)
Radiology	42,002	41,500	502
Prepaid practice—outside referrals	5,224	6,500	(1,276)
Reception and appointments	9,600	9,650	(50)
Medical records	16,755	17,000	(245)
Occupancy	66,600	66,600	0
Administration	60,674	61,000	(326)
Total expenses	$656,270	$655,400	$ 870
Net income (loss)	$ (19,752)	$ (39,984)	$(20,232)
Fee-for-service patient visits—medical	16,300	17,340	1,040
Fee-for-service patient visits—ancillary	24,500	25,004	504
Prepaid patient visits—medical	250	207	(43)
Prepaid patient visits—ancillary	380	298	(82)

When the pediatrics department head reviews the operating statement for his responsibility center (Exhibit 20-1), it should be no surprise to discover that fee-for-service production is $722 below the level planned. Further analysis of the operating statement however, raises a number of questions. For example: Are the assumptions underlying the budget for 19X5 still valid? Were the operating plans on which the budget was based for the first quarter of 19X5 actually followed? Are there any areas that require immediate corrective action, such as an increase in promoting the services of the group? Similar questions should be raised for other responsibility centers. The fee-for-service equivalent of services rendered to pediatric prepaid patients is, however, $954 above the level planned. This would appear to be due to 59 more prepaid visits than had been planned. Were these visits due to increased enrollment or did the prepaid patients simply use more services than planned? The analysis of Exhibit 20-1 also shows that supplies expense, which should be higher because of a higher level of activity, actually exceeds the budget by $219. The favorable variance in the physician benefits of $450 is assumed to be due to the cancellation of a continuing education conference, which may be rescheduled later in the year.

When the operating statement for the entire group is analyzed (Exhibit 20-2), the loss is $20,232 larger than planned. It appears that the primary loss is due to production falling $23,616 below plan. The operating statement, like the profit plan in Chapter 19, focuses upon responsibility centers. Operating expenses are presented in total for each responsibiity center. As an alternative presentation, the expenses could be presented by expense classifications (for example, salaries or supplies). The emphasis here, however, is upon cost control through responsibility centers.

The group should prepare a responsibility center operating statement for the prepaid component. The statement relates capitation payments to the fee-for-service equivalent for service provided inside the medical group and to the cost of outside referrals. The prepaid practice operating statement (Exhibit 20-3) shows a loss or deficiency of $242 for the first quarter.

This dimension of analysis was hampered because the variances from budget mixed the effects of activity changes with those of efficiency and price changes. The performance budget addresses this issue.

Performance Budget. One of the difficulties with attempts to evaluate performance through either a comparison with the prior year's experience or a static budget is the combination of effects due to changes in activity and deviations due to changes in prices and efficiency. The impact of changes in activity may be isolated by adopting the concept of a performance budget, that is, a budget prepared to reflect what revenues and costs should have been at the actual level of activity during the period.

EXHIBIT 20-3
OPERATING STATEMENT—PREPAID PRACTICE
ACTUAL VS. BUDGET
Quarter 1, 19X5

	Budget	Actual	Variance
Revenues:			
Capitation—inside services	$ 7,495	$ 8,896	$ 1,401
Capitation—outside referrals	5,224	6,200	976
Total revenues	$12,719	$15,096	$ 2,377
Expenses:			
Inside services to prepaid patients (fee-for-service equivalent)	$ 6,963	$ 8,838	$(1,875)
Outside referrals	5,224	6,500	(1,276)
Total expenses	$12,187	$15,338	$(3,151)
Contribution to common costs and income	$ 532	$ (242)	$ (774)

Inherent in the preparation of a performance budget is the concept of fixed and variable costs. In Chapter 19 of this volume, a flexible budget applying fixed and variable cost behavior patterns was developed for the group in the continuing example. That flexible budget must be adjusted for programmed fixed costs that are seasonal and for a different time period (quarterly rather than monthly).

The performance budget in Exhibit 20-4 shows that of the $20,232 unfavorable variance in income (see Exhibit 20-2), $18,547 is due to a change in activity and $1,685 is due to changes in prices and efficiency. The performance budget can be a very useful tool in helping to isolate and explain the reasons for variances.

External Comparisons/Performance Evaluation
The final dimension of analysis involves a comparison of current data for the group with data from other groups. The Medical Group Management Association offers a comparative report, the Performance Efficiency Evaluation Report (PEER), that provides productivity and efficiency statistical standards. The performance evaluator provides trend data, comparison with budget, and an external comparison with peer groups on over 200 indicators of performance. It is much more than a comparative data service; this tool provides important trend data for 17 key variables evaluating prepaid practice. The indicators for the first quarter of activity are presented in Exhibit 20-5.

EXHIBIT 20-4
OPERATING STATEMENT—BEST MEDICAL CENTER
ACTUAL VS. PERFORMANCE BUDGET
Quarter 1, 19X5

	Budget	Performance Budget	Actual	Prices and Efficiency Variance
Fee-for-service gross charges	$663,616	$639,418	$640,000	$ 582
Adjustments and allowances	(39,817)	(38,365)	(39,680)	(1,315)
Fee-for-service net revenues	$623,799	$601,053	$600,320	$ (733)
Capitation—inside service	7,495	8,896	8,896	0
Capitation—outside referrals	5,224	6,200	6,200	0
Total revenues	$636,518	$616,149	$615,416	$ (733)
Expenses by responsibility center:				
Family practice	$180,433	$179,833	$180,000	$ (167)
Internal medicine	67,487	67,087	68,000	(913)
Pediatrics	63,331	63,450	63,150	300
Obstetrics/gynecology	84,738	84,390	82,000	2,390
Laboratory	59,426	58,906	60,000	(1,094)
Radiology	42,002	41,552	41,500	52
Prepaid practice—outside referrals	5,224	6,200	6,500	(300)
Reception and appointments	9,600	9,600	9,650	(50)
Medical records	16,755	16,655	17,000	(345)
Occupancy	66,600	66,600	66,600	0
Administration	60,674	60,175	61,000	(825)
Total expenses	$656,270	$654,448	$655,400	$ (952)
Net income (loss)	$ (19,752)	$ (38,299)	$ (39,984)	$(1,685)

Nonfinancial Measures of Performance

One who deals with budgets, performance reports, and financial statements often considers financial performance measures to be the only significant measures of performance. When a medical group has very limited financial information (possibly only a checkbook), assessing performance is difficult. In these cases the administrator usually relies on a few key nonfinancial measures of performance that show activity generated and resources used.

EXHIBIT 20-5
ILLUSTRATION OF PERFORMANCE EFFICIENCY EVALUATION REPORT

PAGE 1

MEDICAL CENTER PC

	CURRENT	INTERNAL TREND			BUDGET COMPARISON		EXTERNAL COMPARISON COMPARE GROUP CG. 1		
	QTR 1 1985	QTR 4 1984	QTR 1 1984	AVG PAST 4 QTRS	ESTIMATE QTR 1	VARIANCE	MEDIAN	RANK	N
*** EXECUTIVE SUMMARY ***									
FEE FOR SERVICE &/OR PREPAID									
1. OUTPATIENT ENCOUNTERS PER FTE PHYSICIAN			1102.39	1100.55			933.95		40
2. HOSPITAL ADMISSIONS PER FTE PHYSICIAN	58.63	35.93	32.48	32.53			41.67	8	34
3. NEW PATIENT REGISTRATIONS PER FTE PHYSICIAN	199.87	99.80	98.60	104.75			63.60	1	37
4. TOTAL GROSS CHARGES PER FTE PHYSICIAN	83414.95	75222.31	77111.43	77322.98			84966.46	23	42
5. TOTAL CASH COLLECTIONS PER FTE PHYSICIAN	81480.42	78195.54	77563.47	75533.17			70550.99	16	42
6. ADJUSTMENTS AS % OF GROSS FEE-FOR-SERVICE CHARGES	3.82	1.15	9.16	3.26			5.58	29	39
7. ALLOWANCES/WRITE-OFFS AS % OF GROSS FEE-FOR-SERVICE CHARGES	2.12	5.86	4.65	9.66			3.95	22	29
8. TOTAL NONPHYSICIAN EXPENSES PER FTE PHYSICIAN	43698.93	41663.36	41038.82	40464.13			40011.76	15	42
9. TOTAL NONPHY EXPENSES AS % OF TOTAL CASH COLLECTIONS	53.63	53.28	52.91	53.58			54.12	24	42
10. GROSS COLLECTION RATIO	0.97	1.04	1.00	0.98			0.81	4.5	41
11. ADJUSTED COLLECTION RATIO	1.01	1.05	1.10	1.01			0.88	5.5	41
12. MONTHS REVENUE IN ACCOUNTS RECEIVABLE	3.00	3.25	2.69	2.96			3.52	27	36
13. TOTAL NONPHYSICIAN SALARY EXPENSE PER OUTPATIENT ENCNTR			15.66	15.72			17.12		40
14. TOTAL NONPHYSICIAN BENEFIT EXPENSE PER OUTPATIENT ENCNTR			2.83	2.93			3.68		38

PAGE 2

MEDICAL CENTER PC

	CURRENT	INTERNAL TREND			BUDGET COMPARISON		EXTERNAL COMPARISON COMPARE GROUP CG. 1		
	QTR 1 1985	QTR 4 1984	QTR 1 1984	AVG PAST 4 QTRS	ESTIMATE QTR 1	VARIANCE	MEDIAN	RANK	N
FEE FOR SERVICE &/OR PREPAID (CONT)									
15. TOTAL MEDICAL SUPPLY EXPENSE PER OUTPATIENT ENCOUNTER			1.94	2.17			2.51		40
16. TOTAL BUILDING AND GROUNDS EXPENSE PER OUTPATIENT ENCNTR			2.31	1.47			5.42		39
17. TOTAL GEN'L AND ADMINISTRATIVE EXPENSE PER OUTPATIENT ENCNTR			4.76	5.12			6.33		39
18. TOTAL DATA PROCESSING EXPENSE PER OUTPATIENT ENCOUNTER			1.30	1.26			0.95		39
19. TOTAL LABORATORY GROSS CHARGES PER FTE PHYSICIAN	6563.52	5074.89	5768.06	5864.26			8168.11	27	37
20. TOTAL LABORATORY EXPENSE PER FTE PHYSICIAN	1419.22	1580.94	1277.07	1507.97			1800.82	27	37
21. TOTAL RADIOLOGY GROSS CHARGES PER FTE PHYSICIAN	6848.01	6591.37	6342.74	6891.59			6860.62	20	37
22. TOTAL RADIOLOGY EXPENSE PER FTE PHYSICIAN	1037.72	833.32	1006.82	857.92			1505.46	28	39
PREPAID ONLY									
23. PREPAID CHARGES (FFS EQUIV) PER MEMBER PER MONTH							30.52		10
24. TOTAL PREPAID INCOME AS % OF PREPAID CHARGES (FFS EQUIV)	99.62	94.54	81.31	89.30			105.21	9	12
25. INPATIENT DAYS PER 1,000 MEMBERS (ANNUALIZED)							317.63		5
26. PHYSICIAN OUTPATIENT ENCNTRS PER 1000 MEMBERS (ANNUALIZED)							3676.75		8

As long as they are acceptable, the group is assumed to be performing well so there is no need for investigation or intervention.

There are different types of nonfinancial performance measures. The easiest to obtain examples include number of patient visits, number of procedures performed, number of physicians, number of physician days, number of employees, number of employee days, number of hours worked, number of laboratory procedures, and quantity of supplies used (or purchased). Standing alone, any one of these indicators is not very useful; however, over time and in combination with other information important trends appear.

A more useful type of performance measure combines two separate indicators to show their relationship. The most common relationship involves level of activity and use of resources per full-time-equivalent physician. Another involves resources used per patient visit or procedure. Some of the more common indicators are:

Collection ratio

Number of scheduled physician office hours (and related measures)

Number of various procedures performed

Number of missed appointments

Turnover of employees

Number of calls completed to patients reminding them of regular checkups

Number of patients referred to medical specialties outside the group

Data related to promotion; for example, results of using advertisements

Monthly average number of prepaid plan members

New enrollees: Total during quarter

Disenrollees: Total during quarter

Prepaid capitation payment per 1,000 members per month

Prepaid charges (fee-for-service equivalent) per 1,000 members per month

Outside physican referral expense per 1,000 members per month

Outside laboratory referral expense per 1,000 members per month

Outside x-ray referral expense per 1,000 members per month

Inpatient admissions per 1,000 members per month

Average length of stay per inpatient admission

Physician outpatient encounters per 1,000 members per month.

Summary

This chapter presented an extended illustration of performance evaluation. The data depicted relationships found in an actual group. Several dimensions of analysis were examined. Reporting activity by responsibility center was discussed. The usefulness of comparing performance to the prior year's results, to a static budget, and to a performance budget was examined, and an illustration of each was given. The need to evaluate the overall performance of the group was discussed. The chapter concluded with a discussion about comparing the group with its peers. The chart of accounts presented in Part I enhances the comparability of financial measures. It must be remembered that nonfinancial indicators are also important in assessing performance.

Chapter 21

Managing Cash and Other Short-Term Resources

The cash budget is the second portion of the comprehensive budget that was developed in Chapter 19. In this chapter, the cash budget is refined and illustrated as a management tool. It is almost impossible to talk about cash management, however, without also talking about other short-term resources, including receivables, payables, inventories, and short-term investments. For example, cash flows tend to speed up when receivables decrease or when payables increase; cash flows tend to slow down when receivables increase or when payables decrease. Inventories and short-term investments also can involve either sources or uses of cash. The focus in the second half of this chapter is on the management of these other short-term resources.

Cash Management

Cash planning for the entire year is accomplished through the cash budget described in Chapter 19. The day-to-day control of cash, however, requires two major tools.

- The short-term cash plan that schedules planned cash inflows and outflows for the immediate future. This may be by day for the current week, and by week for the remainder of the month.

- The daily cash report that monitors the actual cash position by showing the daily balance of cash in each bank account.

These two tools will be illustrated, followed by a discussion of concepts and techniques designed to achieve strong internal control over cash. Such control involves protecting cash from misappropriation and providing accurate cash records. Useful internal controls for protecting the cash position and records described in this chapter are the internal control checklist and the bank reconciliation.

The Short-Term Cash Plan

The short-term cash plan is a dynamic tool for short-term cash management. The period covered and detail of projection depend upon fluctuations of cash and the precision with which management wishes to manage cash. The short-term cash plan identifies shortages and excesses of cash for a short period of time (a week or month) that call for immediate decisions.

For most medical groups, a cash flow projection by day for the next week, and by week for the remainder of the month, should provide excellent short-term cash management. For example, the short-term cash plan presents four weeks of data showing daily cash flows for Week 1 and weekly cash flows for Weeks 2, 3, and 4. At the end of each week the short-term cash plan is "rolled over." A new short-term cash plan will show daily cash flows for Week 2 and weekly cash flows for Weeks 3, 4, and 5. In this manner the short-term cash plan always remains current.

Exhibit 21-1 illustrates a short-term cash forecast for a medical group with a prepaid component. This exhibit makes the assumption that the longer-term cash budget showed that the month of January would produce a net cash drain. Low cash collections in January, resulting from low production in November and December, coupled with the semiannual lease payment, higher cash outlays related to a higher anticipated level of production in January, and high seasonality of the cash needs for payment of claims on the prepaid component cause a net cash outflow for the month. As can be seen from the tentative forecast in Exhibit 21-1, Weeks 2 and 4 contribute to the overall expected deficiency in cash of $11,400. The group needs to raise approximately $21,400 to cover the net cash outflow and restore the $10,000 minimum cash balance maintained by the group. The illustration assumes that the group had generated, but not distributed, $20,000 in earlier months to meet this type of need. The group invested these funds in marketable securities and, as an added precaution, established a line of credit at the bank.

The major purpose of Exhibit 21-1 is to present the most accurate forecast of cash before considering how potential cash deficiencies will be financed or surpluses invested.

Exhibit 21-2 illustrates the revised and final short-term cash plan for the month of January. It was developed from the tentative short-term forecast after revision for decisions involving financing the deficiencies in cash and investing the surpluses in cash. For example, in Week 2 it is planned that $15,000 of marketable securities will be sold and in Weeks 1 and 3 $2,000 cash will be transferred to savings. During Week 4, $10,400 of cash needs will be met by selling $9,000 of marketable securities and borrowing $1,400. An alternative plan for January would use the line of credit at the bank rather than sell $24,000 of marketable securities. During months when outflows are particularly heavy, both sources may have to be used.

EXHIBIT 21-1

TENTATIVE SHORT-TERM CASH FORECAST

By Week for the Month of January

	Week 1[1]	Week 2	Week 3	Week 4
Cash inflows:				
Private pay	$ 4,000	$ 9,000	$ 7,000	$ 5,000
Third-party payers	3,000	4,000	0	2,000
Capitation payment from HMO	15,000	0	0	0
Total inflows	$22,000	$ 13,000	$ 7,000	$ 7,000
Cash outflows:				
Payroll	$ 0	$ 12,000	$ 0	$ 12,000
Taxes	0	0	0	1,800
Accounts payable	8,000	2,000	4,000	3,600
Lease payment	12,000	0	0	0
Claims payment	0	14,000	0	0
Other	0	0	1,000	0
Total outflows	$20,000	$ 28,000	$ 5,000	$ 17,400
Increase (decrease) in cash	$ 2,000	$(15,000)	$ 2,000	$(10,400)
Beginning cash balance	10,000	12,000	(3,000)	(1,000)
Ending cash balance before financing	$12,000	$ (3,000)	$(1,000)	$(11,400)

[1]Cash forecasts for the first week would be shown on a daily basis but have been omitted here to simplify the exhibit.

The short-term cash plan in Exhibits 21-1 and 21-2 presents cash flows only by week for January. Daily projections may have indicated the need for additional cash if cash payments are scheduled early in the week and cash receipts are expected late in the week. Daily projections will show cash needs that "wash out" in longer periods. These timing problems lead to a brief discussion of speeding up inflows and slowing outflows.

Improving Cash Flows

A group may improve the timing of cash flows in several ways. These include:

- Presenting the patient with a bill at the time of service

EXHIBIT 21-2

FINAL SHORT-TERM CASH PLAN

By Week for the Month of January

	Week 1[1]	Week 2	Week 3	Week 4
Cash inflows:				
Private pay	$ 4,000	$ 9,000	$ 7,000	$ 5,000
Third-party payers	3,000	4,000	0	2,000
Capitation payment	15,000	0	0	0
Sale of investments or from savings	0	15,000	0	9,000
Borrowings	0	0	0	1,400
Total inflows	$22,000	$28,000	$ 7,000	$17,400
Cash outflows:				
Payroll	$ 0	$12,000	$ 0	$12,000
Taxes	0	0	0	1,800
Accounts payable	8,000	2,000	4,000	3,600
Lease payment	12,000	0	0	0
Claims payment	0	14,000	0	0
Other	0	0	1,000	0
To short-term investments or savings	2,000	0	2,000	0
Total outflows	$22,000	$28,000	$ 7,000	$17,400
Increase (decrease) in cash	$ 0	$ 0	$ 0	$ 0
Beginning cash balance	$10,000	$10,000	$10,000	$10,000
Ending cash balance	$10,000	$10,000	$10,000	$10,000

- Having suppliers time their billings to follow peak collection periods
- Deferring payment of bills until the end of discount periods
- Arranging deferred payments for major purchases
- Controlling the timing of claims payments
- Arranging for earlier payment of the HMO's capitation to the medical group.

Billing at Time of Service. Encouraging fee-for-service patients to pay at the time of service or within a few days of service will speed up cash inflows and spread cash collections more evenly.

Timing of Billing by Suppliers. Request that suppliers invoice the group at dates that fit the group's cash flow schedule. Ideally, bills would be paid after collections have been made from patients. Although it may not be possible to achieve the ideal, many suppliers will cooperate in setting more convenient payment dates.

Payment at the End of Discount Periods. There is no reason to pay bills early. Payments should be made at the end of discount periods and all discounts should be taken. Missing a discount, however, results in the group paying a very high effective interest rate. If a cash discount of 2/10, net 30 (two percent discount if paid in 10 days or full amount due in 30 days) is missed, it costs the medical group two percent for use of the supplier's money for an additional 20 days. Since there are 18 20-day periods in a year, the effective annual rate is approximately 36.5 percent.

Arranging Deferred Financing. Negotiations with suppliers to make major purchases may result in extending payments over several months. Many suppliers will extend payments for 90 to 120 days without additional cost. In other cases the added interest cost a supplier may charge often is below the group's borrowing cost.

Controlling Claims Payments. Pay claims once or twice a month so as to routinize the payment process, keep cash levels high as long as reasonably possible, and earn income on short-term investments. The desire to control claims payments to the maximum extent must be balanced by any needs for favorable relations with physicians and other providers outside the group.

Arranging for Earlier Payment of Capitation. The timing of the payment should be part of the group's negotiation with the HMO. The HMO itself is normally paid by employer groups in the first half of the month.

The Daily Cash Report

Information contained in the daily cash report is as important to a medical group as the fuel gauge is to an automobile. This report permits the administrator to monitor the cash position on a current basis and to see that the projection in the short-term cash plan actually is achieved. Deviations from the short-term cash plan may require corrective action. It may be necessary to shift cash from one bank account to another, to sell or purchase short-term investments, or to borrow on or repay the line of credit.

The daily cash report is even more important for the group that does not prepare a formal cash budget or short-term cash plan. Through informal planning of cash needs and monitoring the daily cash position, the group may be able to manage cash satisfactorily without a formal cash budget. Exhibit 21-3 contains more information than the typical daily cash report. Three different types of information may be reported daily: first, the balance of each cash account; second, daily receipts and disbursements; and third, a 7 to 10-day projection of cash needs.

Some groups may desire only the information on account balances presented at the bottom of Exhibit 21-3. In addition to the book (or checkbook) balance, the bank balance may be obtained by phone. This information serves at least two purposes: determining the float position of each account and the adequacy of compensating balances. Inadequate compensating balances may result in additional service charges, difficulty in obtaining loans, or higher interest rates.

The upper portion of Exhibit 21-3 displays cash collections by payer type and major expenses by category. Medical groups increasingly want to encourage payment at the time of service. Note that the illustration provides a line for recording cash receipts on the day of service.

A section providing for a cash forecast for the next few days could be included in the daily cash report for groups that do not maintain a cash budget or short-term cash plan. Many administrators believe cash budgets and short-term cash plans are too sophisticated and involved for their needs. Through good planning, however, cash crises may be averted and desired distributions to doctors accomplished. Administrators who feel they do not need to plan for cash needs probably are maintaining too much cash. By adopting good cash management practices and maintaining appropriate levels of cash, the group will operate at a lower cost. In addition, the credit standing of the group will be stronger and the doctors will be more satisfied.

Internal Control of Cash

The study of dental practices, medical groups, and prepaid plans indicates that one of the most important objectives of a financial information system is to provide proper internal control over cash. An internal control system provides a set of controls to safeguard the assets of the organization, to provide reliable and accurate information, and to ensure compliance with organizational objectives and procedures.

An internal control system for cash is intended to:

- Establish custody over cash
- Protect cash from theft or fraud

EXHIBIT 21-3
ILLUSTRATION OF DAILY CASH REPORT

DAILY CASH REPORT

Beginning daily cash balance	$ ________
Cash receipts:	
Medical insurance	$ ________
Public assistance	________
Private pay for today's services	________
Private pay for previous services	________
Capitation payment	________
Other	________
Total receipts	$ ________
Total receipts and beginning balance	$ ________
Cash disbursements:	
Payroll	$ ________
Accounts payable	________
Taxes	________
Claims payment	________
Other	________
Total disbursements	$ ________
Ending daily cash balance	$ ________

Bank Account Number	**Book Balance**	**Bank Balance**
xxx xxx General operating account	$ ________	$ ________
xxx xxx Payroll account	$ ________	$ ________
Other accounts	$ ________	$ ________

Limit employee temptation

Provide a check on accuracy and reliability of cash records.

Specific procedures should be developed to provide a system of internal control.

- Specific persons should be designated to handle and be responsible for cash.

- Accounting records must be kept by persons who do not handle or have access to cash.
- No one person should have complete authority over the entire sequence of transactions involving cash, for example, from purchase of a resource through to payment.
- All cash receipts should be deposited intact daily. No payments should be made out of undeposited cash receipts. Only the petty cash or change fund should remain on the premises overnight.
- A verifiable record should be made immediately after each cash receipt.
- Cash payments should be made by check unless specifically authorized to be paid from petty cash.
- No payment should be made without proper authorization and verification of the amount due.
- For the protection of the medical group, the cashier and others who handle cash regularly should be bonded.
- Cash balances should be verified daily through the daily cash report.
- A monthly reconcilation of each bank account should be made by a person who neither maintains the records nor has custody over cash.
- Multiple signatures should be required on all high dollar checks, for instance, checks for amounts over $2,000.

These procedures should be modified to accomodate the needs of specific groups. Smaller groups will have difficulty in segregating duties to separate cash handling, record keeping, and verification functions. It is particularly important that all receipts be deposited intact and that all payments be made by check. By depositing all cash receipts and making all payments by check, the group has two accounting systems recording the same transaction. This procedure permits the group to validate its cash records every time a monthly bank reconciliation is prepared.

An important part of any audit involves an evaluation of the internal control system of the entity. Exhibit 21-4 presents a condensed internal control checklist. A "No" answer to an item indicates a possible weakness and should be examined.

EXHIBIT 21-4
INTERNAL CONTROL CHECKLIST

YES	NO	
		Cash Fund
[ ]	[ ]	Petty cash or change fund is maintained (imprest system)
[ ]	[ ]	A custodian is responsible for this fund
[ ]	[ ]	Fund reimbursement is made directly to this custodian
[ ]	[ ]	Custodian has no access to accounting records
[ ]	[ ]	Custodian has no access to cash receipts
[ ]	[ ]	Physically secure place is provided for fund storage
[ ]	[ ]	Surprise audits are conducted periodically
[ ]	[ ]	Rule: no employee check cashing
		Cash Receipts
[ ]	[ ]	All cash custodians are bonded
[ ]	[ ]	All cash receipts are deposited daily
[ ]	[ ]	Daily list is maintained of mail receipts
[ ]	[ ]	Daily reconciliation of cash collections is required
[ ]	[ ]	Cashier personnel are separated from accounting duties
[ ]	[ ]	Cashier personnel are separated from credit duties
[ ]	[ ]	Cash is separated from negotiable instruments
[ ]	[ ]	Bank account is properly authorized
[ ]	[ ]	Comparisions are made between duplicate deposit slips and detail of accounts receivable
[ ]	[ ]	Comparisions are made between duplicate deposit slips and cash book
		Cash Disbursements
[ ]	[ ]	Recording, authorization and check-signing functions are completely separate
[ ]	[ ]	Support is required for check signature
[ ]	[ ]	Control is exercised if check-signing machine is used
[ ]	[ ]	Authorization to sign checks is limited
[ ]	[ ]	There is no access to cash records or receipts by check signers
[ ]	[ ]	Detailed listing of checks is required
[ ]	[ ]	Check listings are compared with cash book
[ ]	[ ]	No checks payable to cash are allowed
[ ]	[ ]	Checks are prenumbered
[ ]	[ ]	There is physical control over unused checks
[ ]	[ ]	Mutilation of voided checks is required
[ ]	[ ]	All disbursements are made by check unless specifically authorized from petty cash
[ ]	[ ]	Control over and prompt accounting for interbank transfers is exercised

[ ] [ ] Bank is instructed not to cash checks made by the group to the group
[ ] [ ] All check signers are bonded
[ ] [ ] All payments must have prior written authorization
[ ] [ ] All employees must take vacations annually

Bank Reconciliation

[ ] [ ] Reconciliation between bank and books is conducted at least monthly
[ ] [ ] Person responsible for reconciling bank statement is independent from accounting or cashier duties
[ ] [ ] Bank statement is sent directly to the person responsible for reconciliation

---

A critical part of control over cash transactions is the monthly reconciliation of every bank account. Because it constitutes the verification of two independent accounting systems, it is important that the bank reconciliation be performed by a person who does not have responsibility for cash or by a person who does not maintain the accounting records. In a smaller group, bank reconciliations could be performed by a doctor. In larger groups, bank reconciliations should be performed by the group treasurer or chief fiscal officer. Exhibit 21-5 provides a simplified illustration of a bank reconciliation. This form provides double proof of the correct cash balance.

EXHIBIT 21-5
BANK RECONCILIATION

Balance per books	$xxxx	Balance per bank statement	$xxxx
Add: Amounts that have been added by the bank to the account but have not yet been recorded on the books, e.g., proceeds from from a bank loan	xxxx	Add: Amounts that have been recorded on the books but have not yet been recorded by the bank, e.g., deposit in transit	xxxx
Total	$xxxx	Total	$xxxx
Subtract: Amounts that have been deducted by the bank but have not yet been recorded on the books, e.g., bank service charges	xxxx	Subtract: Amounts that have been deducted on the books but have not yet been recorded by the bank, e.g., outstanding checks	xxxx
Corrected book balance	$xxxx	Corrected bank balance	$xxxx

Managing Short-Term Resources Other Than Cash

The second half of this chapter pertains to the concepts and techniques related to the management of the short-term resources of a medical group other than cash. One of the objectives of this part is to demonstrate how each of these resources is directly related to cash and cash management. For example, the first section deals with short-term investments that are a use of cash when they are acquired and a source of cash when they are sold. This brief section is followed by a discussion of accounts receivable and some of the tools to be used in improving cash collections. The next section spends considerable time on the concepts and techniques that may be used in controlling the cash investment in supplies inventories. Tools introduced in this section are the ABC method of inventory classification, the receiving report, the perpetual inventory system, and the economic order quantity (EOQ).

The chapter closes with a discussion of management of accounts payable and claims payable. Accounts and claims payable provide temporary financing that can be rolled over from month to month if the group maintains its good credit standing.

Short-Term Investments

When the cash position is being built up to meet a large expenditure later in the year, the cash that is in excess of normal needs should be invested. Temporary excesses in the cash account can be transferred to high interest accounts or other short-term investments and returned to cash when needed. It is beyond the scope of this volume to evaluate which short-term investments are best.

From a financial control standpoint, an investment report should list:

- Each investment—showing
  - Current market value
  - Purchase and maturity value
  - Income to date
  - Yield percentage

- Total investment balance for
  - Current month
  - Previous month.

This information can be used effectively in preparing the short-term cash forecast if investments are to be liquidated within the month. If they are not, their proceeds should be included in the cash budget for the month in which they are liquidated.

Accounts Receivable from Patients

Accounts receivable are considered to be one of the most important assets by the majority of medical groups. Billings of $40,000 per month that are outstanding for an average of 90 days create a necessary, but non-interest-earning, asset of $120,000. If the collection period could be reduced by only three days, however, $4,000 would be freed for other uses. On the other hand, a slowdown in collections causing a three days' increase in the collection period would require an additional investment of $4,000 to maintain the business. It is extremely important in cash management, therefore, to control accounts receivable. The first step toward assuring the timely collection of accounts receivable is to grant credit only to private pay patients who have a responsible credit record and who also fully accept the terms granted.

The addition of a prepaid component to the group should not change any of the fundamental considerations discussed here. The amount of receivables from the prepaid component should be nominal, as the payment for the capitation is made in advance by the HMO. This prepayment accelerates the collection of cash and avoids the administrative costs of billing and collecting.

Systematically, a listing of past due accounts should be prepared and classified by appropriate collection procedure categories. The steps taken to collect the accounts and the results attained should be recorded to determine the need for follow-up. A listing of accounts written off also should be prepared showing reasons for the write-off, with both monthly and year-to-date summaries.

Reports should be developed that monitor the status of outstanding accounts for third-party payers. These reports also should list action necessary to expedite the receipt of payments. Such monitoring should include an assessment of the status of incomplete claims that the group must correct to qualify for the payment.

Statistics about bill payers are important, but there is no substitute for devoting individual attention to slow accounts, because it is people who pay bills. The following section addresses a new approach for analyzing the overall financial control of accounts receivable. Called the payments-pattern approach, it is compared with traditional methods such as the aging schedule and collection ratios.

Care should be taken to exclude prepayment revenues from the analysis, as these revenues by definition are not outstanding in the sense that revenues from fee-for-service patients are outstanding. If prepayment revenues are included, the data generated are potentially misleading in terms of how well accounts receivable are being managed.

Payments-Pattern Approach

Within the last few years a new tool has been introduced to help managers plan and monitor collection of accounts receivable. This tool is called the payments-pattern approach. The idea behind this method is demonstrated in the following example. Assume a medical group records $50,000 of fee-for-service billings in October, $40,000 in November, and $30,000 in December (to simplify the illustration, billings for prepaid service are excluded). These amounts are then collected as follows:

	Collections from October Billings	Collections from November Billings	Collections from December Billings
October	$25,000	$ 0	$ 0
November	15,000	20,000	0
December	5,000	12,000	15,000
January	2,500	4,000	9,000
February	0	2,000	3,000
March	0	0	1,500

Collections expressed as a percentage of billings are:

	Percentage of October Billings Collected	Percentage of November Billings Collected	Percentage of December Billings Collected
October	50%	0%	0%
November	30%	50%	0%
December	10%	30%	50%
January	5%	10%	30%
February	*	5%	10%
March		*	5%

*Remaining 5% written off as a bad debt.

As the data indicate, the pattern of collections for each month is identical. Once an historical collection pattern is established, this information can be used to plan and control receivables. For example, if the 50%-30%-10%-5% pattern is typical, these percentages multiplied by the billings forecasted for each of the next 12 months will provide the receipts for the cash budget. These percentages, if established over a 12-month period, can be compared with recent collection experience. This comparison will identify any control problems that have developed and require corrective action.

Another way to view the payments-pattern approach is to determine what percentage of billings from each month are uncollected and remains in accounts receivable.

	Percentage of October Billings Uncollected	Percentage of November Billings Uncollected	Percentage of December Billings Uncollected
October 31	50%	0%	0%
November 30	20%	50%	0%
December 31	10%	20%	50%
January 31	5%	10%	20%
February 28	*	5%	10%
March 31		*	5%

*Remaining 5% written off as a bad debt.

Other Accounts Receivable Control Methods

Four other methods used to provide control over the collection of fee-for-service accounts receivable are:

(1) Adjusted Collection Ratio:

$$\text{Adjusted collection ratio} = \frac{\text{Collections for the period}}{\text{Billings for the period (adjusted gross charges)}}$$

(2) Months Billings (Revenues) Outstanding:[1]

$$\text{Accounts receivable ratio} = \frac{\text{Accounts receivable/Monthly billings (annualized)}}{\text{12 months}}$$

or

$$= \frac{\text{Accounts receivable/Year-to-date billings (annualized)}}{\text{12 months}}$$

(3) Accounts Receivable Turnover:

$$\text{Accounts receivable turnover} = \frac{\text{Billings for the period (annualized)}}{\text{Accounts receivable}}$$

(4) Aging Accounts Receivable:

Age of patient receivables = Percentage of patient accounts receivable in each age category multiplied by the age category in days

[1]Also called accounts receivable ratio.

Exhibits 21-6 and 21-7 are presented to compare these traditional methods with each other and with the payments-pattern approach. It will be noted in column three of Exhibit 21-6 that collections for each month are different. This is due to the fact that the production data on which they are based also fluctuate from month to month during the year. However, the payments-pattern built into Exhibit 21-6 is a constant 50%-30%-10%-5%, with five percent written off as uncollectible. As can be observed, the traditional measures used to control accounts receivable provide misleading and conflicting information, especially when they are applied on a monthly basis. For example, the collection ratio improves when billings for the current month decrease, whereas the days billings outstanding (monthly) may worsen for the same reason. Actually, the payments pattern has neither improved nor deteriorated, because the collection pattern in this case is constant. The medical group using these traditional methods to measure accounts receivable should seriously consider the payments-pattern approach.

EXHIBIT 21-6
TRADITIONAL METHODS USED TO CONTROL ACCOUNTS RECEIVABLE

	Accounts Receivable End of Month Balance	Billings	Collections	Collection Ratio	Accounts Receivable Turnover
January	$27,140	$32,700	$29,890	91%	14.6
February	$30,450	$38,900	$33,720	87%	14.9
March	$35,375	$45,900	$39,215	85%	14.3
April	$34,905	$40,400	$39,495	98%	13.5
May	$32,965	$36,700	$37,005	101%	13.8
June	$33,375	$39,400	$37,045	94%	14.1
July	$37,270	$47,400	$41,210	87%	13.7
August	$41,955	$53,400	$46,695	87%	12.7
September	$40,790	$46,800	$46,130	99%	12.3
October	$37,940	$41,200	$42,350	103%	12.9
November	$34,440	$37,700	$38,560	102%	13.9
December	$29,150	$30,300	$32,920	109%	15.4

Patient Receivables Aging Schedule

As mentioned previously, an aging schedule that identifies patients having overdue accounts is obviously an excellent tool in managing patient accounts. It can be integrated with the best control concepts, including management by the exception.

Improved collection of cash will be accomplished through follow-up with these patients. A distortion in the age of patient receivables may arise when age is evaluated as days billings outstanding or when the aging schedule is presented as a percentage of accounts in each age category. For example, Exhibit 21-7 indicates substantial changes in percentage of patient receivables in each age category reported over a 12-month period. Actually, the data are based on the first three columns of Exhibit 21-6, which maintained a constant payments pattern of 50%-30%-10%-5% for each month. This distortion is caused by fluctuations in billings from month to month, which consequently cause fluctuations in collections and receivables from month to month. Because of this problem, it is possible for the collection pattern to deteriorate without being detected when an increase in billings more than offsets a slowdown in collections.

EXHIBIT 21-7
PATIENT RECEIVABLES AGING SCHEDULE

	Age of Patient Receivables			
	0-30 Days	31-60 Days	61-90 Days	91-120 Days
January	60%	20%	13%	7%
February	64%	22%	9%	5%
March	65%	22%	9%	4%
April	58%	26%	11%	5%
May	56%	24%	14%	6%
June	59%	22%	12%	7%
July	64%	21%	10%	5%
August	64%	23%	9%	4%
September	57%	26%	12%	5%
October	55%	25%	14%	6%
November	54%	24%	14%	8%
December	52%	26%	14%	8%

Control of Supplies Inventory

Medical groups have recognized a number of problems in controlling supplies inventory. Among the most common are:

- Too many people have authority to order supplies from vendors.
- Supplies are stored in a variety of locations resulting in duplicate and excessive stocks of similar items.
- Neither the dollar amounts nor the physicial quantities of supplies inventory is known.

- There is no formal process for charging responsibility centers with the cost of supplies used.
- There is no systematic way to identify obsolete supply items.
- There is no formal process for determining that the types and amounts of supplies ordered are received.
- The group does not know which supply items account for the largest dollar volume of inventory.

These problems add up to wasted space, unwarranted carrying costs, unknown investment in inventory, and an inability to trace the cost of supplies to users. To meet these problems, several steps may be taken by the medical group. First, one individual must have both the authority and responsibility for purchasing supplies. Second, stores of supplies should be centralized and charged out to responsibility centers as needed. The charge-out method must be simple, quick, and accurate. It also should facilitate tracing supply costs to responsibility center expense accounts in the ledger. Third, a study should be made to determine which items account for most of the dollar volume. This procedure will enable the group to put its inventory control where it will be most effective.

Inventory Control Tools

For the medical group taking steps to improve its control over supplies, several tools deserve serious consideration. Among the most common are:

The ABC classification of supplies inventory

The receiving report

The perpetual inventory system

The economic order quantity (EOQ) formula

The ABC Classification of Supplies Inventory. The ABC method classifies supplies (inventories) by their importance in terms of annual dollar usage. This is done by listing individual supply items and their annual dollar usage in descending order and then classifying them into three groups according to dollar value. Exhibit 21-8 shows a typical situation in which five percent of the supply items (Type A) accounts for 70 percent of the annual dollar usage. Because this five percent of the items has the greatest potential for savings, these items should receive the bulk of the control effort. Type C items, on the other hand, account for only 10 percent of the dollar usage and hence warrant only simple, low-cost control procedures.

EXHIBIT 21-8
ILLUSTRATION OF ABC CLASSIFICATION METHOD OF SUPPLIES INVENTORY

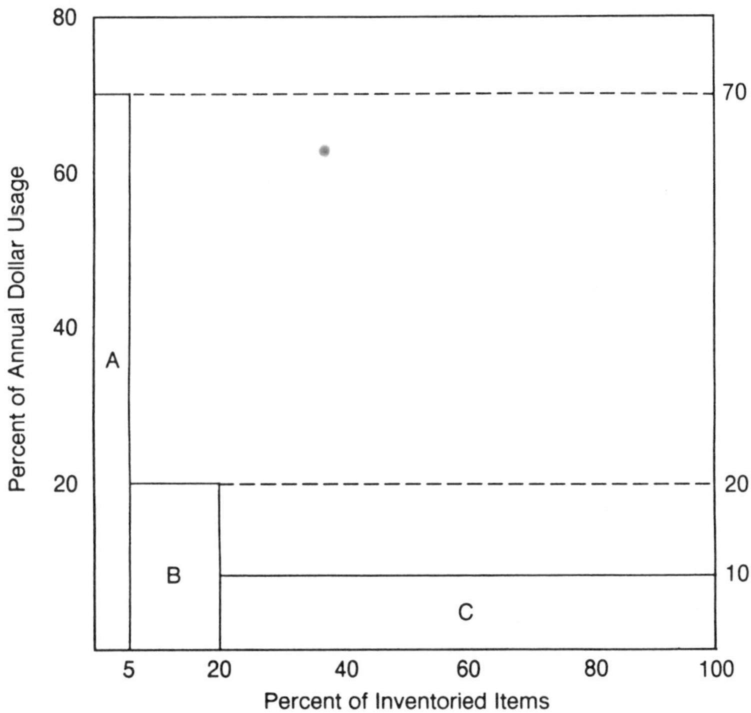

	Annual Usage	% Items	% Dollars
A Items	$100 and over	5%	70%
B Items	$50-99	15%	20%
C Items	$0-49	80%	10%

The Receiving Report. The receiving report provides the medical group with a form to compare what was received with what was ordered in terms of quantity, quality, price, and delivery date. If any of these specifications is not substantially met, without corrective action the group will not be obtaining the appropriate value for the dollars it spends on supplies. The receiving report need be no more than a hand-stamped format on the vendor's invoice or packing slip that provides appropriate specifications such as those shown in Exhibit 21-9. If a group is not using a formal receiving report, it should at least cover each point included in Exhibit 21-9 in a systematic manner.

EXHIBIT 21-9
ILLUSTRATION OF A RECEIVING REPORT

RECEIVING REPORT

Date________________ Purchase Order No.________________ Initial

	YES	NO	
Invoice compared with purchase order	( )	( )	_____
Quantity checked with invoice	( )	( )	_____
Quality as ordered	( )	( )	_____
Prices same as PO or lower	( )	( )	_____
Delivery date acceptable	( )	( )	_____
Payment terms as agreed	( )	( )	_____
Inventory placed in storeroom	( )	( )	_____
Amount recorded on inventory cards	( )	( )	_____

The Perpetual Inventory System. The perpetual inventory system maintains an up-to-date record of receipts, issues, and inventory balance for individual inventory items. To minimize clerical costs, the system must be simple, quick, and accurate. The stock control card shown in Exhibit 21-10 is a facsimile of the perpetual inventory record card currently in use in many groups. Regardless of the physical form the record takes, the information included in this exhibit is typical of what is desirable for every inventory item included in the system. The requisition for supplies by a responsibility center should be the basis for both charging the department for the supplies and updating the perpetual inventory system. Items with low unit value (Type C) should be issued in sufficient quantity (by the dozen, gross, box, etc.) to justify the cost of a perpetual record.

Although the perpetual inventory system involves significant clerical costs, it also has major advantages. Among these are:

EXHIBIT 21-10
ILLUSTRATION OF STOCK CONTROL CARD

STOCK CONTROL CARD

	Delivery Time/Wks	Unit Cost
Vender 1		
Vender 2		
Vender 3		

Order Number Vender: 1   2   3

ORDERED				RECEIVED						ISSUED				BALANCE		
DATE	PO NO	VEN	QUAN	DEPT RECP	DATE	INV NO	QUAN	UNIT COST	TOTAL COST	DATE	QUAN	DEPT REC	COST CHARGES	QUAN	UNIT COST	INVTY VALUE

Unit of Issue   Unit per Case   Reorder Level   Stockage Level

ITEM DESCRIPTION	SIZE	SHELF NUMBER	LOCAL STOCK NUMBER

- An up-to-date record of how much is invested in inventory
- A source of information to indicate items that are no longer used
- A comparison with the physical inventory that reveals the amount of theft, spoilage, or pilferage
- An accurate basis for charging responsibility centers with supplies used
- An indication of the days of supply on hand that can be determined by dividing the current balance into the past usage data.

The Economic Order Quantity (EOQ) Formula. In preparing the cash budget, the annual requirements for supplies as a whole must be determined. High dollar usage items (Type A) should receive individual attention. For example, 304 cans of anesthetic (each can containing 50 individual cartridges) are needed during a year at an invoice price of $50.00 per can. Once this requirement is established, the next question to be addressed is how many cans should be purchased at one time. If the annual needs are met by a single purchase, order costs are kept low but carrying costs over the year are high. On the other hand, if anesthetic is purchased a can at a time, order costs are extremely high but carrying costs are at a minimum. The optimum size of an order allows the total of order costs plus carrying costs to be at a minimum. If we assume that it costs $5 to place and receive an order and 24 percent of the inventory cost to carry the inventory, the data below indicate that the optimum order size is 16 cans of anesthetic.

	Size of Order in Cans					
	6	**11**	**16**	**21**	**26**	**31**
Total order costs for year	$255	$140	$ 95	$ 75	$ 60	$ 50
Total carrying costs for year	36	66	96	126	156	186
Total order and carrying costs	$291	$206	$191	$201	$216	$236

Using an order of six cans as an example, the total order costs for each order size are determined as follows:

$$\frac{\text{Annual requirement}}{\text{Size of order}} \times \text{Assumed order costs per order} = \text{Total order costs}$$

$$\frac{304}{6} = 51 \text{ (rounded from 50.67)} \times \$5 = \$255$$

Again, using an order of six cans as an example, the total carrying costs for each order size are determined as follows:

Average dollar inventory × 24% = Carrying costs per year

$$\frac{6 \times \$50}{2} = \frac{\$300}{2} \times 24\% = \$36$$

A formula is available that will provide the optimum number of units that should be purchased at any one time. It is called the economic order quantity (EOQ) formula.

$$\text{EOQ} = \sqrt{\frac{2 \times \text{Annual requirements} \times \text{Order costs per order}}{\text{Carrying costs for one unit per year}}}$$

When applied to the data in our example, the EOQ (16 boxes) is the same amount as determined above.

$$\text{EOQ} = \sqrt{\frac{2 \times 304 \times \$5}{24\% \ (\$50)}} = 16 \text{ (rounded from 15.92)}$$

Exhibit 21-11 shows these relationships graphically.

In order to apply the EOQ formula, order costs and carrying costs must be identified and quantified.

Order costs include:
- Preparation of purchase orders
- Postage and handling
- Recording purchases and payables
- Check payment costs.

Carrying costs include:
- Out-of-pocket storage costs
- Obsolescence, deterioration, theft, and pilferage
- Deterioration, or expiration, of potency-dated medicines

EXHIBIT 21-11
ECONOMIC ORDER QUANTITY CHART

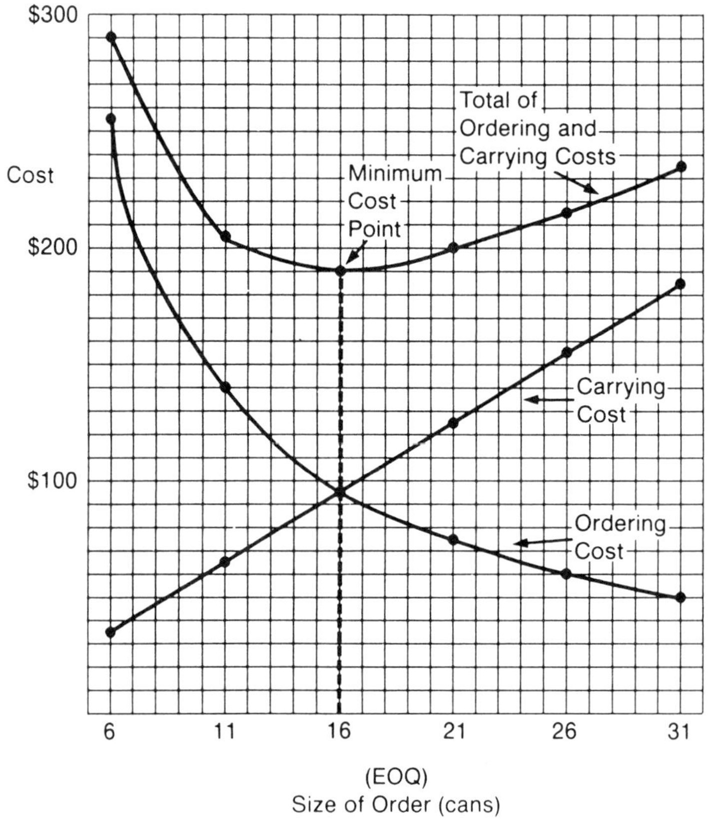

Interest costs (which may be the return foregone by having money invested in inventory)
Insurance
Property taxes.

One obvious conclusion is that for every application of EOQ, the above costs must be estimated. This conclusion reinforces the earlier statement that this method should be used only for Type A items. Results obtained from EOQ for items with usage patterns that fluctuate widely over the year may be misleading and should be used with care.

Control of Accounts Payable

The medical group that prepares a receiving report for supplies has a head start in controlling accounts payable. Bills will be paid only once, in the correct amount, and according to the terms agreed upon.

A subsidiary ledger of accounts payable should be maintained by vendor, and a tickler file by calendar days should show the names of all vendors who must be paid on a given date. This information about each account payable is essential for preparing the monthly short-term cash forecast. It also prevents the group from missing cash discounts.

As mentioned earlier in this chapter, suppliers may honor requests for a given billing date. By this method it is possible to keep payments from bunching up. Another possibility to explore with vendors is a discount for paying cash at the time of purchase rather than being billed at a later date. Discounts of up to five percent are sometimes obtained.

Control of Claims Payable

Control of health care services required by prepaid plan members and performed outside the group can be accomplished by assigning each prepaid plan patient to a primary care physician who acts as "gatekeeper" for access to the health care delivery system and by using preprinted and appropriately signed forms for referral services and hospital admissions. The forms typically are signed by the primary care physician. In a number of groups the authorization is not complete until the medical director countersigns the approval given by the primary care physician. The forms are normally multiple-copy, with the original and a copy sent to the referral physician who, in turn, returns the copy with a written report. A second copy is sent to the claims management department where it is held as an open claim in a tickler file. Most groups implementing this control do not pay the claim until both the claim and the report on the services rendered are received from the referral physician.

Most groups have either the medical director or the primary care physician review the claim in at least a cursory fashion. All claims are normally scrutinized by a clerk who ascertains, at a minimum, that the claim was authorized, the price charged is reasonable, and that all services billed are appropriate for the facts and circumstances.

A more extensive discussion of control of claims payable follows in Chapter 22.

Summary

In this chapter, the management and control of cash and other short-term resources were emphasized. Unless the group maintains an excessive amount of cash, it must have a reasonably accurate picture of both the amount and timing of expected cash flows and their relation to the acquisition and disposition of other short-term resources.

Chapter 21 began with two major tools of day-to-day cash management: first, the short-term cash plan that schedules the planned cash inflows and outflows for the immediate future—by day for the current week and by week for the remainder of the month; second, the daily cash report that monitors the actual cash position by showing the amount in each bank account and a summary of the cash activity for the day. This section was followed by concepts and techniques used to achieve the objective of strong internal control over cash. Cash management controls introduced were the bank reconciliation and an internal control checklist.

The second half of the chapter concentrated on the management of short-term resources other than cash. A brief section listed the information needed by management with respect to the group's current holdings of marketable securities. This was followed by financial planning and control tools used to manage patient receivables. When billings fluctuate from month to month, the payments-pattern approach provides a better measure of the overall effectiveness of collecting patient receivables than traditional methods.

Four inventory control tools were examined briefly: the ABC system, the perpetual inventory system, the receiving report, and the EOQ formula. The ABC method classifies purchased supplies into three annual-dollar-usage categories and thus indicates where control effort should be placed. A perpetual inventory system should be used for items that account for a high dollar volume because its advantages in these instances outweigh clerical costs. Receiving reports should be used to ensure that the medical group is actually receiving what it has ordered and on the terms established with its vendor. The EOQ formula may be used to determine the optimum order quantity for large dollar volume items that exhibit a stable usage pattern over the year.

The final section of the chapter presented a discussion of the management of accounts and claims payable.

Chapter 22

Estimating Claims Outstanding

It is a rare medical group that can provide within the group all of the services that it is committed to provide through its agreement with an HMO. The medical group must, then, arrange for the needed services outside of the group. Two general problems tend to arise when services are purchased outside of the group:

(1) Exerting adequate control over the outside services

(2) Estimating the financial liability of the medical group for the outside services rendered.

Reliable data on the experience of the medical group, and all other health care providers included in the HMO program, is vital to monitoring ongoing operations. An important factor in obtaining reliable experiential data is a valid and consistent method for estimating the claims outstanding.

The illustrations in the remainder of this chapter are based on examples contained in *Actuarial Issues in the Fee-for-Service/ Prepaid Medical Group*, a monograph in the *Going Prepaid* series.[1]

Accrual Basis

Premiums are paid by employers to the HMO, which, by contract, covers all necessary health care services provided to the enrolled employees and dependents on an accrual basis during the period of the contract. The accrual basis means that the HMO has a contractual obligation for all qualified services rendered during the contract period even if the claim is presented after the time period is past. The medical group that has a capitation arrangement with the HMO to provide some or all of the services is in a similar position. Thus, it is

[1]*Actuarial Issues in the Fee-for-Service/Prepaid Medical Group,* Center for Research in Ambulatory Health Care Administration, Denver, Colorado, 1983.

important for both the medical group and the HMO, preferably at the end of each month but at least quarterly, to make accurate estimates of all potential liabilities resulting from the provision of health care services.

In brief, an estimate of health service expenses or claims outstanding "incurred but not reported" (IBNR) is one of the accounting means of adjusting from a cash to an accrual basis. Hospitals, physicians, and patients frequently take lengthy periods of time to submit bills for services to the HMO for reimbursement. In the case of a prepaid medical group, which usually is on a total capitation basis for all medical services, the bills from referral physicians (which are the medical group's financial responsibility) may similarly lag a number of weeks (or even months) in being received and processed for payment and entered into the accounting system of either the HMO or the medical group, depending on processing responsibility.

Exhibit 22-1 illustrates the time lag involved in receiving and processing claims for medical services. It displays the physician referral bills processed and paid in the month of March 19X5 by the medical group. It is important to note that in the example it takes eight months for all bills from outside physicians to be received. Once the referral physicians are used to the payment mechanism, the lag between the service date and the submission of a claim may shorten.

EXHIBIT 22-1

REFERRAL COSTS: ANALYSIS OF CLAIMS RECEIVED/PAID MARCH 19X5

Month of Incurral[1]	
March	$ 9,551
February	9,829
January	1,959
December	1,360
November	1,082
October	165
September	410
August	702
Total claims processed in March	$25,058

[1]Month that service was actually provided.

Nonstatistical Method

A nonstatistical method of estimating the outstanding claims liability is workable until the volume of claims is large enough to be more effectively estimated by the use of summary data generated by a computer. The manual methods usually use either copies of forms (referral and hospital admission), logs of activity such as inpatient admissions, or telephonic confirmations with key providers such as a hospital. The units of service indicated are multiplied by the standard costs for the more common referrals and admissions to arrive at an estimate of the financial liability for those claims not yet received. Frequently, several methods of estimating claims are employed at the same time so that the results from one method can be validated by another.

Exhibits 22-2 and 22-3 are examples of a referral form and hospital log headings, respectively. The log in Exhibit 22-3 should be set up in such a manner that claims not yet received are readily apparent. The copy of the referral form in Exhibit 22-2 would be maintained in a claims payable tickler file until the actual claim is received. At month end the forms in the claims tickler file would be the starting point for estimating the claims liability for referral services.

EXHIBIT 22-2
SAMPLE REFERRAL FORM—BEST MEDICAL CENTER

---

1. Patient Name ____________________ 3. Date ________________

2. Identification Number ______________

4. Referred to ______________________
____
____

5. For ________ Consultation Only
________ Treatment Only
________ Other

6. Scheduled Date of Appointment ____________

7. Description of Problem ______________________________________
____
____

8. The following test results are available ______ Laboratory
______ X-ray
______ Other

EXHIBIT 22-2 (continued)

9. Note: a. The referral is for one visit only.
   b. All laboratory and radiology tests must be performed within Best Medical Center.
   c. No further referrals are possible without the written approval of the medical director.

10. Signed by

____
Primary Care Physician

____
Medical Director

Distribution of copies:
Original - Referral Physician
Copy 1 - Referral Physician - Return with report
Copy 2 - Claims Tickler File

EXHIBIT 22-3
SAMPLE HOSPITAL LOG HEADINGS

Patient Name	Date Admitted	Date Discharged	Admitting Diagnosis	Admitting Physician

Expected Length of Stay	Name of Hospital	Date Claim Received	Actual Amount of Claim	Estimated Amount of Claim

Statistical Method

The time lags vary substantially between HMO programs and could vary significantly for affiliated medical groups, depending on the closeness of their relationships to referring physicians. Emergency referrals will also occur. These must also be considered in estimating liabilities.

Conceptually, it is important to understand the difference between the HMO's liabilities and the medical group's liabilities where the medical group has contracted with the HMO to provide all medical services for patients assigned to the group. Since the HMO has contracted with the medical group on a capitation basis, it normally has no liability for these services. Therefore, the HMO financial statements will not have pending or unreported medical services claims other than any unpaid capitations. The medical group, on the other hand, may have substantial liability for outside referrals already authorized and performed but for which no payment has been made. The medical group must include an estimate of these liabilities to reconcile its actual operating expenses with the capitations received. Since many medical groups operate their fee-for-service practices on a cash basis comparing cash income to operating expenses (and generally have no liability for referrals), the change of situation with the prepaid environment must be carefully considered. For the medical group, prepaid income is handled on an accrual basis, but expenses paid (unless adjusted) may still be handled on a cash basis. It is very important for the medical group to estimate its referral claim liabilities on its monthly operating statements to protect the medical group's financial viability.

In terms of limiting the HMO's risk, a case could be made for it to retain a portion of the medical group's monthly capitation to accrue for the group's IBNR claims. This protection device is one about which the medical group and the HMO need advice and counsel.

The size of the liabilities of the medical group can vary substantially depending on the specialty makeup of the group. For a primary care group which is on a total capitation arrangement, referral physician costs may amount to 50 percent or more of the capitation revenue. Thus, accruing liabilities accurately is critical. For a large multispecialty group with minimum outside referrals, referral revenue could be 10 percent or less of its total capitation revenue and, in the short range, not important to the financial well-being of the group.

A detailed statistical analysis and explanation of methods to develop estimates of IBNR claim liabilities is beyond the scope of this text. However, a number of simple examples will give the medical group manager an understanding of the concepts involved and some idea of the importance of accurate accruals of liabilities as they may apply to the medical group and its sponsoring HMO.

Examples of Data and Estimating Methods

Exhibits 22-4 through 22-7 are examples of the typical lag involved in receipt by a medical group of claims from referral physicians where the group is financially liable. As noted, this lag varies considerably by plan.

Exhibit 22-4 illustrates the typical triangular lag table generally used in evaluating claim liabilities by insurers and HMOs. The table depicts the actual claims received and paid by month of incurral, that is, the month in which the service is actually provided and the expense incurred. The column under the month of March is the same as the dollars shown in Exhibit 22-1. Exhibit 22-4 shows that for referral expenses incurred in August, $4,302 was paid in August, $6,355 was paid in September, $1,613 was paid in October, etc.

Exhibit 22-5 shows the numbers included in Exhibit 22-4 on a cumulative basis. For example, for referral claims incurred in August, $4,302 was received and paid in August; by the end of September, $10,657 had been received and paid during the two-month period ($4,302 + $6,355). At the bottom of each column is the sum of the dollars received or paid from the top of the table to the last month of claim processing. As noted, there is a second sum that is the total from the top to the bottom of the column, excluding the last month. These sums will be related between columns to produce a statistical estimate of the lag patterns.

In Exhibit 22-6, the ratios of the "a" total for each column to the "b" total of the following column (from Exhibit 22-5) are used to determine the percentage of claims paid during each month related to the cumulative amount paid one month later. These ratios are accumulated from the end of the table forward to produce estimates of the lag factors or completion factors for each month from the date of incurral.

In Exhibit 22-7, the final estimate of incurred claims is calculated together with the total estimated incurred but not reported claims. The IBNR is the difference between the incurred claim estimates and the cash claims paid to date. The lag or accrual factors are divided into the paid claims to produce the incurred estimate. This computation is sometimes called the completion method.

The last column in Exhibit 22-7 converts the dollar claims into expense per member per month. This experienced claim cost per member month might be compared with the estimated referral budget. At the end of the eight months in the exhibit (as of the end of May), it is estimated that the claim liabilities are approximately 25 percent of the claims paid. If this amount is not included in the medical group's year-end reconcilation, the group may well negotiate a referral capitation that is lower than its actual accrued expenses. It might also be noted that the trend in referral expenses seems to be slightly up, although the May month in the exhibit is certainly the figure with the least statistical validity due to possible short-term fluctuations in claims processing.

EXHIBIT 22-4
REFERRAL COSTS: CLAIMS BY MONTH OF INCURRAL AND MONTH PAID

Month of	Month in Which Claims Were Paid									
Incurral	August	September	October	November	December	January	February	March	April	May
August	$4,302	$6,355	$1,613	$ 428	$ 467	$ 481	$ 236	$ 702	$ —	$ —
September		5,242	4,752	510	478	705	152	410	—	22
October			6,409	4,876	708	3,322	136	165	—	108
November				5,364	5,626	2,520	257	1,082	655	190
December					4,894	6,807	3,014	1,360	585	86
January						9,409	6,856	1,959	3,205	1,093
February							6,473	9,829	2,809	744
March								9,551	7,739	2,075
April									7,686	6,839
May										11,427

EXHIBIT 22-5

REFERRAL COSTS: CUMULATIVE CLAIMS RECEIVED/PAID BY MONTH OF INCURRAL

Month of Incurral	Month of Incurral	1 Month Following	2 Months Following	3 Months Following	4 Months Following	5 Months Following	6 Months Following	7 Months Following	8 Months Following
August	$ 4,302	$ 10,657	$ 12,270	$ 12,698	$13,165	$13,646	$13,882	$14,584	$14,584
September	5,242	9,994	10,504	10,982	11,687	11,839	12,249	12,249	12,271
October	6,409	11,285	11,993	15,315	15,451	15,616	15,616	15,724	
November	5,364	10,990	13,510	13,767	14,849	15,504	15,694		$14,584[1] $26,855[2]
December	4,894	11,701	14,715	16,075	16,660	16,746		$26,833[1] $42,577[2]	
January	9,409	16,265	18,224	21,429	22,522		$41,749[1] $57,441[2]		
February	6,473	16,302	19,111	19,855		$56,605[1] $73,351[2]			
March	9,551	17,290	19,365		$71,812[1] $94,334[2]				
April	7,686	14,525		$90,266[1] $110,121[2]					
May	11,427		$100,327[1] $119,692[2]						
		$104,484[1] $119,009[2]							
	$59,330[1] $70,757[2]								

[1]Sum August through April, etc.
[2]Sum August through May.

EXHIBIT 22-6

REFERRAL COSTS: ESTIMATE OF CLAIMS RECEIVED/PAID AS PERCENTAGE OF TOTAL INCURRED BY DURATION

	Month of Incurral	1 Month Following	2 Months Following	3 Months Following	4 Months Following	5 Months Following	6 Months Following	7 Months Following	8 Months Following
Claims received	$59,330[1]	$104,484	$100,327	$90,266	$71,812	$56,605	$41,749	$26,833	$14,584
Claims received following month	$119,009[2]	$119,692	$110,121	$94,334	$73,351	$57,441	$42,577	$26,855	$14,589
Percentage	49.9[3]	87.3	91.1	95.7	97.9	98.5	98.1	99.9	100.0
Percentage	35.9[4]	71.9	82.4	90.4	94.5	96.5	98.0	99.9	100.0

[1] Exhibit 22-5, Column 1, footnote 1

[2] Exhibit 22-5, Column 2, footnote 2

[3] Ratio of footnote 1 divided by footnote 2 in Percentage

[4] Cumulative ratio in Percentage, e.g., 35.9 = 71.9 × 49.9

EXHIBIT 22-7
REFERRAL COSTS: ESTIMATE OF GROSS INCURRED REFERRAL LIABILITY

Month of Incurral	Cash Claims To Date	Accrual Factor	Estimates Incurred	Number of Members	Capitated Expense
October	$ 15,724[1]	.999	$ 15,740	5,940	$2.65
November	15,694	.980	16,014	6,200	2.58
December	16,746	.965	17,353	6,500	2.67
January	22,522	.945	23,833	8,100	2.94
February	19,855	.904	21,963	8,250	2.66
March	19,365	.824	23,501	8,250	2.85
April	14,525	.719	20,202	8,450	2.39
May	11,427	.359	31,831[2]	9,750	3.26
	$135,858		$170,391[3]	61,440	$2.77

Note: August and September are assumed to be complete and omitted from table.

[1]Exhibit 22-5: October—7 months following cumulative
[2] 31,831 = 11,427/.359
[3]Estimated claims liability is $170,391 – $135,858 = $34,533 or 25.4% of cash claims paid to date.

Summary

Claims liability needs to be estimated monthly or at least quarterly. A nonstatistical method of estimation may be used as long as the volume of claims is not too cumbersome. A statistical method is more efficient at some point in the prepaid practice's growth. An example of each method was given.

The statistical method shown is only one of many statistical analyses that could be used to make estimates of claim liabilities. It should be noted that the statistical system should be able to completely reconcile the emerged liability after the fact by following similar tables to the end on a continual basis.

During the first year or two of prepaid operations, or with a low number of prepaid plan patients, there can be severe fluctuations in the lag factors, and results can be distorted by a few large bills. Nevertheless, a reasonable estimate must be made of the extent of incurred but not reported claims.

Chapter 23

Short-Range Decisions

Decisions made by a medical group, or any other type of business, can be judged efficient if the benefits arising from the decisions exceed the costs of the decisions. It is important that a medical group be able to identify, measure, and compare the benefits and costs attributable to particular kinds of decisions.

The decisions facing a medical group fall into two general classifications—long-range decisions, involving addition or replacement of capacity, and short-range decisions involving the use of existing capacity. The information needs and decision criteria for long-range decisions are different from those for short-range decisions.

The most common short-range decisions include: What fees should be charged? What procedures should be performed? What volume of services should be provided? Because these activities recur each month, the group tends to perform much as it did in the previous period and considers a change only when necessary. Other short-range decisions do not recur every month and involve a potentially sizeable financial commitment. An example, when providing care on a prepaid basis, is deciding whether to provide a needed service within the group or purchase it outside the group.

Different Information for Different Decisions

To make any decision, the decision-maker needs to know the relevant benefits and costs of each alternative. A relevant benefit is the change in revenue directly attributable to a decision. A relevant cost is the change in costs directly attributable to a decision. Benefits and costs that are relevant to one decision will not necessarily be relevant to another decision. Different classifications of costs have been developed to explain the ways that costs change as a result of different decisions. Several concepts of cost have been identified in this text, particularly in Part II, *Cost Accounting for Prepaid Medical Groups*. Three concepts of cost are used in this chapter when illustrating short-term decisions: fixed and variable costs, avoidable costs, and full costs. All have one characteristic in common, namely, relevance to the specific decision under consideration.

Fixed and Variable Costs

For many decisions, such as those involving volume and mix of services, the group must know which costs will change with changes in activity. Here, the concept of fixed and variable costs is important. Variable costs are costs that change as activity changes and include such items as medical supply costs and laboratory costs. Fixed costs, on the other hand, are costs that do not change as activity changes. Fixed costs are often called capacity costs and include such expenses as rent, insurance, property taxes, and administrative salaries.

Because a change in activity will change both revenues and variable costs, a quick and simple measure of the change in profit resulting from a change in activity is called the contribution margin (revenue less variable costs). For those decisions that involve a change in activity, the measurement of contribution margin provides a criterion for evaluating the decision. Assuming that fixed costs do not change, the group should select the alternative that will maximize contribution margin.

The concept of fixed and variable costs is useful in assessing when an activity will reach the break-even point; in deciding whether to perform a procedure, such as a lab procedure, inhouse or purchase it outside; and in making a wide range of decisions involving changes in activity.

Avoidable Costs

Another classification of costs relevant to some short-range decisions is avoidable costs. When an activity, such as a laboratory, is discontinued, some costs will be eliminated or avoided. While fixed costs are generally considered irrelevant for most short-range decisions, any costs, including fixed costs, that would change as a result of a decision are relevant to that decision. As an example of avoidable costs, assume a medical group is considering eliminating its own laboratory and purchasing its laboratory services from a reference laboratory. If equipment for the inhouse laboratory is rented on a cancellable lease, the equipment rent expenses would be avoided and the avoidable cost is relevant to the decision. The rental cost of space occupied by the laboratory would not decrease and is therefore not an avoidable cost.

Full Costs

In Part II, the process of determining the full cost of a responsibility center or procedure was explained and illustrated. The full cost of a procedure includes both the direct costs traceable to the procedure, such as lab services, and a fair share of all indirect costs that cannot be traced and therefore must be allocated to the procedure. The full cost of a procedure is useful as an aid in setting fees. Because full cost is not a good measure of the effect of changes on total costs, the concept of full cost is of limited use in short-range decisions.

Illustrations of Short-Range Decisions

In this section, several types of short-range decisions will be illustrated using the concepts introduced briefly in the previous section of this chapter. The situations presented are not intended to fully encompass all short-term decisions made in medical groups but rather to provide examples of different types of short-range decisions made by medical groups.

Break-even Analysis

If a decision involves changes in activity, the concept of fixed and variable costs is relevant. In Chapter 10, identification of fixed and variable costs was discussed and three approaches to cost behavior identification were illustrated. Using the scattergraph approach, the following flexible budget for a laboratory was developed.

$$TC = \$8{,}500 + \$2.80(x)$$

TC is total cost and (x) represents the number of laboratory tests performed. Monthly fixed costs are $8,500. Each laboratory test will require $2.80 in variable costs, leaving a contribution margin of $3.20 if laboratory fees average $6.00 per test. To reach the break-even point, sufficient revenue must be generated to cover both fixed costs and variable costs. Each laboratory test will produce $3.20 of contribution margin to cover fixed costs and provide income. The break-even point is determined by dividing the $8,500 of fixed costs by the $3.20 of contribution margin. As shown below, the laboratory must produce 2,656 tests each month to cover all costs, or break even.

$$\text{Break-even point} = \frac{\text{Fixed costs}}{\text{Contribution margin per test}}$$

$$= \frac{\$8{,}500}{\$3.20} = 2{,}656 \text{ laboratory tests}$$

If the physician-owners were to decide that the laboratory should be providing $1,000 per month for administrative services performed by the group, in addition to covering the direct costs of the laboratory, the break-even point would be determined as follows.

$$\text{Break-even point} = \frac{\text{Fixed costs} + \text{Allocated costs}}{\text{Contribution margin per unit}}$$

$$= \frac{\$8,500 + \$1,000}{\$3.20} = 2,969 \text{ laboratory tests}$$

In order for the laboratory to meet the desired objective of management, it must now produce 2,969 tests each month.

Through break-even analysis it is also possible to test the impact of anticipated changes in costs or fees to determine the volume necessary to achieve the objectives of management. It is particularly useful in assessing the volume needed to cover the incremental costs of going prepaid.

Adding a Physician

Another area of decision making where break-even analysis (or cost-volume-profit analysis) is frequently (often only informally) applied is in the decision to add a physician in order to avoid outside referrals for services to prepaid patients. If additional facilities and equipment are required, the decision should be evaluated by long-range decision techniques which include consideration of the time value of money as well as incremental revenues and costs.

Earlier in this text (Chapter 19), projections of prepaid plan enrollment and resulting patient visits were prepared for Best Medical Center. Assume that Best Medical Center wants to determine when to add a general surgeon to the group.

There are a number of policy questions that must be answered before the financial implications of the decision are considered. These deal with such issues as: Does the group wish to remain a primary care group? Will any new physician serve fee-for-service patients as well as prepaid patients? What impact will the addition of specialists, such as surgeons, have on the income distribution formula? After the most basic policy issues are answered, the group may consider the financial issues.

The decision framework would include the incremental revenues and incremental costs, which are determined from the membership and utilization projections. The group should determine the point at which capitation revenue for general surgery will exceed the cost of maintaining a general surgeon. Assuming the following costs, the break-even point for adding a surgeon will be reached between the twelfth and fifteenth months.

Costs of general surgeon:	
Salary and benefits	$ 8,333 per month
Support staff and benefits	2,880 per month
Equipment rental	200 per month
Professional liability insurance	500 per month

Space (1,500 sq. ft. x $1.50 per month)	2,250 per month
Total costs	$14,163 per month
Supplies and other variable expenses	$5 per patient visit

The flexible budget for the cost of a general surgeon is determined to be $14,163 per month plus $5 per patient visit. The revenue of the general surgeon will be the portion of the monthly capitation payment that is for general surgery. Assume that $3.44 of the monthly capitation payment per member is for surgery.

Enrollment projections, surgery patient visits (now referred out), incremental costs, and incremental revenues are presented for selected months in Exhibit 23-1.

EXHIBIT 23-1
ANALYSIS OF WHEN TO ADD A DOCTOR
BEST MEDICAL CENTER

Month	Enrolled Members	Surgery Patient Visits	Incremental Costs	Incremental Revenues
1	130	1	$14,168	$ 447
3	328	4	14,183	1,128
6	1,875	21	14,268	6,450
9	2,590	30	14,313	8,910
12	3,850	44	14,383	13,244
15	5,330	61	14,468	18,335

The incremental revenues will cover the incremental costs in about the thirteenth month. This conclusion is based upon a number of assumptions including: there will be no change in the "gatekeeper" role of the primary care physician, utilization rates will continue as projected, and enrollment projections will be reached.

Break-even analysis provided the decision framework for this decision. While the reader may argue with the specific numbers in the illustration, the decision framework is sound. The importance of accurate planning and projections cannot be overemphasized.

Dropping an Activity
In this section it is assumed that the group opened a satellite clinic in anticipation of member growth in a particular geographic area. It is also assumed that the satellite clinic has been unprofitable and the group is asking, "How much will the group save by eliminating the unprofitable satellite clinic?"

The most recent operating statement for the satellite clinic is presented in Exhibit 23-2. The satellite clinic has shown a loss since it was opened. The combination of increased competition from other medical groups, a downturn in the economy of the area, and the inability to provide proper supervision of the clinic—all contributed to the loss. It is doubtful that the satellite clinic could produce additional revenue without substantial additional resources.

EXHIBIT 23-2
OPERATING STATEMENT FOR SATELLITE CLINIC
Current Month

Revenues		$12,000
Operating expenses:		
Associate physician's salary	$4,000	
Associate physician's benefits	800	
Staff salaries	2,400	
Staff benefits	280	
Lab and x-ray services	3,000	
Supplies	1,200	
Occupancy	1,400	
Administrative services for main clinic	1,000	$14,080
Net loss		$ (2,080)

Although the concept of fixed and variable costs is useful in this situation, it is not sufficient. The group must know which costs will be avoided if the satellite clinic is closed and which costs will continue.

The associate physician is on a contract that is dependent upon the continuation of the satellite clinic. The staff is assumed to be working on an hourly basis, only as needed. Space is rented on a five-year noncancellable lease. The best the group can do with the space is to sublease it for $1,000 per month, thereby losing $400 per month in rent. The administrative services represent allocated costs from the main clinic. Closing the satellite clinic will have little, if any, effect on administrative costs. Exhibit 23-3 identifies the avoidable and unavoidable costs of closing the satellite clinic. The exhibit shows that $12,680 of the $14,080 total costs are avoidable and $1,400 would continue if the satellite clinic is closed.

EXHIBIT 23-3

ILLUSTRATION OF AVOIDABLE COSTS RELEVANT TO DECISION TO CLOSE SATELLITE CLINIC

Type of Expense	Fixed or Variable	Monthly Costs	Avoidable Costs	Unavoidable Costs
Associate physician's salary	Fixed	$ 4,000	$ 4,000	
Associate physician's benefits	Fixed	800	800	
Staff salaries	Variable	2,400	2,400	
Staff benefits	Variable	280	280	
Lab and x-ray services	Variable	3,000	3,000	
Supplies	Variable	1,200	1,200	
Occupancy	Fixed	1,400	1,000	$ 400
Administrative services	Fixed	1,000		1,000
Total		$14,080	$12,680	$1,400

The effect of closing the satellite clinic can now be determined as follows:

Decrease in revenues	$12,000
Decrease in costs	$12,680
Savings by closing satellite clinic	$680

At this level of activity, the group will save $680 per month by closing the clinic. The group now knows that continuing the clinic is costing at least $680 per month. The $1,400 of unavoidable costs will continue regardless of what the group decides to do with the satellite clinic.

The relevant data in this example are revenues, variable costs, and avoidable fixed costs. Variable costs should always be avoidable in a decision of this nature. The occupancy and administrative costs that continue are unavoidable and therefore irrelevant to this decision.

The data in this example may suggest other decision possibilities, such as reducing costs or changing staff. These decisions will require cost concepts other than avoidable and unavoidable costs.

Setting Fees

Until recently, many medical groups set fees based on the going market rate or on what other physicians in the area were charging. Fee increases generally occurred whenever costs increased in the group. While such approaches may have provided satisfactory results in the past, the ability of medical groups to continue setting fees in this manner is becoming less possible as patients become more sensitive to fee increases, as public law regarding allowable maximum fees are enacted, and as competition among medical groups increases.

The full cost of a procedure is a useful concept of cost as an aid in setting fees. To determine cost-based fees for services provided, the group must be able to establish the full cost of each procedure or class of procedure, including direct costs of each procedure or procedure class and a fair portion of allocated costs. Because of fluctuations in the mix of services and number of procedures performed from month to month, quarterly or annual costs, rather than monthly costs, provide a better basis for measuring the full costs of procedures.

The mechanics of determining the full cost per procedure or patient visit were illustrated in Chapter 14. The cost per patient visit for the four specialties and two ancillary responsibility centers were as follows:

Family practice	$21.83
Pediatrics	$26.05
Internal medicine	$21.88
Obstetrics/gynecology	$40.29
Laboratory	$ 3.74
X-ray	$18.33

Based on these costs per patient visit, the cost per member per month for physician services provided to prepaid patients was determined to be $9.95.

The costs may be based on historic or projected data. The fees, however, must be sufficient to cover future costs. If the cost per member per month is based upon historic costs, this cost must be adjusted for anticipated changes in utilization and inflation.

By adjusting past costs for expected increases, fees can be compared with expected costs of each procedure class. The result should be more equitable fee adjustments based on expected actual costs. Of course, the group must also determine that the resulting cost-based fees are acceptable in the market. If actual costs for any or all procedures greatly exceed the fees being charged by other groups in the area, the medical group should evaluate the efficiency of its operations before fee adjustments are considered. Some questions that might be asked include: Are buying habits for supplies leading to higher costs? Are laboratory services purchased at comparative prices? Is the group efficiently using its human and physical resources?

Establishing a Capitation Rate

A medical group providing care to patients who are members of an HMO or other prepaid plan is typically paid a capitation (a fixed amount per prepaid plan member per month) to cover the cost of services rendered by the medical group and usually all outside referral services. The monthly capitation may include emergency room care and normally does not include hospital inpatient care.

In some instances the medical group also will assume responsibility for hospital inpatient costs as part of its capitation contract. The accounting for the capitation for hospital inpatient costs is normally kept separate from the capitation for the range of medical group services. The capitation for the range of physician services is typically based on something less than 100 percent of the fee-for-service equivalent value (usually 85-95 percent) because of certain financial advantages accruing to the clinic out of the arrangement with the prepaid plan.

Financial advantages of capitation include the following:

- Payment is typically made by the prepaid plan to the medical group by the middle of the month. On the average, the group receives payment two months or more earlier than if the group has to bill the individual patients for services rendered. This prepayment represents a significant cash flow advantage to the group which may be expressed in terms of several months' interest at the prime rate.

- Billing is eliminated for any services rendered to prepaid patients, unless the medical group is responsible for collecting any copayments payable by prepaid patients that were not collected at the time of service. The group will not incur bad debts with respect to prepaid plan patients, except perhaps with regard to copayments. Copayments for medical group prepaid services are usually nominal—for example, $3.00 or $5.00 per clinic visit—and billing costs and bad debt problems can be minimized by collecting the copayment at the point of service. If the medical group must bill for the copayment, the prepaid plan could allow the group to charge an additional billing fee to cover the costs related to billing and collection of copayments. Computation of the prepaid plan's total capitation payment to the medical group should be reduced to reflect the overall bad debt rates experienced on fee-for-service business—typically three percent to seven percent.

A careful analysis of the projected cost of prepaid health care services is an essential part of evaluating the impact on the contracting medical group. Cost analysis helps to establish the capitation paid to the medical group for the delivery of prepaid services or can be used to evaluate the capitation proposal of an HMO or umbrella organization with which the group contracts. Cost analysis covers certain parameters of operation—including utilization of health care services and fee levels or cost per unit of health care service—within which the medical group must operate if the prepaid venture is to be successful on a long-term basis.

The medical group must determine to its satisfaction that it can operate a prepaid mode within the parameters established by the prepaid plan's cost assumptions. Making this decision requires input from an actuary or competent financial consultant who can assist the fee-for-service medical group with an analysis of its existing group patterns, inform it regarding the operational experience of other prepaid plans, and review any changes that must take place in the delivery of health care services to make the prepaid component successful.

There are at least two methods used to establish capitation payments for services rendered by the medical group and by referrals outside the medical group. These methods are called:

(1) Fee-for-service or actuarial method

(2) Cost or budgetary method.

A combination of the two methods also may be used. Following is a brief description of each method.

Fee-for-Service Method. The fee-for-service method bases the capitation payment for prepaid services rendered by the medical group or by referral physicians on the fee-for-service equivalent charges for all covered services. The variables involved include the frequency of services rendered per prepaid patient per year and the fee-for-service charge equivalents for those services derived from the medical group's or other providers' fee schedules. If the group lacks good cost data or if the prepaid component is small, this method should provide a capitation rate that approaches the contribution revenue of similar fee-for-service practices. It is important that the medical group has available monthly and year-to-date summaries of fee-for-service charge equivalents for medical care services rendered to prepaid plan members for negotiating purposes.

Cost Method. There are several approaches to projecting costs for developing capitation rates. They range from a marginal or incremental cost approach to a full cost approach. The medical group may want to analyze its true incremental costs of providing services to a large number of prepaid plan members (for example, 10,000) based on staffing requirements, supply and equipment costs, and additional facilities expenses. If the medical group's fee-for-service revenues are covering costs of operation and providing a desired level of profit (and assuming that the group can add physicians as needed to render services to prepaid members without expanding facilities), then something less than 100 percent of the fee-for-service equivalent of charges will be adequate to cover the incremental costs of rendering services to prepaid plan members. The capitation amount may be reduced, because revenue from the prepaid plan will not be required to cover certain fixed costs, or because fixed cost coverage requirements change with the increase in patient population realized through the prepaid plan.

Another cost approach (sometimes called the budgetary method) projects prepaid costs by analyzing prepaid demand for health care services and translating this demand into terms such as the number of full-time-equivalent physicians (or laboratory technicians, x-ray technicians, medical records staff, etc.) required per 1,000 prepaid members. This method is used when the group lacks good cost data on the cost per member per month for the prepaid practice.

Separate measures of demand are established for each specialty. The demand measures define the staffing requirements for physicians and other health care personnel for the prepaid plan. The staffing requirements can be combined with an average cost per physician (including base compensation, fringe benefits, malpractice premiums, education allowances, etc.) to determine the cost of physician services. Additional provision is made for the medical group's support staff, laboratory and x-ray services, supplies, equipment, and occupancy. The costs for some of these factors may be determined using a procedure analogous to fee-for-service equivalent charges.

An illustrative calculation of a prepaid capitation rate for medical group services using the budgetary method is outlined in Exhibit 23-4. The key underlying basis of the budgetary method is the productivity level of health care personnel (particularly physicians) and the utilization patterns of prepaid members. For example, an assumed utilization rate of three primary care physician office visits per prepaid member per year and an assumed productivity rate of 5,000 office visits per primary care physician translates into the need for one primary care physician per 1,667 prepaid members (5,000/3). This need is equivalent to .6 physicians per 1,000 members, which may be further split among family practice, pediatrics, obstetrics/gynecology, and internal medicine physicians. Depending on the medical group's delivery system for surgical specialties, productivity estimates should consider allocation of time to hospital and clinic settings.

The capitation for a medical service category depends on a combination of two variables—frequency of utilization per member per year and average cost per unit of service. A capitation cost factor, or cost per member per month, is the product of the annual frequency and average charge divided by 12. Such factors must be developed for each of the service categories. Once determined, these factors are used to develop a capitation cost schedule.

Once the prepaid practice comprises more than 25 percent of the medical group's patient population, a more detailed cost study should be considered for arriving at the capitation payment. This study should be designed to accurately determine the medical group's expenses associated with the delivery of health care services to both the fee-for-service and prepaid populations—and indeed each section of the prepaid population (employer group, Medicare, Medicaid, private pay individuals, etc.). A capitation could be better defined in terms of these actual expenses. Such a cost study should allocate expenses on a departmental basis between the prepaid plan members by market sector and the fee-for-service patient population. The allocation might be done according to the fee-for-service equivalent of services rendered or according to the number of units of services rendered using a standardized relative value study. Once costs have been allocated to each department, the cost per member per month can be determined for prepaid patients according to the prospective budget of the medical group.

EXHIBIT 23-4

ILLUSTRATION OF BUDGETARY METHOD FOR DETERMINING COST PER MEMBER PER MONTH FOR PREPAID SERVICES

	Cost per Member per Month
Primary care	
.6 FTE physician per 1,000 members	
Average total compensation = $120,000[1]	
Cost per member per month = $\frac{.6 \times 120{,}000}{1{,}000 \times 12}$ =	$ 6.00
Specialty care	
.3 FTE physician per 1,000 members	
Average total compensation = $150,000[1]	
Cost per member per month = $\frac{.3 \times 150{,}000}{1{,}000 \times 12}$ =	3.75
Support staff	
3.0 per FTE physician	
Average total compensation = $20,000[1]	
Cost per member per month = $\frac{.9 \times 3.0 \times 20{,}000}{1{,}000 \times 12}$ =	4.50

Medical supplies[2]	
Assume 3.5 visits per member per year	
Average cost per visit = $2.00	
Cost per member per month = $\frac{3.5 \times 2.00}{12}$ =	.58
X-ray supplies	.20
Laboratory supplies	.40
Depreciation of equipment[3]	.24
Occupancy[4]	
Assume 1 square foot per member	
$23 per square foot per year	
Cost per member per month = $\frac{23}{12}$ =	1.92
Miscellaneous overhead[5]	.50
Profit, capital allowance (10% of total costs)	2.15
Subtotal	$20.24
Referrals: Mental health services	1.23
Total cost per member per month for medical group services	$21.47

Note: The cost of services rendered by physicians not included on the group's staff can be estimated using the fee-for-service method or the above method for staff physicians.

[1]Includes base compensation, fringes, individual malpractice, continuing education allowance, memberships, and dues.

[2]Includes cost of disposable medical supplies and medical records.

[3]Assumes $600,000 of medical equipment and furniture depreciated over seven years. Assume equipment can handle demands of 30,000 patients.

[4]Includes depreciation on building or lease, amortization of improvements, utilities, taxes, insurance, janitorial/maintenance.

[5]Includes malpractice insurance for group, telephone, memberships for group, administrative staff expenses related to prepaid operations, postage, clinic supplies.

Part II of this text illustrated the development of cost per member per month, methods for allocating costs for negotiating or evaluating the performance of a capitation contract, and determination of cost for each procedure or service.

For medical groups that offer prepaid programs, projecting unit costs of procedures is critical, especially when renegotiating capitation payments and the amount of copayments required for specific procedures. By projecting the expected utilization rate of the prepaid members at the full cost per procedure, the approximate cost per member can be established. Once full costs have been estimated, the required capitation payments can be set or negotiated.

Comparison of Methods

The fee-for-service method has a definite advantage over the budgetary or cost method in that it incorporates factors that are very familiar to the medical group—fee-for-service charges. However, fee-for-service charges are not necessarily a fair representation of the cost of services rendered, since they tend to understate the cost of physician/nursing services and overstate the cost of ancillary services such as lab tests and x-rays. The budgetary or cost method may seem more abstract to the medical group's management and physicians, but it does approach the development of prepaid costs from a pure expense standpoint.

An understanding of these factors is important to the medical group and the prepaid plan as partners in the prepaid venture, since cost, rather than a fee-for-service charge that approximates cost, should be the final common denominator.

Summary

Short-range decisions involve deciding how to use existing capacity over a short period of time. The relevant revenues and costs for a particular decision are those revenues and costs that change as a result of the decision. Each short-range decision is different and, to some extent, the relevant costs are different.

The cost concepts considered in this chapter were: fixed and variable costs, avoidable and unavoidable costs, and full costs. Because most short-range decisions involve a change in activity, the most widely used cost concepts in short-range decisions are fixed and variable costs. Since variable costs change with activity and fixed costs do not, a quick and very useful measure of the impact of many short-range decisions on profit is the contribution margin (revenues minus variable costs). In short-range decisions the group should seek to maximize total contribution margin.

Short-range decisions illustrated in this chapter include: break-even analysis, adding a physician, dropping a satellite clinic, setting fees, and establishing a capitation rate for the group. An example of determining the cost per member per month for prepaid services illustrated the need for good cost information in setting capitation rates.

Chapter 24

Summary of Part III

The purpose of planning is to reduce uncertainty and achieve the goals and objectives of the organization. The purpose of control is to achieve conformity to plan. The addition of a prepaid component to a fee-for-service medical group involves different methods for financial planning and control.

Part III of this text has addressed the need and techniques for continuous planning on a short-term basis. Chapters 16 and 17 discussed goals and objectives as the starting point of the group's planning. To provide prepaid services in a cost effective manner and maintain the group, it is crucial that the group's goals and objectives include clear directives for the involvement in prepaid care. After the primary goal has been established, supporting goals lead to the formation of key objectives that are the framework for developing operating plans for the coming year. Objectives bridge the gap between the long-range goals and the short-term operating plans. Budgets are the result of expressing these operating plans in terms of dollars.

Chapter 18 provided an overview of budgeting. The main advantage of budgeting is that it requires management personnel to plan in an organized and concentrated way. Most fee-for-service medical groups do plan, but informally. To move from an informal plan to a comprehensive budget requires preparation of a profit plan (or operating budget), a capital expenditures budget, a cash budget, and a projected statement of financial position. The major purpose of this chapter was to provide an overview of the comprehensive budget, its various parts, and how these parts fit together.

Chapter 19 discussed and illustrated the development of the comprehensive budget introduced in Chapter 18. The example in this chapter involved a bottom-up approach to budgeting. After goals and objectives are developed and communicated throughout the group, each responsibility center plans its activities and prepares a profit plan. The responsibility center is the focal point of the budgeting process in Chapter 19 and the control process in Chapter 20.

Chapter 20 presented an extended discussion of performance evaluation. The results of the group's activities should be analyzed in terms of responsibility centers, goals and budget/performance evaluation, and comparative external sources. Nonfinancial measures are also important in assessing performance.

Chapter 21 focused on the management and control of cash and other short-term resources. The first half of Chapter 21 examined tools for day-to-day management of cash. The cash budget for the year may show that the group is achieving its overall objectives, but day-to-day control is critical to make certain that the group will actually have the right amount of cash at the right time. The second half of the chapter concentrated on the management of marketable securities, patient receivables, supplies, and payables.

Because of its importance in prepaid practice, Chapter 22 was devoted to a discussion of estimating incurred but unreported claims for referrals and hospitalization. Two major problems that arise in the management of outside claims for medical services are: exerting adequate control over medical services purchased outside the group, and estimating the financial liability of the medical group for the claims for the services rendered. Because fee-for-service groups generally use the cash basis of accounting and are not responsible for fee-for-service patients' use of hospital or referral services, this area is particularly difficult for the fee-for-service group just entering prepaid group to understand.

Chapter 23 examined a number of short-range decisions faced by a fee-for-service/prepaid medical group. These decisions included break-even analysis, when to add a doctor, dropping an unprofitable service, setting fees, and negotiating capitation payment. The cost concepts involved in these examples are fixed and variable costs, avoidable costs, and full costs. To make any decision, the decision maker needs to know the benefits and costs relevant to each decision. Benefits and costs that are relevant to one decision will not necessarily be relevant to another decision.

Management Accounting for Fee-for-Service/Prepaid Medical Groups is set in 10 pt. Helvetica digitized phototypography. The authors entered the original manuscript directly onto the DEC 10 computer at Pacific Lutheran University, Tacoma, Washington. The magnetic data were transferred onto Wang diskettes and edited at the Center for Research. Final manuscript copy was telecommunicated to Network Graphics, Inc. and typeset utilizing a Compugraphic MCS10/8400 digitized phototypesetter.

Telecommunications: Castle Key Corporation.
Typesetting, layout, and design: Network Graphics, Inc.
Printing and binding: Interstate Book Manufacturers, Inc.
Published by: The Center for Research in Ambulatory Health Care Administration.